An American Legend

Zippo

A COLLECTOR'S COMPANION

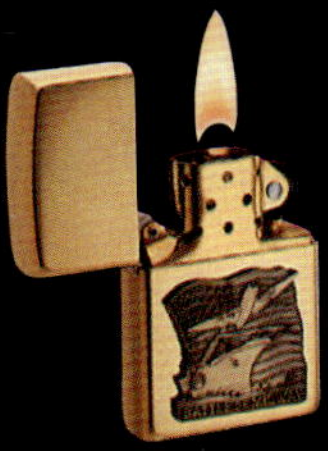

Avi R. Baer
Alexander Neumark

MJF BOOKS
NEW YORK

DEDICATION

For Wesley Oliver Baer

Published by MJF Books
Fine Communications
322 Eighth Avenue
New York, NY 10001

Zippo
LC Control Number 2005936862
ISBN-13: 978-1-56731-768-8
ISBN-10: 1-56731-768-5

Cover Designed by Mary Ann Liquori and Alex Van Riper
Interior Designed and Produced by Frank Ainscough @
Compendium Design and Production Ltd.

This special edition published by MJF Books in arrangement with Running Press, A Member of the Perseus Books Group.

Printed in Thailand.

SIP 10 9 8 7 6 5 4 3 2 1

CONTENTS

ACKNOWLEDGEMENTS

Our sincerest thanks for hospitality, help, and cooperation to Patrick Grandy, James Baldo, Kevin Spoor, and all the employees of the Zippo Manufacturing Company who gave us their precious time and attention and provided the bulk of the photographs.

To our publishers, Alan Greene and Martin Windrow, our appreciation for your patience and accessibility is beyond words.

Our thanks too, to all those Zippo owners and enthusiasts who showed us their collections, and fed us with information and stories that are new and wonderful.

Our appreciation to all those web surfers on the Internet who fed us with their stories and pictures and scans of personal Zippos.

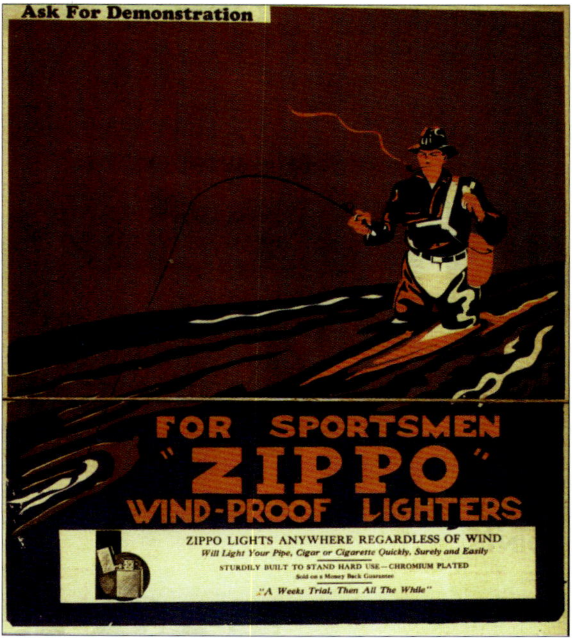

INTRODUCTION

Little did I know that the receipt of a small gift so many years ago would result in an exciting and fact-finding hobby that would eventually lead to this book. I was given a Zippo lighter nearly 15 years ago by my mother, Shoshana Baer, in Cape Town, South Africa. She told me that it had belonged to my father and that for many years she had kept it to give either my brother or myself. The lighter, a Slim Zippo dating back to 1964, has the emblem of the Balboa Bay Club, Newport Beach, California. The hinge was broken, and the lighter was in need of some care. I set about finding the Zippo agent in South Africa. One call to a local tobacconist that stocked these lighters soon put me in touch with the Zippo agent for Southern Africa.

I was living in the city of Durban at the time and I called the Cape Town-based Zippo agents. I spoke with Mr. Bernard Lange, who informed me that the lighter was guaranteed for life, and that I was to send it to him. I duly sent the lighter on to Cape Town, and as the weeks went by I forgot all about it, until one day a parcel arrived. Lo and behold there was my lighter in pristine condition – and what's more there were no charges associated with the repair! When I called Bernard to thank him, he told me that the lighter had been all the way to the United States and back. I was truly amazed, and this event started a lifelong passion for Zippo Lighters.

In the last five years I have traveled extensively and have consistently found unusual and exciting Zippos all over the world. It never ceases to amaze me that wherever I may be, I am assured of meeting people through these lighters. The familiar sound of a Zippo opening and closing has often been the entry point for many a long and interesting discussion.

Since their invention in 1933, Zippo lighters have enthralled millions of owners around the world. These pocket wonders with their hundreds of uses have managed to enter into history books the world over, have been the subject of many tales, and have even saved some lives. Did George G. Blaisdell the inventor of the Zippo lighter ever imagine that, in less than 65 years, 300 million Zippos would leave the Zippo Manufacturing Company in the town of Bradford, Pennsylvania ? He may not have imagined the incredible demand for the Zippo lighter, but he certainly went about promoting his product to his utmost ability.

In the 67-year history of the Zippo lighter, the design of the lighter has remained basically the same. Call it a legend, call it a design masterpiece – it will remain one of those inventions that will always be considered a classic. While some small modifications have taken place they have all added to the efficiency of this unique product.

Not only was the Zippo lighter a unique conception, but it was born in a troubled era that undoubtedly must have been one of the harshest in American history – the Great Depression. At a time when millions of people did not have enough money to buy food, this product emerged and was successful. Not only is George G. Blaisdell responsible for the creation of a classic American icon, but he also created a miniature canvas, the Zippo lighter today has become a portable promotional medium for companies and individuals. Like the T-shirt, the Zippo lighter is a highly useful and successful marketing tool. Many Zippo collectors search for specific lighters with special advertisements on them. Zippo collectors all over the world regard Zippos with corporate logos to be the most sought-after collectors' pieces.

While there is no question that the Zippo lighter is a classic design, there are many other factors that have added to its success. The lifetime guarantee that accompanies each and every lighter that leaves the Zippo Manufacturing Company is another example of what makes this product so great. Today, as always, Zippo will repair your lighter free of charge. All you have to do is get it to the nearest Zippo distributor worldwide, and in a few weeks your lighter will be returned in perfect working order. Zippo has never charged a cent to repair any of its lighters, and while many lighters arrive at the Zippo Repair Clinic accompanied by money to cover the cost of repair, the money is always returned with the repaired lighter.

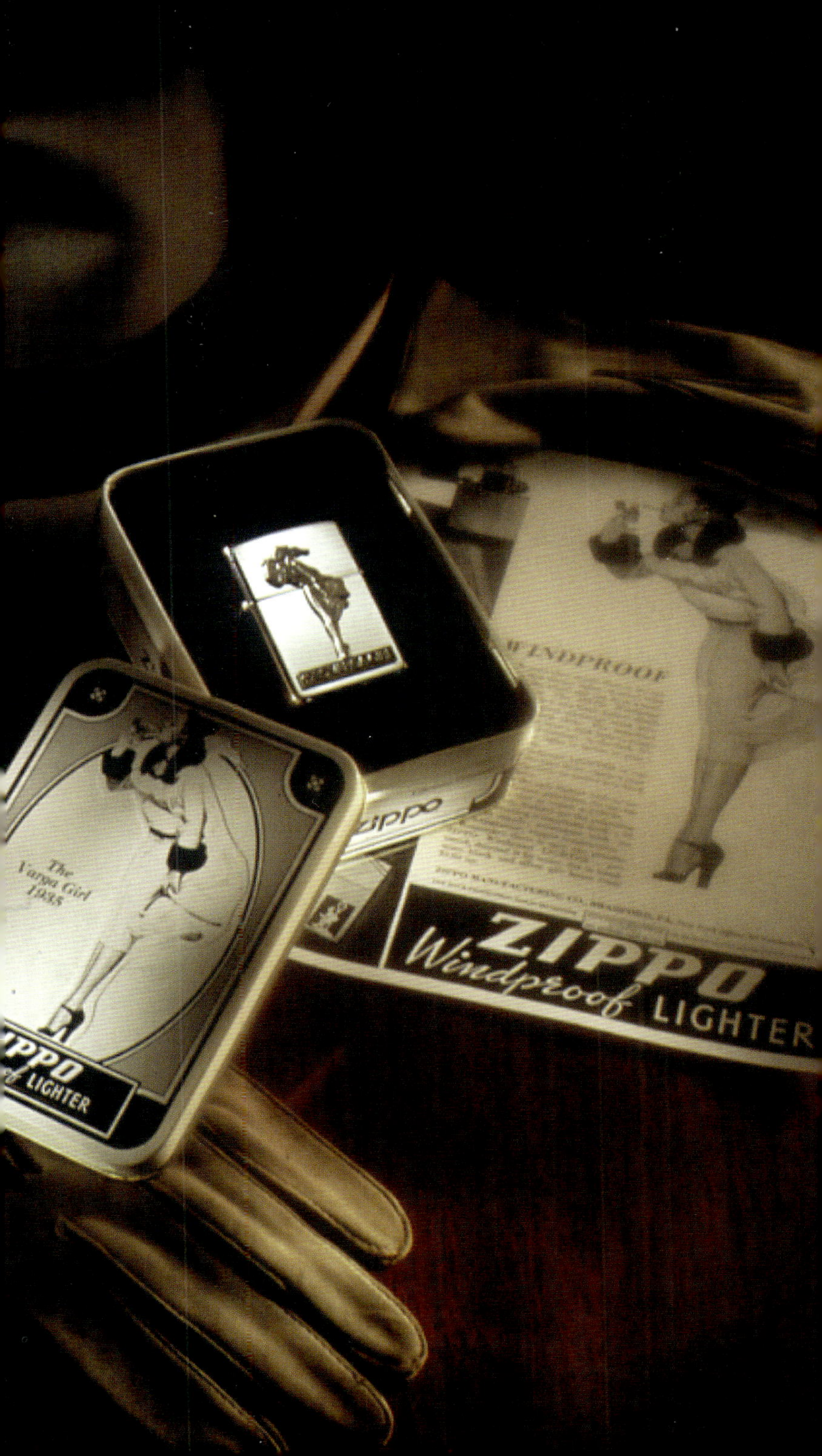
WINDPROOF
ZIPPO
Windproof LIGHTER
The Varga Girl 1935
ZIPPO
LIGHTER
Zippo

Such an icon is the Zippo lighter, that many manufacturers have tried to imitate it. Over the years many fakes have been circulated, but once you are familiar with a genuine Zippo you will be able to spot a fake instantly. The Zippo click, as it has come to be known, is very distinct, and to those Zippo aficionados out there, this sound is also a perfect way to distinguish a Zippo from a fake. The weight of a Zippo and the feel in the palm of the hand are additional sure-fire ways to tell that you have an authentic Zippo lighter.

Although the Zippo lighter is a simple thing, this simple thing has become an important part of our lives and our culture. It certainly is an American legend.

CHAPTER 1

'MR. ZIPPO'

The predominantly red-brick town of Bradford, Pennsylvania, nestles at the foot of the Allegheny Mountains near the New York State border. The town in part owed its foundation and pre-1870s development to the lumber industry which grew up to exploit the surrounding forests of pine, oak, and hemlock.

The main spur to the town's growth was provided by the discovery of a major petroleum reservoir under Hinckey Farm in 1871. Exploitation of this 'black gold' brought some 7,500 new residents into Bradford by 1879. (Although production has declined from its peak of 23 million barrels in 1881, oil and its associated industries still represent the mainstay of Bradford's economy today.)

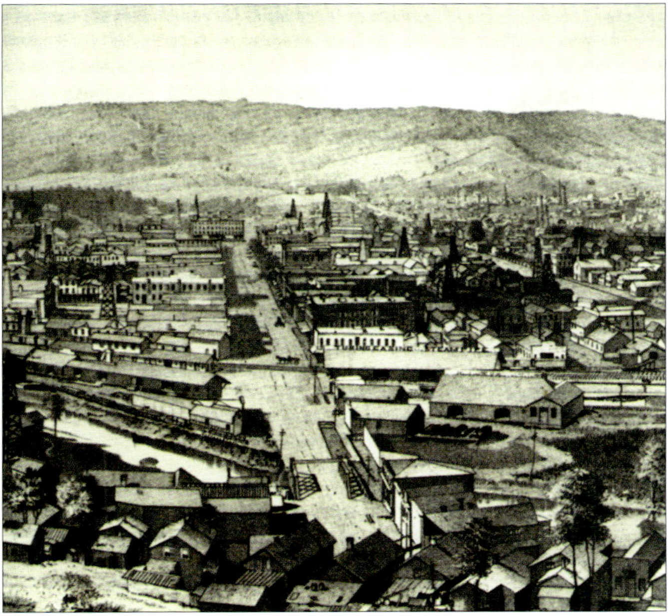

The town of Bradford, Pennsylvania, in the 1870s.

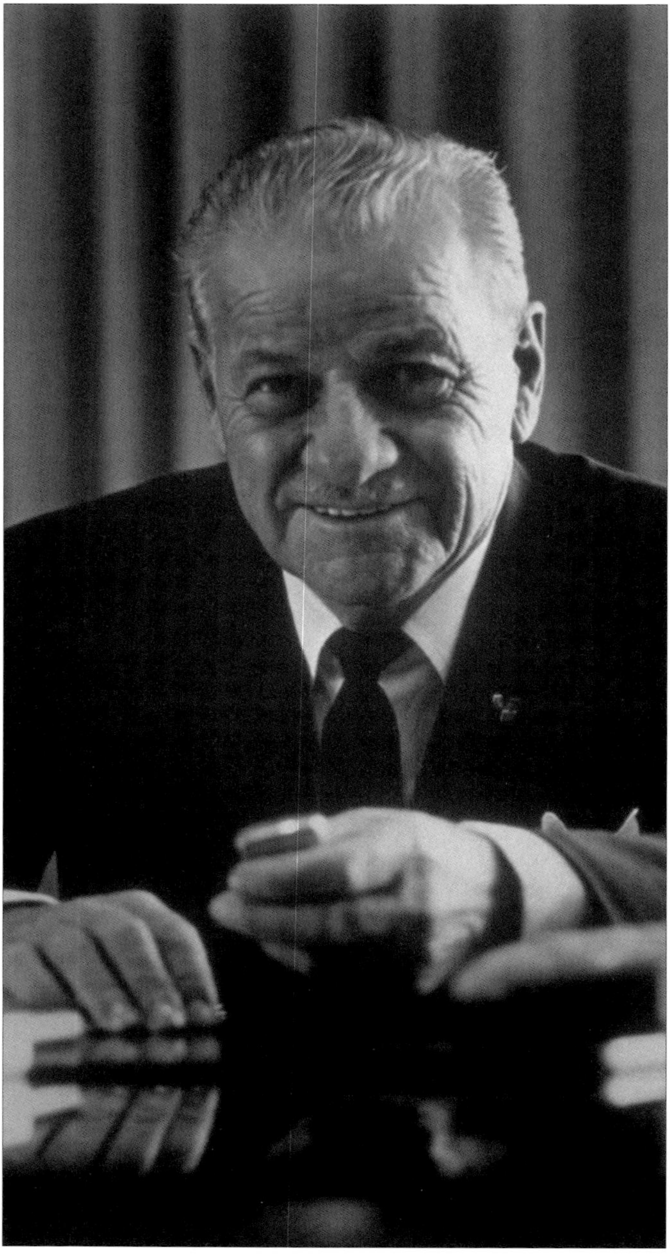

George G. Blaisdell (1895-1978) was born and raised in Bradford, where his father Philo Blaisdell was in the business of manufacturing oil drilling equipment. When he was in the fifth grade young George announced that he did not want to finish school, and would prefer to take a job. His parents reacted by sending him off to military school; but two years later he was back in Bradford, and started work in his father's Blaisdell Machinery Company – the hard way, as an apprentice.

Philo did not believe he should get the easy ride enjoyed by some owners' sons: George worked a 59-hour week, and was paid ten cents an hour. He thrived on hard work, however, and quickly showed a talent for the craft of machining and engineering. When his technical apprenticeship was complete George was transferred onto the sales side. He eventually took over management of the company in the early years of World War I.

In 1920 he sold the engineering company and, with his brother, started up an oil drilling business under the name of the Blaisdell Oil Company. Although this venture initially prospered, the Great Depression brought hard times. Conditions throughout the US economy were at an all-time low, and for the Blaisdell Oil Company, as for so many thousands of struggling firms, the prospects for better revenues seemed bleak. The entrepreneur in George Blaisdell was always looking out for new business opportunities, but nothing obvious had yet presented itself by the warm summer night in 1931 when he happened to attend a gathering at the Bradford Country Club. Little did he know that this was the evening which would transform his life, and launch an American icon.

Legend has it that during the function George stepped outside, and fell into conversation with a very elegantly turned out man. (There have been many conflicting stories as to his identity, but it is believed that he was Dick Dresser, who

George G. Blaisdell – inventor of the Zippo lighter and founder of the Zippo Manufacturing Company.

ran Dresser Industries Inc.) As they chatted, his acquaintance lit a cigarette with a lighter which seemed to George a clumsy and unsightly accessory for such a well-dressed man and he couldn't help remarking,

'You're all dressed up – why don't you get a lighter that looks decent?'

'Because it works,' his friend replied.

This simple answer so impressed the practical-minded George that he applied for, and was granted, the US distribution rights for the one-dollar Austrian-made lighter used by his elegant acquaintance. This consisted of two main pieces – a removable brass lid, and a brass bottom case which held the wick, fuel reservoir and striking mechanism. In an effort to improve its appearance Blaisdell persuaded the Austrian manufacturers to chrome plate the case.

In spite of this cosmetic treatment sales were still disappointing; and Blaisdell soon relinquished his distribution rights for the imported product. However, using the skills and experience gained in his father's machine shop, he set out to design and manufacture a lighter of his own. He rented a small workshop on the second floor above the Rickerson & Pryde garage on Boylston Street, Bradford, for $10.00 a month. Blaisdell's original investment was $800 and he employed six people. The workshop equipment, bought for $260.00, consisted of a kitchen hotplate which was used for soldering, and a variety of second-hand machinery, including a hand motor, a punch press, and a welding machine.

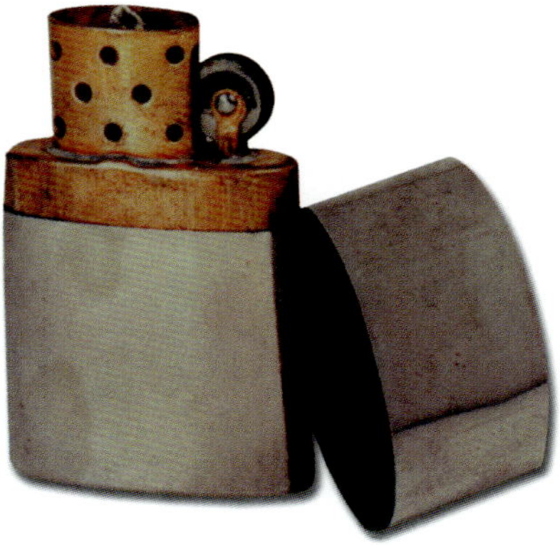

The Austrian lighter for which George Blaisdell acquired distribution rights in 1932.

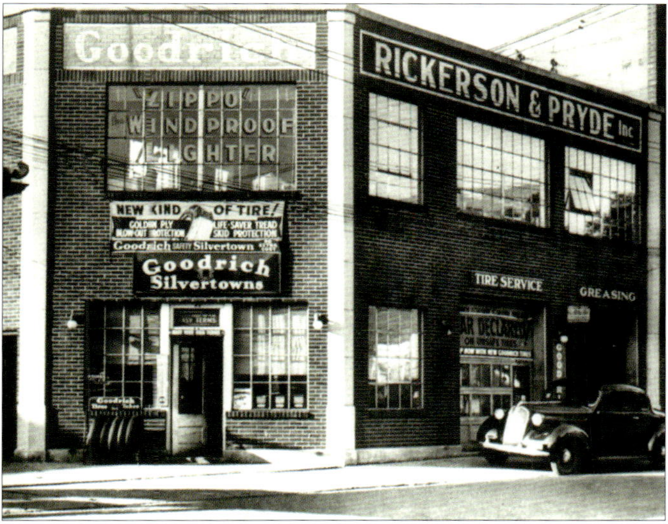

The Rickerson & Pryde building in 1932; the workshop on the second floor was Zippo's first home, and Blaisdell painted the name on the window rather than going to the expense of a signboard.

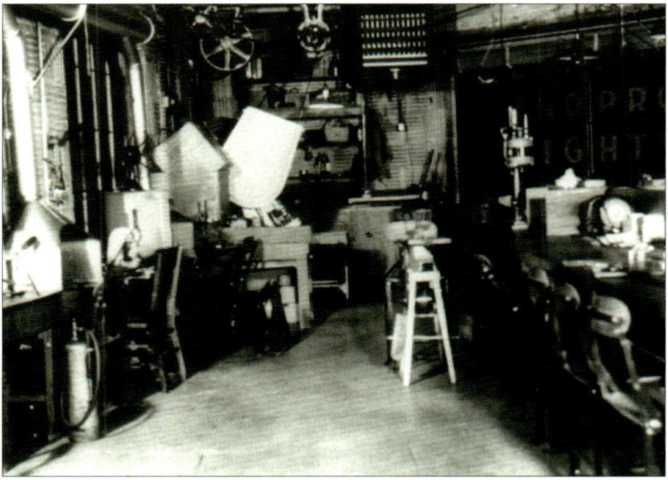

The interior of the first workshop in 1932.

In remodelling the clumsy two-piece Austrian original, Blaisdell gave priority to producing a design for a lighter that would fit comfortably into the palm, and which did not need both hands to operate. Using rectangular brass tubing, he carefully fashioned a case with the lid hinged on the outside, allowing the lighter to be used with one hand. He surrounded the wick with a replica of the Austrian lighter's wind hood, the patent of which he had purchased.

An American legend had been born; indeed, George Blaisdell was so excited by his new lighter that he declared that his product – 'Would not change as long as I live!'

That first 1933 lighter was one quarter-inch taller than the model we know today, and had sharp square corners and an external hinge. Although minor improvements have since been made to the flint wheel and case – and new technology has eased production and reliability – those are the only immediately noticeable changes introduced since 1933: the Zippo purchased today is to all intents and purposes virtually the same as George Blaisdell's original.

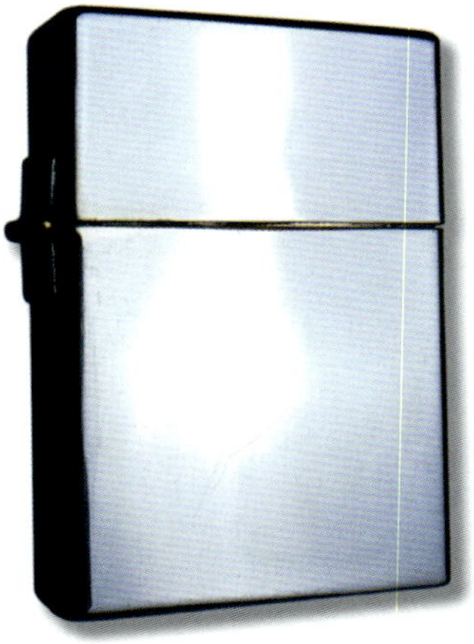

The original Zippo lighter of 1933-34. A quarter inch taller than the 1934-40 type, these so-called 'Phantom Zippos' are now very rare and command enormous prices from collectors.

There was no special significance in the choice of the name 'Zippo'. Shortly before the time of Blaisdell's invention the Talon Company of Pennsylvania had introduced to the market its slide fastener under the name 'Zipper'.

Blaisdell's imagination was caught by the modern sound of this name, which seemed to him to represent all that was new and progressive; so he named his lighter 'Zippo', simply be-

A Zippo advertising leaflet dating from 1935.

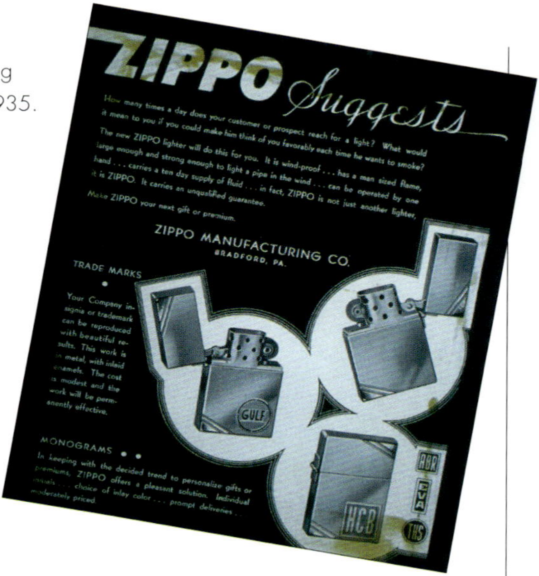

cause it sounded right to him. 67 years later it has become almost a generic name for a lighter.

Indeed, the familiar 'clink-clop' sound of a thumb flipping a Zippo open and shut has itself become universally recognisable. So much so that many of the experienced quality controllers at the Zippo factory can rely upon the sound alone when passing or failing lighters at final inspection.

When, after many years of hard work, Zippo became an undoubted success, Blaisdell set up the Sarah and Philo Blaisdell Foundation in memory of his parents. The foundation underwrites numerous worthy local causes and charities, many of them anonymously. Among the community projects supported have been sports facilities, flood control projects, ambulances, and, in particular, educational projects for the county's mentally challenged children.

George G. Blaisdell remained at the head of his company until he passed away in 1978, when the business was inherited by his daughters, Harriett B. Wick and Sarah B. Dorn. Although the sisters were familiar with the running of the business, they appointed a long-time Zippo employee, Robert Galey, to head the company. Robert Galey retired in 1986,

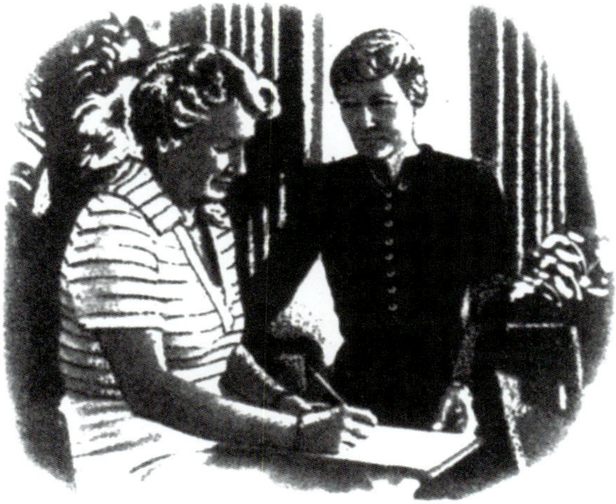

Sarah B. Dorn and Harriett B. Wick, daughters of George Blaisdell and owners of the Zippo Manufacturing Company.

when the Controller, Michael Schuler, was appointed President and Chief Executive Officer, a position he holds today. The children of George G. Blaisdell's daughters hold executive positions in the business.

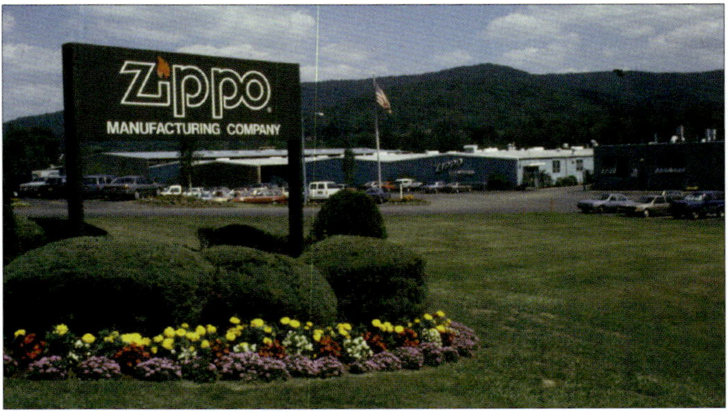

ABOVE Zippo's manufacturing plant as it looked in 1991.

RIGHT Zippo headquarters on Barbour Street, Bradford, Pennsylvania.

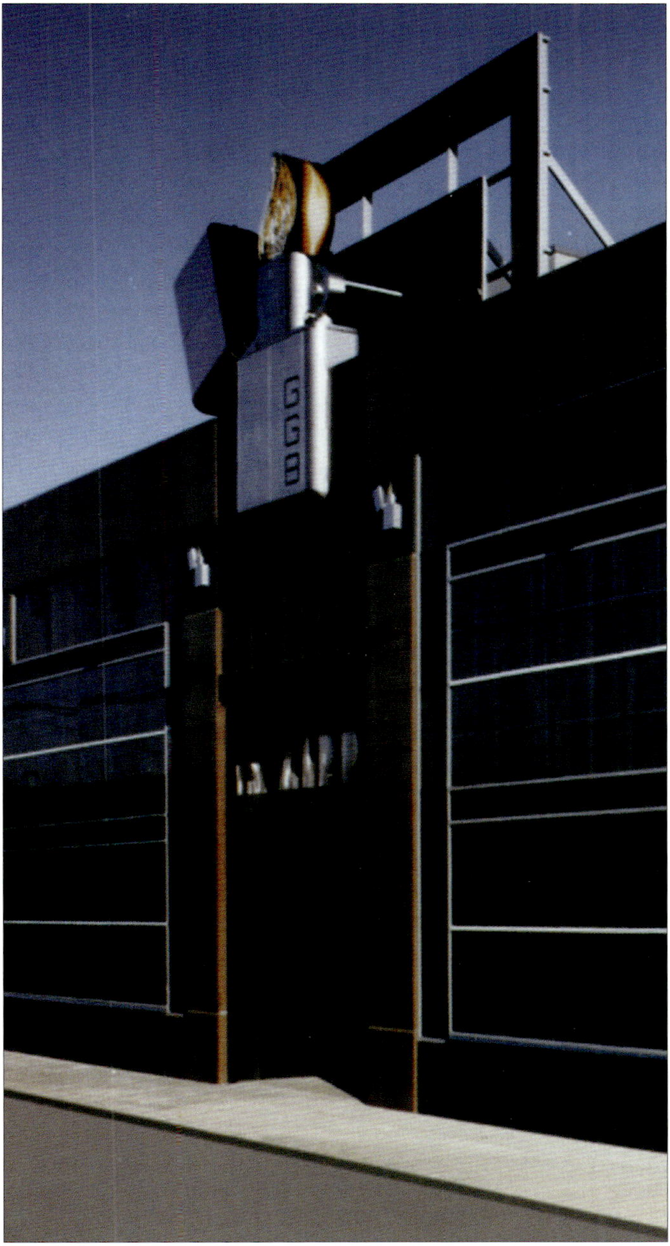
GGB

CHAPTER 2

THE EARLY YEARS

In the Depression year of 1932 George Blaisdell had come up with a promising new product, but he still had to sell it, and he had very little money behind him. Initially he performed simultaneously the functions of factory supervisor, purchasing agent, serviceman, and salesman. In spite of the excellence and simplicity of his lighter, he did not immediately conquer the market. The first few years were very tough, but they served to hone his marketing skills, which were considerable.

The retail price of the first Zippo was $1.95, and Blaisdell sold just 82 units in the first month of business, producing an income of $62.15 . . . He came up with many marketing ideas, some of them successful, others less so. From the start he would hand out his lighters in places that many people frequented. An old friend ran the Bradford Bus Station, so Blaisdell gave lighters to the long distance bus drivers, asking them to demonstrate and recommend them to their passengers – thus starting to spread the word. He also delivered them to tobacconists, jewelers, hardware, and sporting goods stores on a sale-or-return basis – with variable success. Even in those days retailers hesitated to order stock without a commitment from the company to an advertising campaign.

By the second month he produced 367 lighters, and his sales reached the figure of $312.

One of Blaisdell's most significant – indeed, unique –

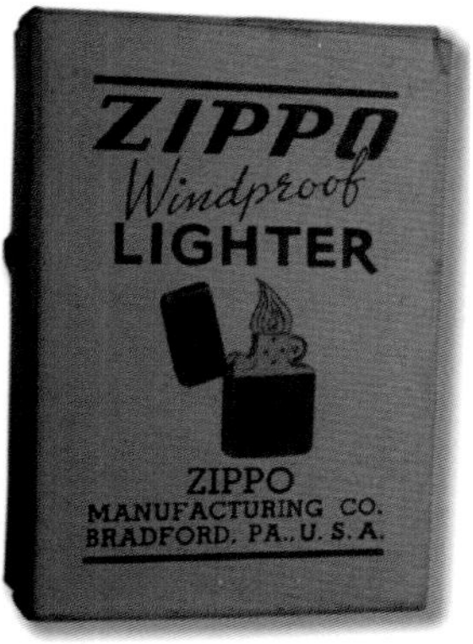

World War II Packaging

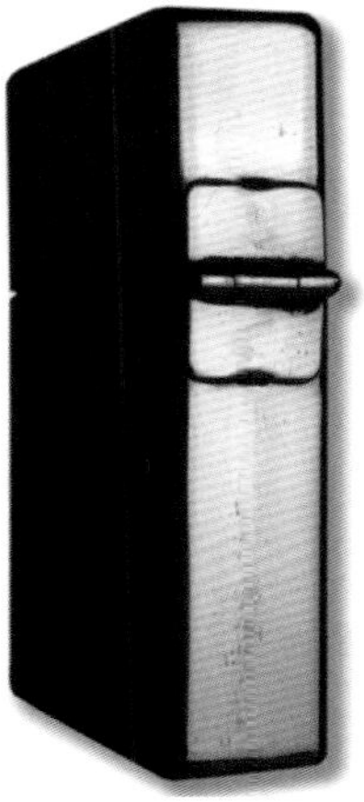

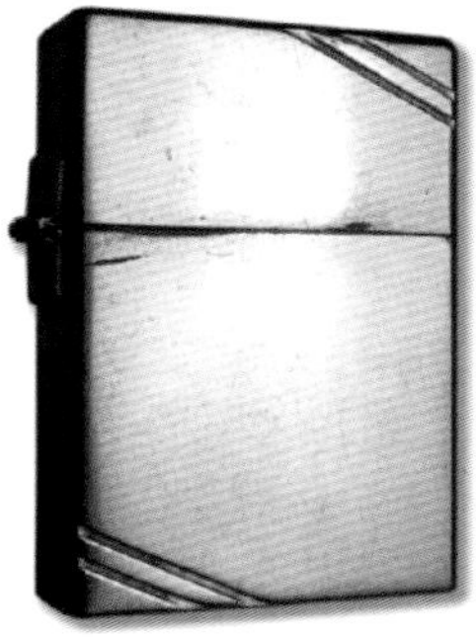

LEFT: The original Zippo lighter of 1933. Note the external hinge. Origninal height was a quarter inch more than the subsequent 1934 models.

ABOVE: In 1934 a second design was added. It incorporated diagonal lines top and bottom and it too was reduced in size by a quarter inch later the same year. This is a replica of the classic 'diagonal line' Zippo, still very popular today as part of the Zippo commemorative releases. These replicas are the only Zippos manufactured with the original patent number on the base. *Photo A. R. Baer*

marketing concepts was the introduction of the extraordinary 'lifetime guarantee'. At that time many companies relied heavily upon revenue generated by servicing the products they sold to consumers. Blaisdell disapproved of this practice and anyway had complete faith in his product. From the first year of business he insisted that it would never cost a customer a penny to have a Zippo lighter repaired by the factory – and it never has. Today, 67 years later, people from all over the world still send their lighters in for free repair. This unusual policy was to become one of the foundations of Zippo's success. In the 1940s and 1950s, when people started giving Zippos as presents, they recognized that they were in fact giving a gift which would last forever.

Minor changes in the lighters appeared at various dates during these early years – insignificant at the time, these have since become identifying details of considerable interest to

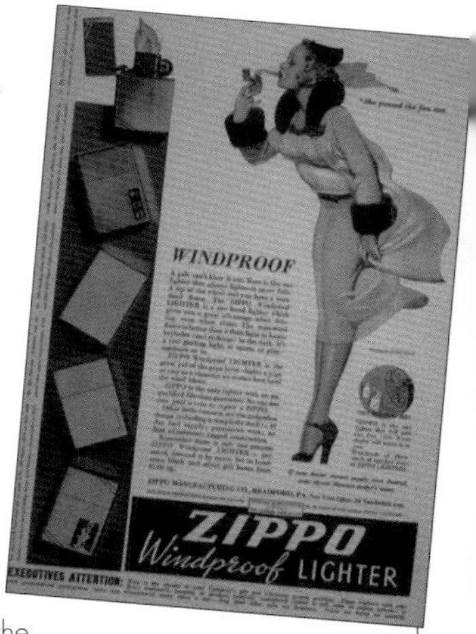

The illustration of a girl by artist Enoc Bowles has for many years been confused with art by Emilio Varga. Due to this error she has often been called the 'Varga Girl.' Today, educated Zippo enthusiasts just call her 'Windy,' as she passed the fan test. In an attempt to encourage retailers to stock his lighters, Blaisdell tried out a full page advertisement in the December 1937 issue of *Esquire* magazine, borrowing most of the $3,000 needed to pay for it. Results were disappointing; the retailer base was still too limited for Zippo to gain the full benefit from such an advertisement.

collectors. In 1934 two diagonal lines were cut into opposite corners of the case and the hinged lid. The original plain model also continued to be manufactured. The lighter now became a quarter inch shorter, and the diagonal lines on this shortened type were placed closer together than on the original taller model.

In May 1934 Zippo applied for a patent on the manufacturing process, which was subsequently granted under patent number 2032695. This number was recorded on the base of all Zippos circa 1936. This was also the year that the hinge was moved from the outside to the inside of the case, which required a change to the width of the insert.

In 1938 there was a change in the manufacturing process from a case made from brass tubing to a drawn case with round corners. This permitted solid molding in a press machine and eliminated soldering, resulting in the case with rounded corners which we know today.

During these years George Blaisdell continued to try out various marketing and promotional ideas. He introduced the catch phrase 'Try the Fan Test', emphasizing the efficiency of the wind hood by challenging people to light a Zippo and other competing products in front of an electric fan. He began to run contests with Zippos as prizes: one required contestants to complete a limerick:

There was an old man named Sinclair
Whose lighter wouldn't work in the air
Then he tried a Zippo
And hollered out 'Yip-po'
. . .

(Well, Mark Twain probably wouldn't have been much good at inventing lighters, either.)

Circa 1936 Blaisdell introduced engraving and insignia on the case; customers could send in $1 to have their initials engraved, or for a standard colored insignia – such as the Scotty Dog and the Drunk design. As engraving was not yet available a thin metallic L, the metallique, frame was cemented to the case and filled with enamel paint; the first colors available were black, red, blue, green, yellow, orange, purple, and white. These Zippos became popular as personalized gifts.

At about this time the Zippo appeared in a mail order catalog for the very first time. The Sports Wholesale catalog from the Sports Company of Minnesota displayed the 'Zippo Wind Proof Lighter' as item no. M250-BRS with a recommended retail price of $2. The sample price advertised was $1.29, or a dozen for $14.40.

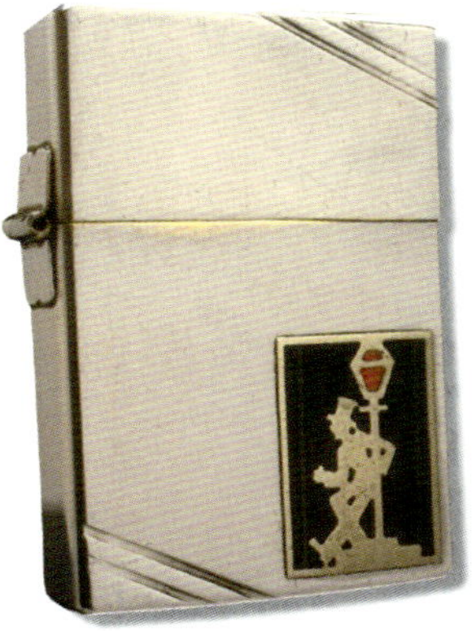

Circa 1935 'Drunk' or 'Reveler' lighter, with an insignia produced by The Probar Co. in New Jersey. The metalliques are metal lace, handcrafted slices of chrome plated brass. Razor thin at .005"

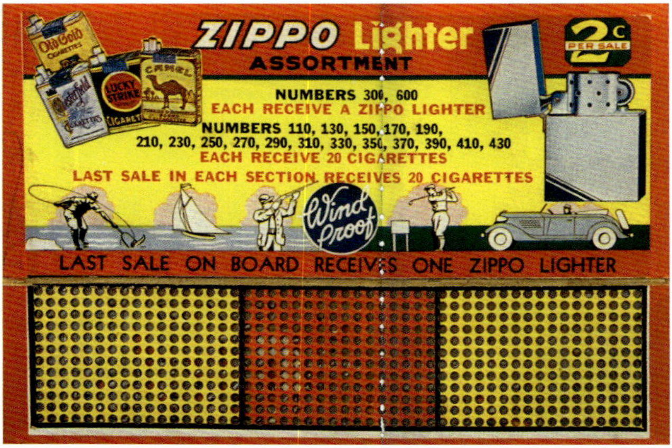

An example of a punchboard as used by George Blaisdell to promote his lighters as prizes during the 1930s.

However, the first really important boost in sales came through association with a popular contemporary product – the punchboard. In the 1930s these were found nationwide, in poolrooms, tobacco and confectionery shops, and cigar stands. The punchboard was a game of chance: it had either 1,000 or 2,000 numbered holes divided into blocks of 250, and for 2c the player could punch any chosen hole. If it matched up with one of the designated lucky numbers the player won a prize – typically a free pack of cigarettes.

Blaisdell was introduced to the punchboard by Ray Johnston, a Pittsburgh tobacco store clerk and one of the first locations he used for a punchboard offering a Zippo as a prize was a poolroom run by an old friend of his, E. G. Holland. So successful was this idea that between 1934 and 1940 – when the punchboard was ruled illegal as a form of gambling – Zippo sold more than 300,000 lighters as punchboard prizes. However, other retailers were still reluctant to stock the lighters without the backing of national advertising.

In 1936 an order from an Iowa insurance company steered Zippo marketing into a new and significant direction. The order was for 200 lighters, to be engraved and given as prizes to the insurance company's salesmen. At almost the same time the Kendall Oil Company ordered 500 lighters with their insignia as gifts for customers and employees. Zippo had entered the specialty and promotional sector.

Before long Zippo's campaign to persuade manufacturers and retailers to use the lighter as an advertising medium began to get a positive response. Famous brand names such as Coca Cola, Texaco, and Lucky Strike led the way for other advertisers to take advantage of this new promotional opportunity.

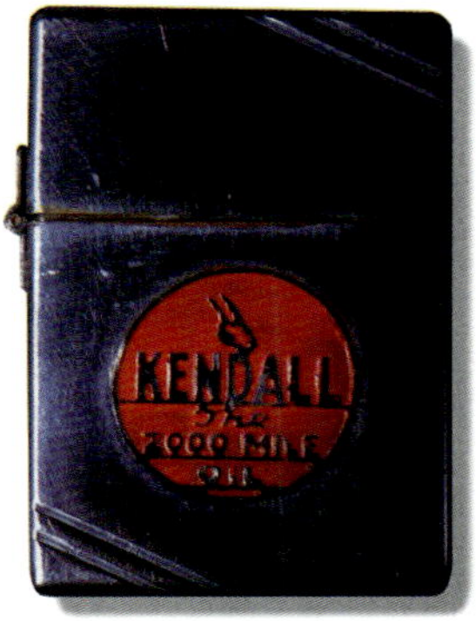

The Kendall Oil Company's commission for 500 of these beautiful lighters as gifts for clients in 1935 was the foundation of the promotional and advertising speciality division of Zippo.

The sales breakthrough provided by the punchboard promotion and the small technical improvements such as the smoother case and new hinge, allowed Blaisdell to investigate new marketing avenues. In 1937 he brought out a series of lighters decorated with designs etched into the case from line drawings and filled with enamels — using pantograph engraving machines. Examples of these designs are the golfer, a hunter, a fisherman, an elephant, a greyhound, and a bulldog, then in 1938 a Scotty was added to the selection.

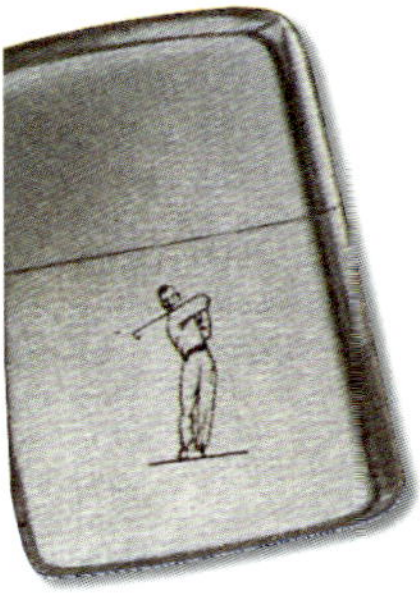

This Golfer sports lighter illustrated the instruction manuals of the late 1940s when $1 would get a Zippo engraved with one of 17 designs. *Photo A. R. Baer*

All these designs were the forerunners of the Sports series available today. Since the Zippo was always marketed as an outdoor lighter it is

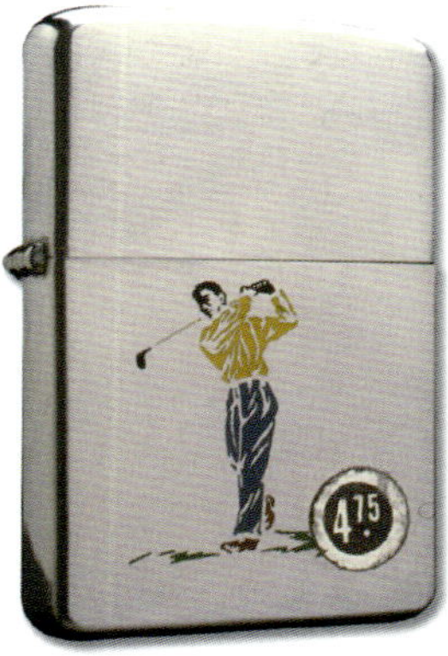

Sport series lighter
c. 1959 based on the
original 1937 series.

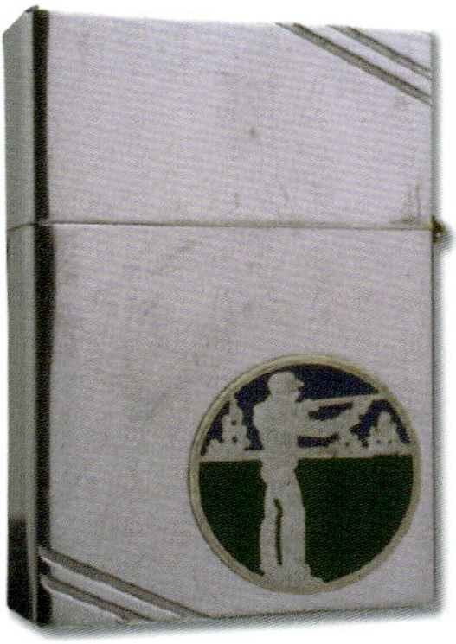

Early model Sport series
lighter depicting
"the shooter" metallique.

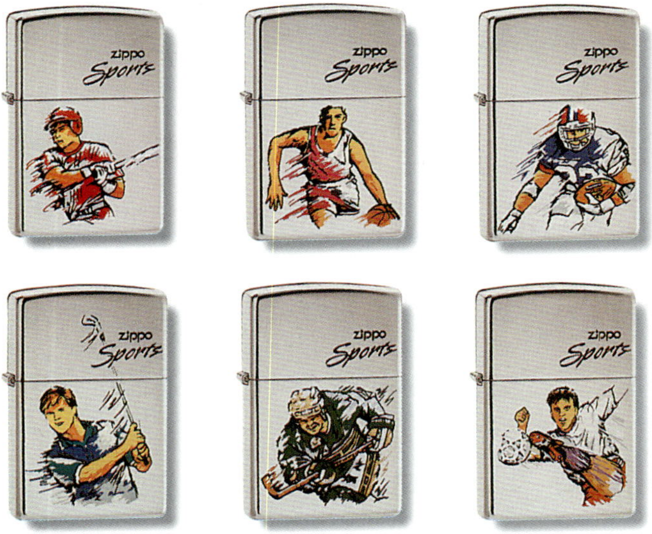

Zippo Sports series, 1997. In the early years, it was impossible to use graphics such as these, but technical advances allow more elaborate designs.

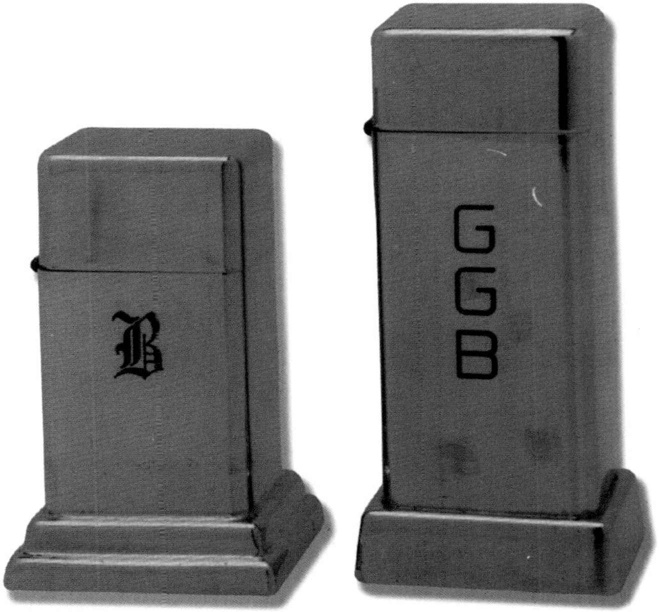

No. 10 Barcroft table lighter, with George G. Blaisdell's initials, standing next to the third model Barcroft introduced during the 1950s.

not surprising that they were well received, and flourishing sales led to many new and exciting designs. The first Sports series lighter had the model number 275, based on the price of $2.75. A later model of this style had a carrying lanyard attached and the model number changed to 180.

The growing volume of business soon obliged Blaisdell to expand his workshops over the whole second floor of the Rickerson & Pryde building, with a new office at 21 Pine Street. In 1938 the factory and offices moved to 36 Barbour Street.

That year also saw Zippo introduce their first table lighter, named the No.10 Barcroft; this was to be the tallest of all the table lighters. It held four times as much fluid as the regular Zippo. It seems from the documentation that these table lighters were not a commerical success, and a letter of

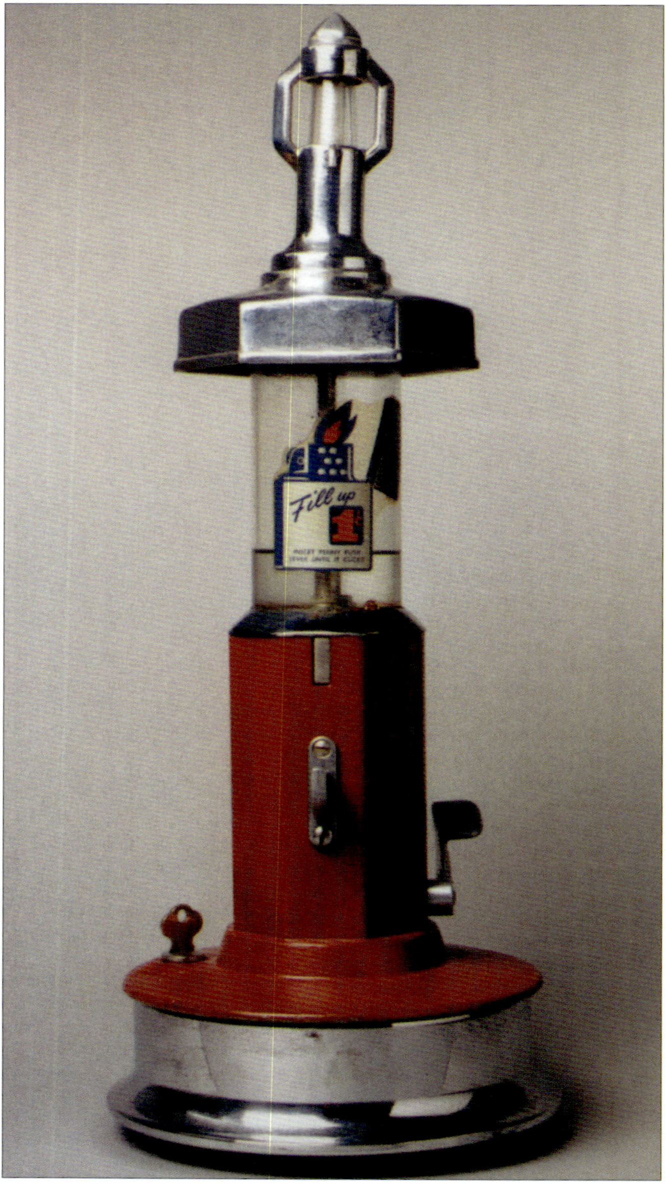

The famous Zippo fuel dispenser that allowed a refill for a cent. *Photo A. R. Baer*

17 October 1941 from George Blaisdell to all his customers announced that the product was being discontinued.

Blaisdell also introduced a cheap and novel method of refuelling lighters by placing lighter fluid dispensers in stores and bars. Zippo owners could then refill their lighters for 1c per fill. Not many of these machines survive, but some can still be seen at the Zippo corporate offices, as well as the Zippo/Case Visitors Center in Bradford, PA.

The 1930s allowed some small measure of individualism with monograms or two images – the Scotty or the Drunk. *Photo A. R. Baer*

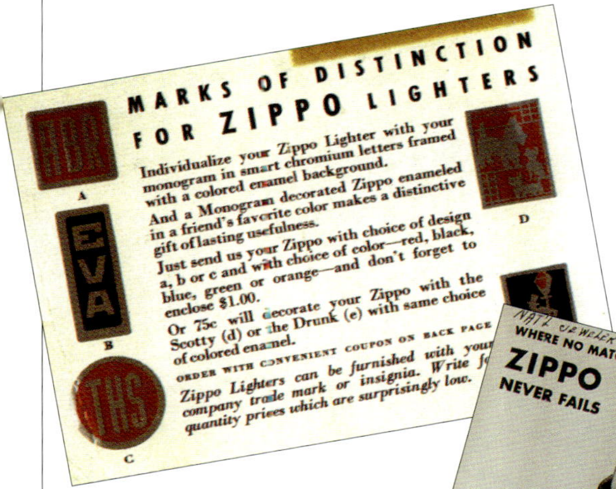

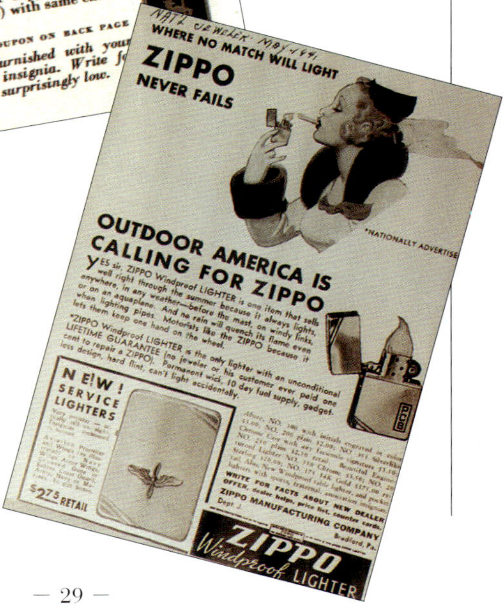

Where no match will light. *Photo A. R. Baer*

CHAPTER 3

THE LIFETIME GUARANTEE

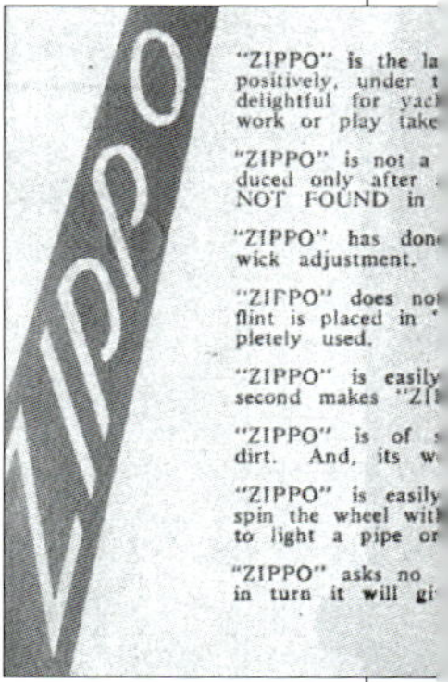

George G. Blaisdell was not only an innovative engineer, but also an exceptionally gifted merchandising promoter. Almost concurrent with the birth of Zippo, he launched his brilliantly conceived lifetime guarantee — an idea unique in American business at that time.

In 1933 Blaisdell presented 25 friends with his new lighters. A few days later one of them returned his lighter for a repair; Blaisdell fixed it then and there, and told his friend 'You don't owe me a penny.' It was this owner's surprised pleasure that made him realize the exceptional appeal of a free repair service — and the lifetime guarantee was born. George Blaisdell's approach to his business lives on today through this policy, which is one of Zippo's most effective marketing techniques.

The lifetime guarantee. This one dates from c1994.

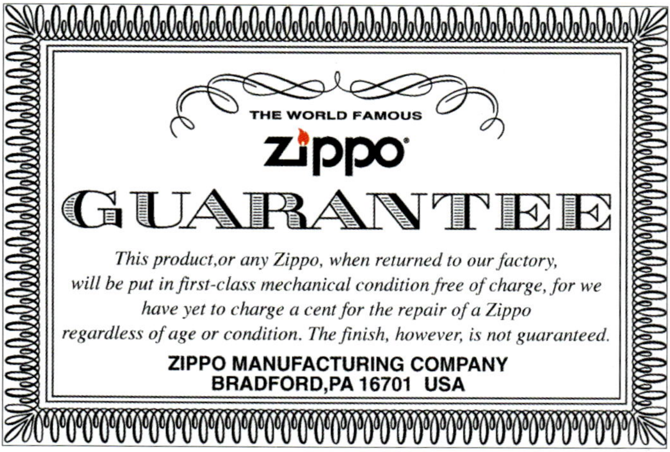

THE WORLD FAMOUS

Zippo

GUARANTEE

This product,or any Zippo, when returned to our factory, will be put in first-class mechanical condition free of charge, for we have yet to charge a cent for the repair of a Zippo regardless of age or condition. The finish, however, is not guaranteed.

ZIPPO MANUFACTURING COMPANY
BRADFORD,PA 16701 USA

The lifetime guarantee conceived by Blaisdell soon after his invention of the Zippo lighter. This guarantee is still packaged with each and every Zippo sold today.

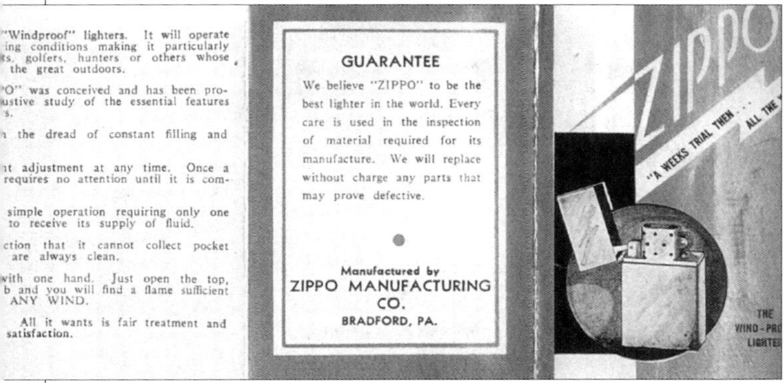

No Zippo owner has ever had to pay for repairs. Although the wording of today's guarantee differs slightly from the original, the sentiments and the integrity remain the same. Very often owners send their Zippos in for repair accompanied by money to cover postage; their lighters are returned repaired, postage paid, and their remittance returned. While the fulfilment of the guarantee is an expensive overhead for Zippo, the trade-off in customer goodwill is immeasurable.

Although most of the lighters returned need only a new hinge (the most abused part), Zippo has on display in their museum examples of lighters which they have replaced after having received them back mangled beyond repair, and sometimes beyond recognition. Some of these Zippos have been crushed by bulldozers or railroad trains, mangled by washing machines, garbage disposals and power mowers, or chewed up by ice crushers.

By 1962 the 'Zippo Repair Clinic' was mending over half a million lighters a year, and picking up the tab. Aproximately 1,000 lighters and other Zippo products, some as old as the company, are received daily at the US repair facility, now housed in the Zippo/Case Visitors Center. Zippo at

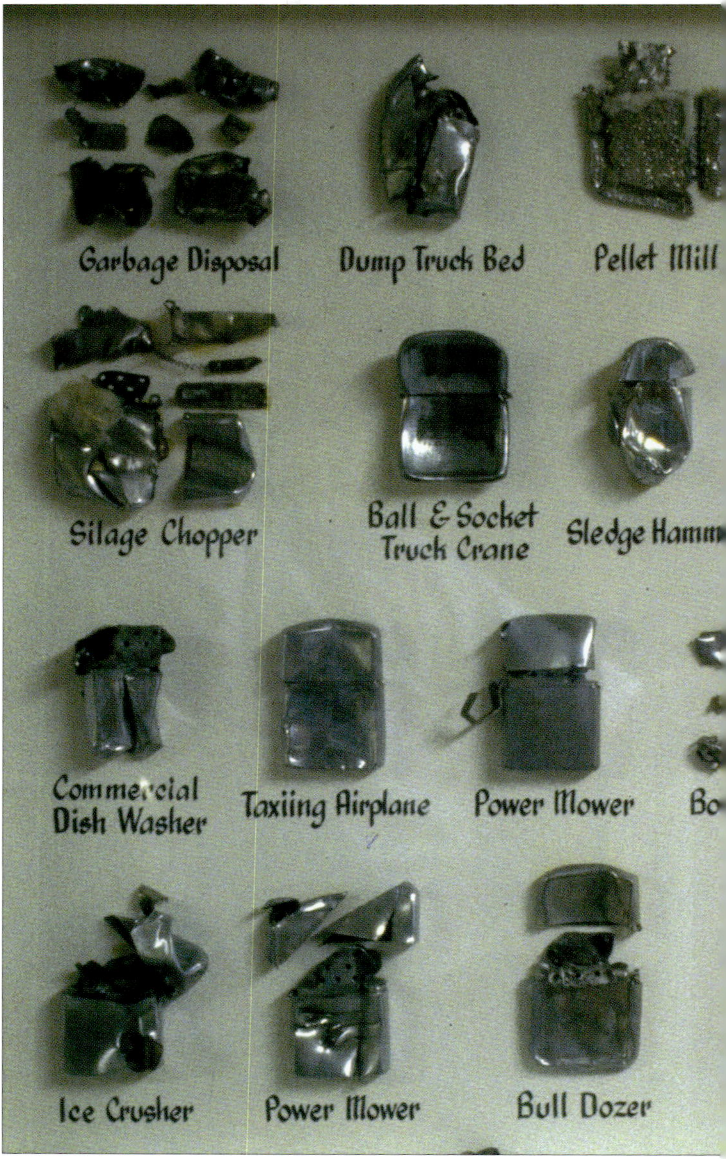

Even the Lifetime Guarantee can only go so far!
Damaged lighters and their fate.

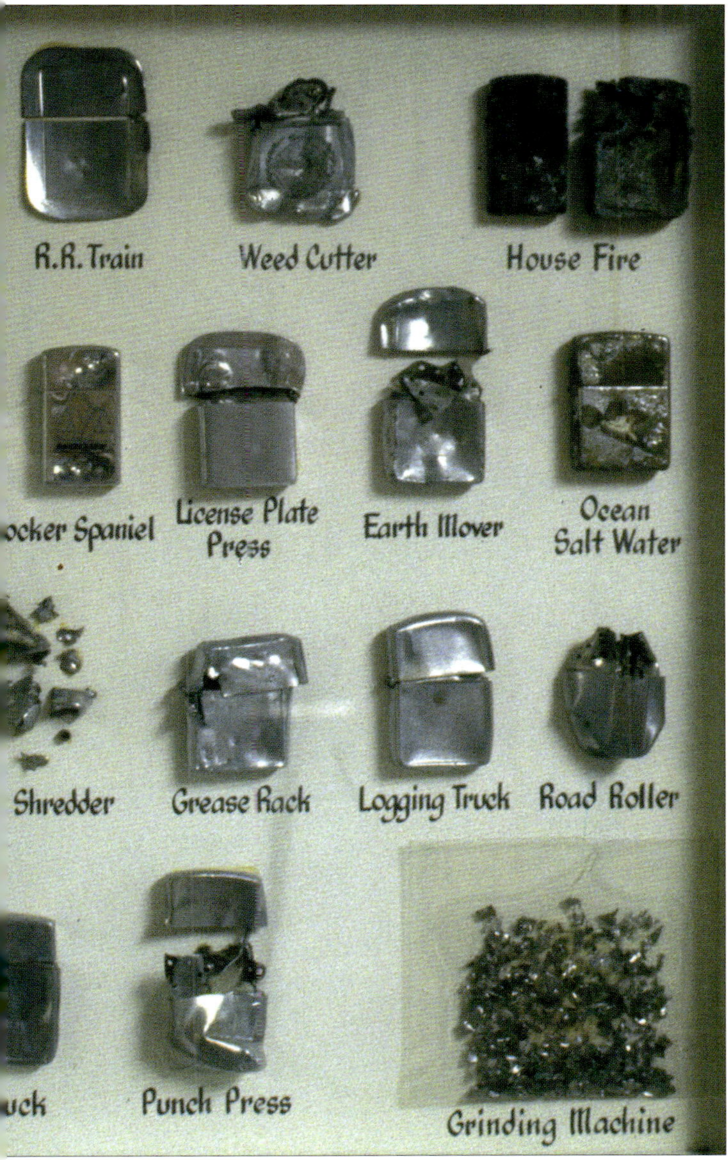

Courtesy Zippo, Bradford, Pennsylvania,
Photo A. R. Baer

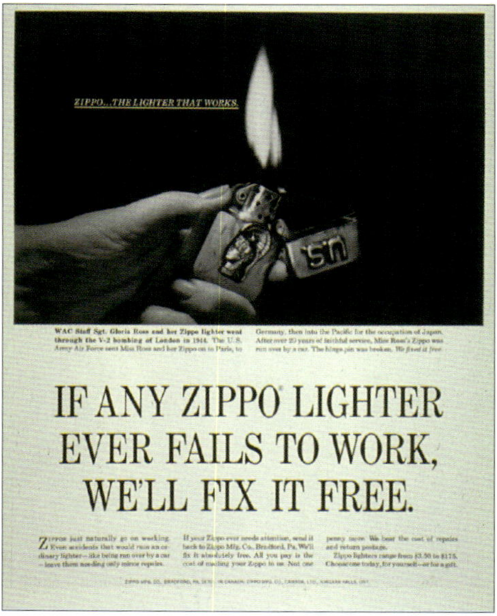

If any Zippo lighter ever fails to work, we'll fix it free. Advertisement placed in 1965, telling the story of WAC Staff Sgt. Gloria Ross and her Zippo lighter. Together they lived through the 'Baby Blitz' – the bombing of London in 1944 by V-2 rockets. Subsequently, the U.S. Army Air Force sent Miss Ross and her Zippo to Paris, to Germany, then into the Pacific for the occupation of Japan. After 20 years of faithful service, when Miss Ross's Zippo was run over by a car and the hinge broken, we fixed it free.

Bradford is currently repairing and returning roughly 1000 lighters every working day; and they keep a data base of all repairs done, by owner's name, for a two-year period. International repair departments also operate in Great Britain, Japan, Canada and several other countries. Many of Zippo's distributors worldwide keep stocks of replacement inside units. If a lighter has a damaged or broken hinge, or an insignia medallion has come off, these will be sent back to the main repair facility at Bradford; all more minor repairs can be carried out in the country of purchase.

Zippo lighters at the repair facility awaiting work. The notes from the owners are wrapped around the lighters. *Photos Avi Baer*

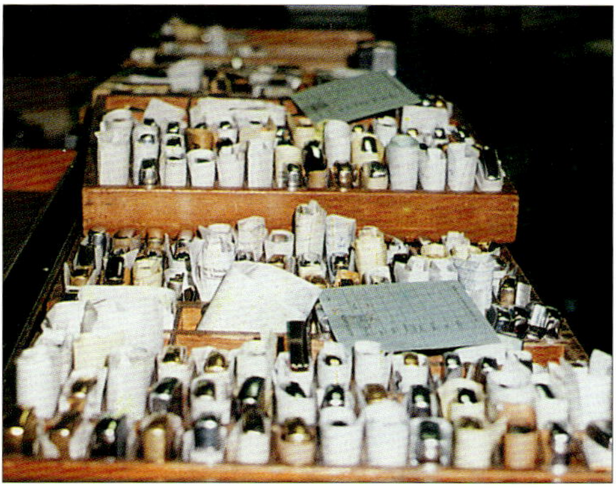

At the Repair Clinic all lighters go through a ten-stage process:

1 Open received parcel; wrap note from owner around lighter, and place in pigeonhole box.
2 Record owner's name and address and apparent problem in computer data base, and print a six digit bar code to identify the lighter.
3 Strip the lighter down into its component parts.
4 Drill out the hinge.
5 Clean the hinge area.
6 Weld on a new hinge.
7 Fit a new insert, and check the wheel and spark action. (New inserts are only fitted to vintage lighters on request; but when a vintage lighter comes in for repair Zippo often send back the repaired lighter with a new insert accompanying the old one.)
8 Reassemble the lighter.
9 Read the bar code, and print a mailing label.
10 Pack, label, and mail the lighter back to the owner.

Should you be sending your Zippo in for repair, please make life easier for the people at Bradford: detail the problem, include a return name and address, and never attempt to do your own repairs.

Many people still wonder how a company can continue offering a free service year after year; but Zippo believes it is the hallmark of their business – the necessary expenditure is not so much a cost to the company as an investment in future success. The hundreds and thousands of pounds weight of mail which pour into Bradford from flabbergasted customers expressing their thanks for the service would suggest that George Blaisdell was right all along.

THE PATENTS

The first patent for the Zippo lighter was applied for on 17 May 1934, and patent number 2032695 was granted on 3 March 1936. Prior to this the words PAT. PENDING were engraved on the bottom of the lighter. The patent was granted to Blaisdell and George Gimera as the inventors, and was registered to Zippo Manufacturing Company – a partnership consisting of George G. Blaisdell, W. G. Blaisdell, Frank W. Calkins, George Gimera, George B. Morris, and their heirs.

The details of their application noted that the lighters were simple in construction, single hand operated, windproof, held more fuel, and were easy to refill. The patent also noted that the lighters were designed in such a way as to have few protrusions, preserving clothing by avoiding snagging. The patent was to last 17 years from the date of the grant.

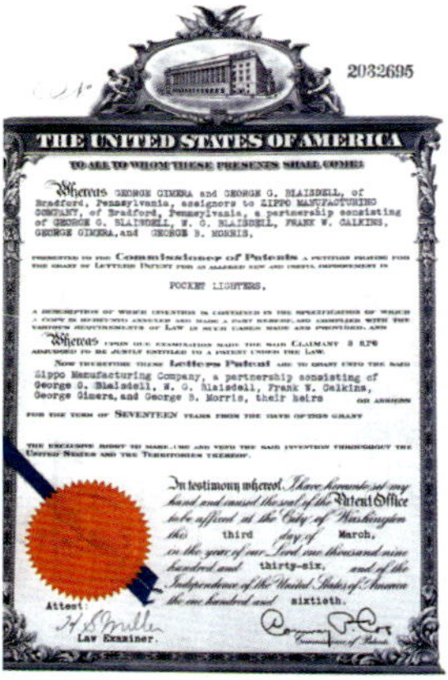

2032695

THE UNITED STATES OF AMERICA

Whereas GEORGE GIMERA and GEORGE G. BLAISDELL, of Bradford, Pennsylvania, assignors to ZIPPO MANUFACTURING COMPANY, of Bradford, Pennsylvania, a partnership consisting of GEORGE G. BLAISDELL, W. G. BLAISDELL, FRANK W. CALKINS, GEORGE GIMERA, and GEORGE B. MORRIS,

Commissioner of Patents

POCKET LIGHTERS.

Whereas

Letters Patent

Zippo Manufacturing Company, a partnership consisting of George G. Blaisdell, W. G. Blaisdell, Frank W. Calkins, George Gimera, and George B. Morris, their heirs

Seventeen

In testimony whereof I have hereunto set my hand and caused the seal of the Patent Office to be affixed at the City of Washington this third day of March, in the year of our Lord one thousand nine hundred and thirty-six, and of the Independence of the United States of America the one hundred and sixtieth.

Attest:

Law Examiner.

Commissioner of Patents.

Patent No. 2032695 granted to George G. Blaisdell and George Gimera as inventors of the Zippo Lighter, March 3, 1936.

Circa 1950 a new patent number, 2517191, was engraved on the bottom of the lighters. This patent, issued on 1 August 1950 and expiring on 1 August 1967, applied to the flint tube bushing. The

Detail views of the Zippo lighter (continued over)

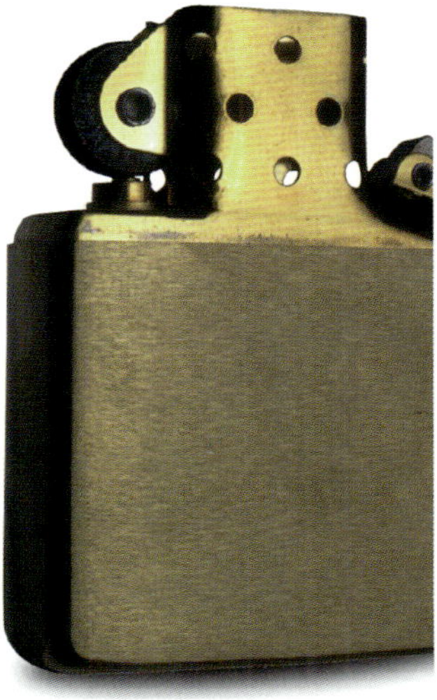

toothed wheel

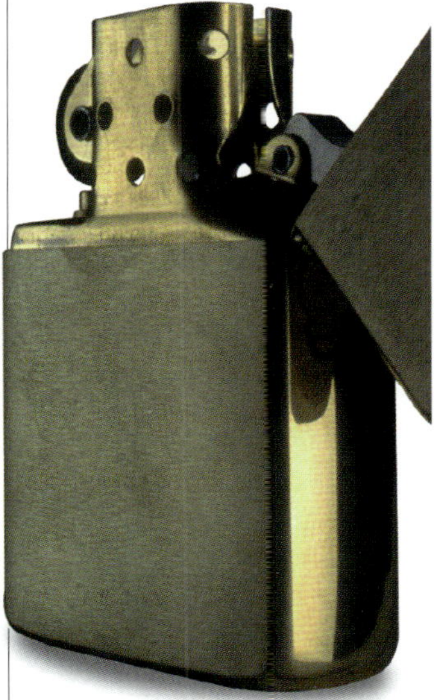

hinge and lever

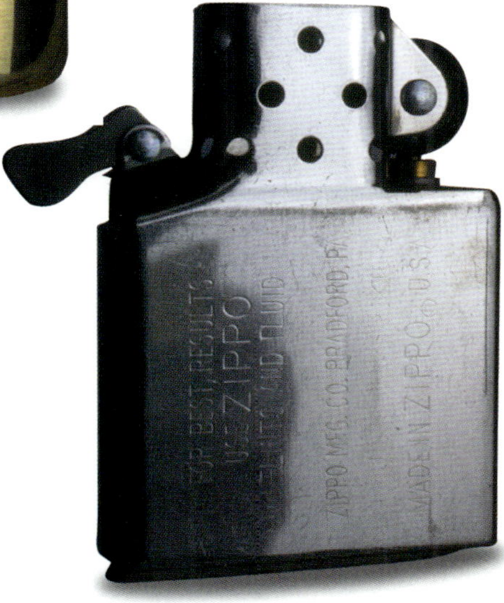

internal unit

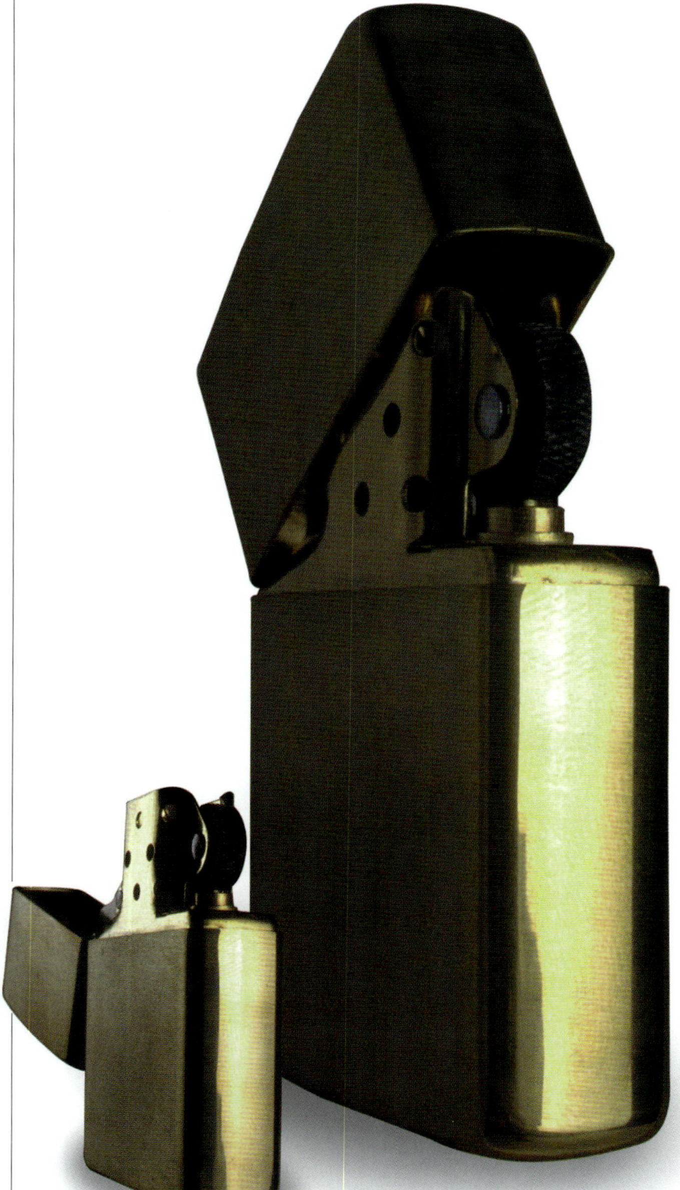

top closure

Patented Mar. 3, 1936

2,032,695
UNITED STATES PATENT OFFICE
2,032,695
POCKET LIGHTER

George Gimera and George G. Blaisdell, Bradford, Pa., assignors to Zippo Manufacturing Company, Bradford, Pa., a partnership consisting of George G. Blaisdell, W. G. Blaisdell, Frank W. Calkins, George Gimera, and George B. Morris

Application May 17, 1934, Serial No. 726,022
1 Claim. (Cl. 67-7.1)

This invention relates to pocket lighters of the hinged cover type. Pocket lighters having covers hinged on their upper ends must have means for holding them closed if they are to be satisfactory, and it is also desirable that they have means for preventing the covers from closing prematurely and extinguishing the flame after they are opened. In lighters known heretofore these means take the form of exposed latches and interior springs and levers which take up space in the lighters and reduce their storage capacity for inflammable lighter fluid. Furthermore, the exposed latches are apt to catch in and wear the clothing, to be accidentally actuated in the pocket, and to accumulate dirt. Such lighters are complex and frequently get out of order, while they must be constructed in a cheap manner in order to be saleable at a low price.

It is among the objects of this invention to provide a pocket lighter having a minimum of projections from its closed case, and in which movement of the cover from either its fully open or its fully closed position is restrained by simple means concealed when the lighter is closed.

Further objects are to provide such a lighter having large storage capacity for lighter fuel, which is easy to fill, is strong and durable, and is simple in design and construction with a minimum of moving parts.

The preferred embodiment of the invention is illustrated in the accompanying drawing, of which Figs. 1, 2 and 3 are, respectively, perspective, side and top views with the cover open; Fig. 4 is a central vertical section through the lighter with its cover closed; and Fig. 5 is a side view with the cover closed.

Referring to the drawing, a casing is provided consisting of two telescopically disposed hollow members, the inner member 1 being substantially coextensive with the outer member 2 and having a very snug sliding fit therewith. The outer member is closed at its lower end. The top plate 3 closes the upper end of inner member 1, which is preferably formed from a section of seamless tubing. This forms in the casing a reserervoir for inflammable lighter fuel, such as gasoline, which is carried by a stufiing of saturated cotton waste.

The upper edges of the side walls of the inner member are provided with upright integral extensions, the central position 4 of each having its sides curved inward over the top plate toward the opposite extension to form a generally elliptical wind screen in which a plurality of draft openings 6 are punched (Figs. 1 and 3). These curved sides are likewise provided with integral extensions on lugs 7 and 8 disposed in spaced parallel relation longitudinally of top plate 3.

In the front pair of lugs 7 there is journalled a toothed wheel 9 which engages the upper end of an elongate flint 11 slidably disposed in an opening through top plate 3. The flint is constantly held in frictional engagement with the toothed wheel by a coiled spring 12 (Fig. 4) compressed between the bottom of the flint and a set screw 13 threaded in the lower end of a tube 14 depending from top plate 3. The toothed wheel is adapted to throw sparks, when rotated by the thumb, from the flint to a wick 16 surrounded by the wind screen and projecting into the fuel reservoir through a hole in top plate 3.

In order to protect the projections at the top of the casing, as well as the clothing, the casing is provided with a cover 18 which is connected at its rear wall to the rear wall of outer telescoping member 2 by means of a small hinge 19. As will be observed in Fig. 5 of the drawing, there are no projections from the lighter other than this hinge when the cover is closed. However, as it is desirable that the cover remain closed except when the operator opens it, means is provided for accomplishing this object without exposing anything which might catch in and wear the pocket or be accidentally actuated.

Accordingly, a lever 21 is pivotally mounted at one end between the rear pair of lugs 8 so as that it can be swung from an upright position, as shown in Fig. 4, to a substantially horizontal position, as shown in Fig. 2, and vice versa. The lever resists movement from both its upright and horizontal position because its pivoted end is provided with a laterally projecting toe portion 22 which must depress a spring-biased plunger 23, slidably disposed in an opening through top plate 3, as the lever moves from one of said positions to the other. The spring 24, which biases the plunger against the pivoted end of the lever radially of its pivot axis, is compressed between the bottom of the plunger and the lower end of a closed tube 26 secured in the inner telescoping member 1. When the lever is substantially upright the pressure of the plunger against the under side of toe 22 biases the lever toward the wind screen (Fig. 4).

When the cover is closed it is held in that position by the upright lever bearing against the rear side of a cross member 27 secured in the cover transversely

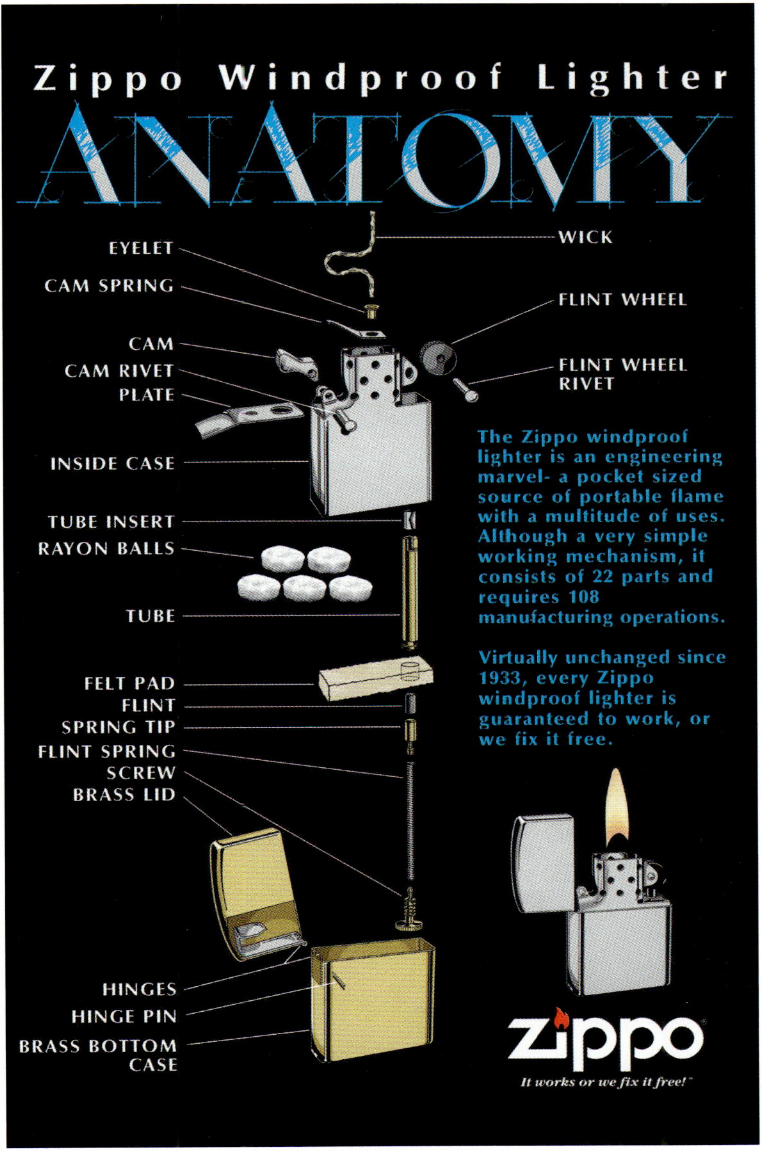

Anatomy of a Zippo.

flint tube, made of brass or copper for resistance to rust, originally caused pressure on the wheel which resulted in stiffness; the new design, covering the top of the flint bushing with solid metal, eradicated this flaw.

After this patent expired on 1 August 1967 the patent number was replaced by the ringed R, except for lighters from the vintage series which still carry the patent number 2032695 and the current date codes for the year of manufacture.

The ringed R denotes that the name Zippo is a registered trade mark; the registration took place within the United States Patent Office on 21 February 1946, under the serial number 436 615.

Zippo applied for a number of other patents as the years went by. In 1953 an application was made to register a patent on the new Zippo flint dispenser, which was granted under number 2,645,335 on 14 July 1953; this illustrated a dispenser holding four flints in a line for ease of insertion into the lighter. The patent registered to Zippo Manufacturing Company listed Walter R. Avis as the inventor.

In 1955 Zippo designed a flame guard for the flint wheel, to prevent carbon deposits from getting onto the wheel. While this guard was not immediately used, a similar device was implemented in the production of the 'slim model' from 1956

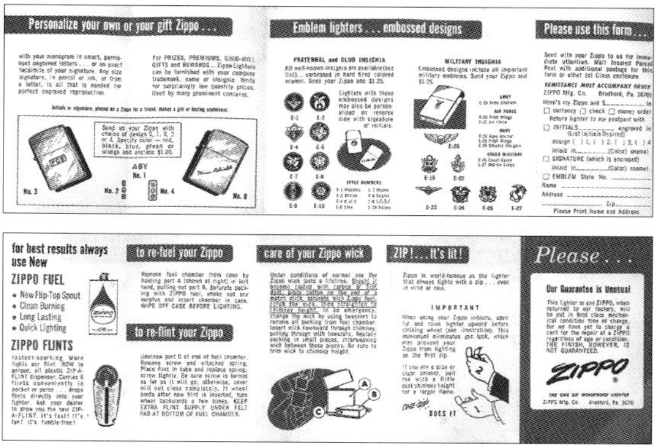

1960s' Zippo lighter insert depicting instructions as well as the newly patented Zippo flint dispenser.

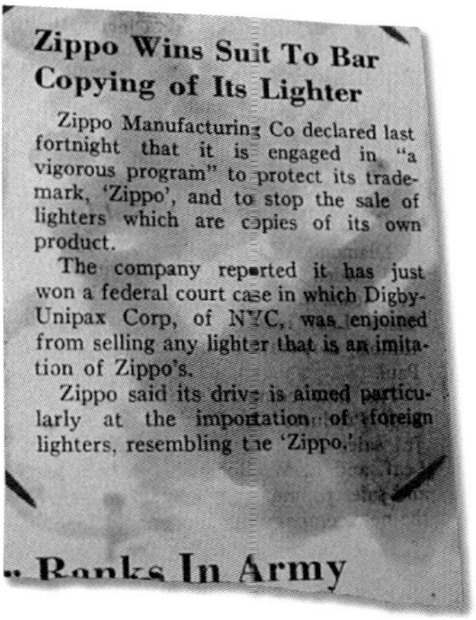

Zippo Wins Suit To Bar Copying of Its Lighter

Zippo Manufacturing Co declared last fortnight that it is engaged in "a vigorous program" to protect its trade-mark, 'Zippo', and to stop the sale of lighters which are copies of its own product.

The company reported it has just won a federal court case in which Digby-Unipax Corp., of NYC, was enjoined from selling any lighter that is an imitation of Zippo's.

Zippo said its drive is aimed particularly at the importation of foreign lighters, resembling the 'Zippo.'

.. Ranks In Army

Newspaper cutting found in the Zippo archives telling of Zippo's hardline attitude with respect to imitation. Even today Zippo will take strong action against a patent or trademark infringement.
Photo A. R. Baer

to 1957.

The patent, number 2,704,447, was granted on 22 March 1955 and named Lester Flickinger and William L. Pierotti as the inventors.

On 20 August 1957 patent number 2,803,123 was granted to the company for additions to the lighters' overall design with respect to the refuelling area; these enhancements, invented by George W. Owen, prevented fuel leakage but were not added to the Zippo lighter production.

In 1959 Zippo came out with a unique design for their flint dispenser, preventing flints from breaking or getting lost and further easing the exchange from dispenser to lighter. Application for a patent was made on 6 October 1953 and it was granted on 24 March 1959, again naming Walter R. Avis as inventor. This enhancement was, also, not implemented to the production of the lighter.

Over many years Zippo has been careful to patent not only all their developments but their trademarks as well. This has been essential in rooting out those companies in various countries which persist in stealing and reproducing features of the patented lighters in 'lookalike' fake Zippos. While to those who have owned and cherished Zippo lighters it is very easy to tell the real thing from the fake, many people do not know the difference. Thanks to the Zippo Manufacturing Company's policy and efforts in respect of patent protection, people all over the world can still be confident of enjoying an authentic Zippo lighter.

CHAPTER 4

ZIPPO IN WORLD WAR II

The sweeping changes which affected the whole nation upon the entry of the United States into World War II brought initial difficulties for Zippo, but also, at last, truly worldwide recognition.

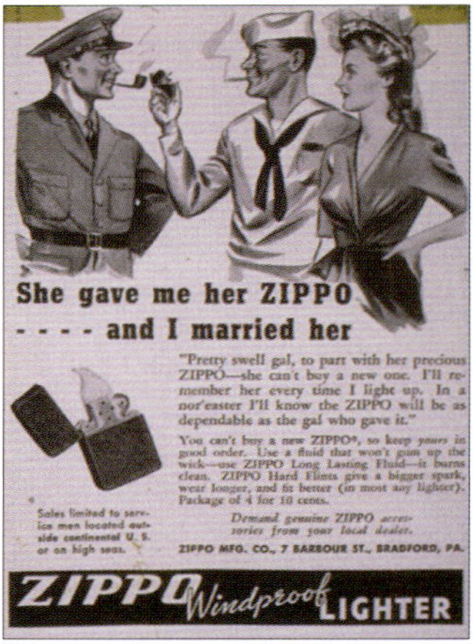

Zippo advertisement placed in *Esquire* in 1943, showing men going off to war and getting the gift of a Zippo. *Zippo Manufacturing Co.*

Brass was now a strategic material needed for the war effort in huge quantities – for one thing, it was used for making all the hundreds of millions of shell and cartridge cases needed by the armed services. Accordingly, Zippo changed their case from brass to steel. In an effort to protect the case from corrosion it received a black paint finish which, when baked, gave a 'crackle' effect. Zippo did draw the steel lighter cases, but subcontracted a local company which had the relevant facilities. During the war they would receive letters from GIs actually praising the dull black finish for its non-reflective qualities in the field. This, and plain steel, were the only base models manufactured during World War II.

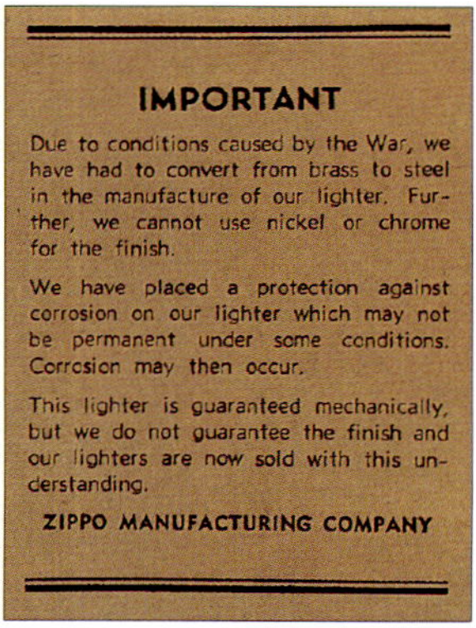

IMPORTANT

Due to conditions caused by the War, we have had to convert from brass to steel in the manufacture of our lighter. Further, we cannot use nickel or chrome for the finish.

We have placed a protection against corrosion on our lighter which may not be permanent under some conditions. Corrosion may then occur.

This lighter is guaranteed mechanically, but we do not guarantee the finish and our lighters are now sold with this understanding.

ZIPPO MANUFACTURING COMPANY

Wartime advertisement, pointing out the lack of brass needed to make the standard Zippo lighter.

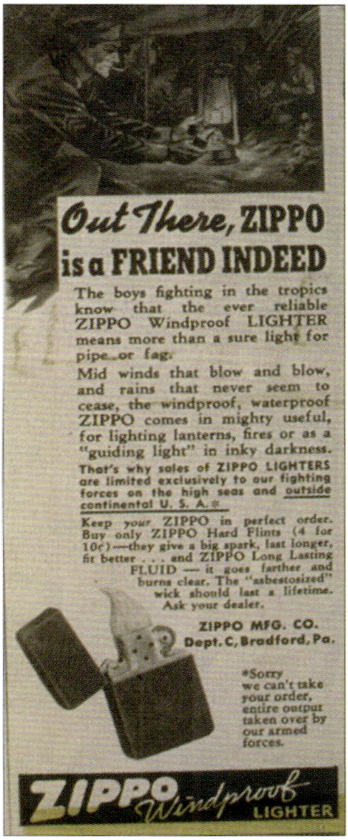

"Out There a Friend Indeed . . ." An advertisement during the war years, emphasizing that the boys out in the tropics could count on a Zippo lighter never to let them down. At bottom right is a note of apology to civilian would-be customers stating that all Zippo production has been taken up for the armed forces.

In 1943 the four-barrel hinge previously attaching the lid to the lower case was replaced by a three-barrel hinge.

Although the Zippo was not officially adopted by the armed forces, Blaisdell shipped thousands of the lighters to many Post Exchanges (PXs). Soon there were hundreds of thousands of men and women in training camps all over the U.S., and when Zippos arrived in the PXs they sold out fast. When the troops were shipped overseas they took their Zippos with them and those without them soon found that they could purchase the lighters in their overseas staging camps.

The demand for Zippos among the armed forces became so great that Zippo Manufacturing's entire production was earmarked for military personnel and they became unobtainable by civilians at home. Indeed, eventually the Zippo was only supplied to overseas Post Exchanges.

Given this level of demand it is hardly surprising that fake Zippos began to appear during the war years. Zippo Manufacturing vigorously opposed the introduction of these fakes to the American market, stressing that only the genuine article had the correct feeling of weight in the hand, and made the distinctive Zippo 'clink-clop' — which has become known today simply as the 'Zippo click'.

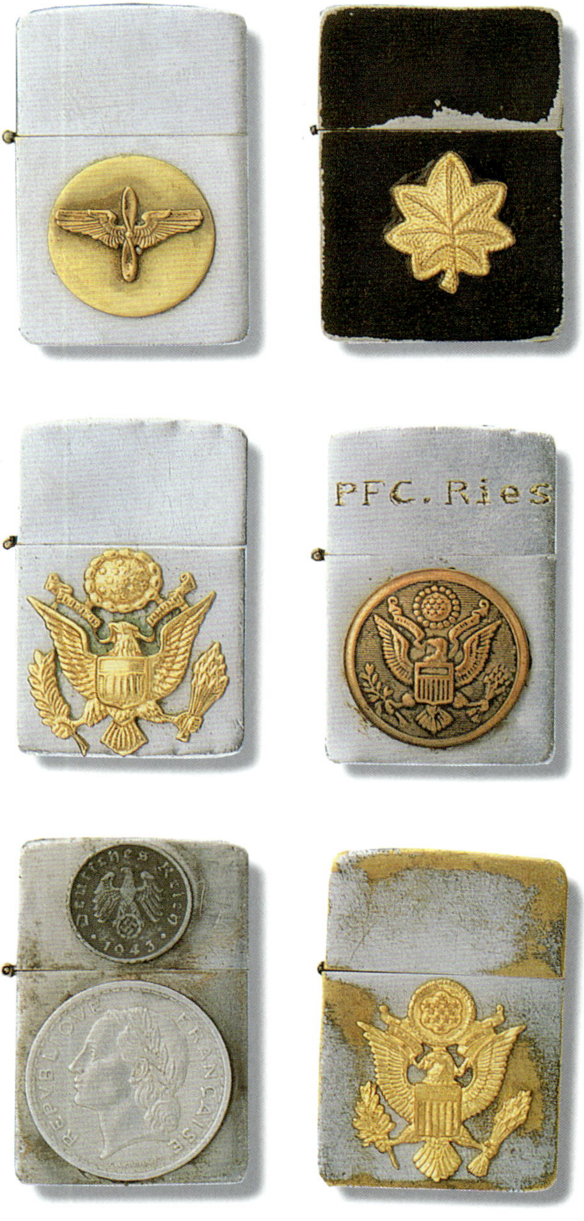

Personalized Zippos from World War II.

In 1942 total sales of the lighter since its introduction ten years previously reached one million units. From then onwards the rate of sales would increase enormously, several million being sold before the end of the war.

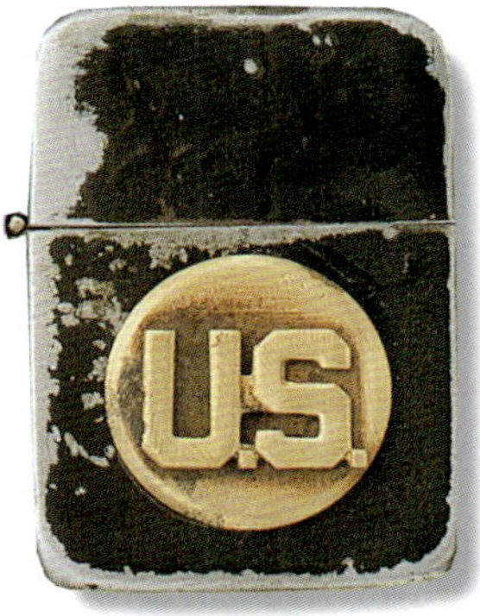

Despite the limitations imposed by availability of materials, Zippo offered nine different designs for sale in the 'crackle' and plain steel finishes:

1 Plain
2 Monograms
3 Replica of owner's signature
4 Crossed rifles
5 Army eagle emblem
6 Crossed rifles on one side, monogram on the other
7 Crossed rifles on one side, signature replica on the other
8 Army eagle on one side, signature replica on the other
9 Army eagle on one side, monogram on the other

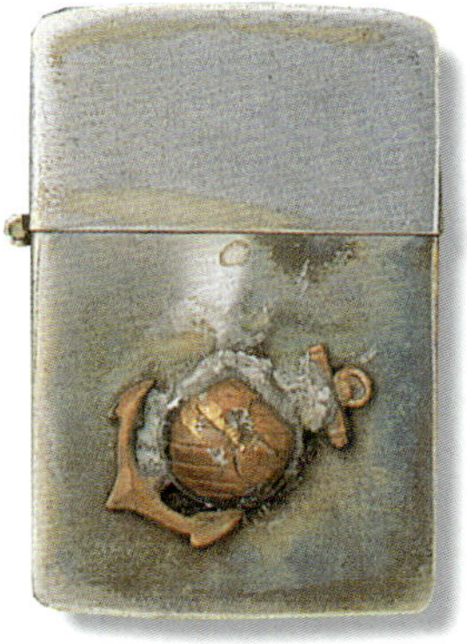

Zippo also offered the option of attaching regimental coats of arms to lighters ordered by Post Exchanges. Moreover, GIs themselves soon began to personalize their lighters with initials, military emblems, or the names of wives and sweethearts, added by unit craftsmen or civilian jewelers where ever they found themselves serving.

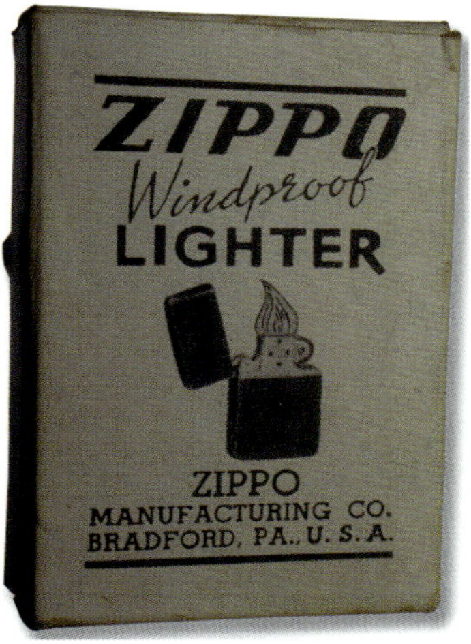

Gift box used between 1942 and 1946. Many Zippos were delivered to the armed forces soaked in protective oil.

These individual touches embellished their constant and reliable companion, which men and women carried with them and handled many times a day, in battle and out, lending them a special sentimental value. Today many veterans proudly display their old Zippos in cabinets with the rest of their wartime memorabilia.

The literally millions of Zippos used by members of the U.S. ground, air, and naval forces became familiar and envied among the populations of the foreign countries where they served in Europe, Asia, and Africa. This tremendous exposure — in the hands of those who were mostly welcomed as comrades and liberators, and at a period when all U.S. military gear was widely admired for its novelty and quality — was almost certainly the basis of Zippo's future success in the export of

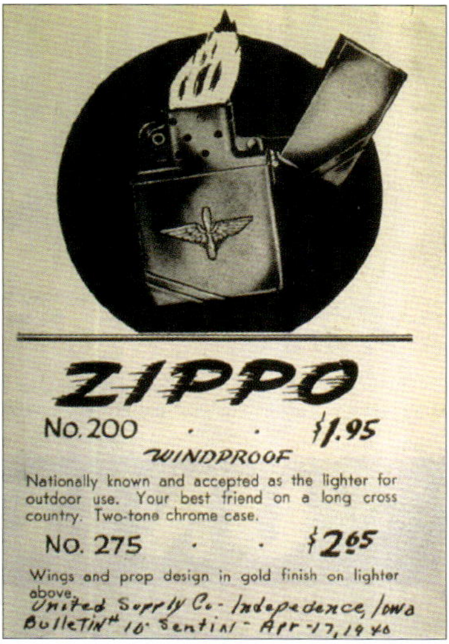

'Your best friend on a long cross-country' a 1940 advert aimed at the military.

these classic lighters. Many soldiers, airmen, sailors, and marines who fought side by side with foreign allies gave away lighters as gifts to mark these new friendships forged in battle. The Zippo became a coveted American icon, eagerly sought after as a gift, trade item, or outright purchase.

The mutual regard shared by George Blaisdell of Zippo and the famous war correspondent Ernie Pyle helped to spread the lighter's fame and popularity.

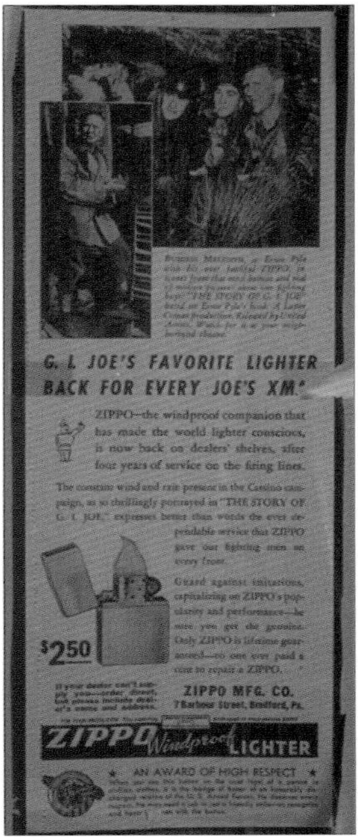

'G.I. Joe's favorite lighter.' Another wartime advertisement.

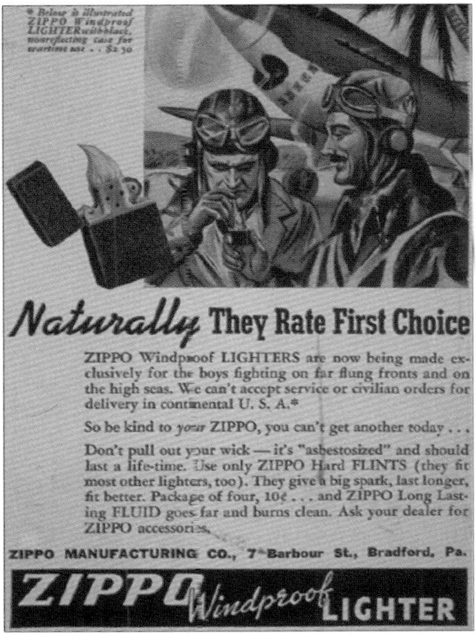

'Naturally they rate first choice.' By 1943 Zippo advertised that orders could not be accepted — from serviceman or civilian — from the Continrental U.S.

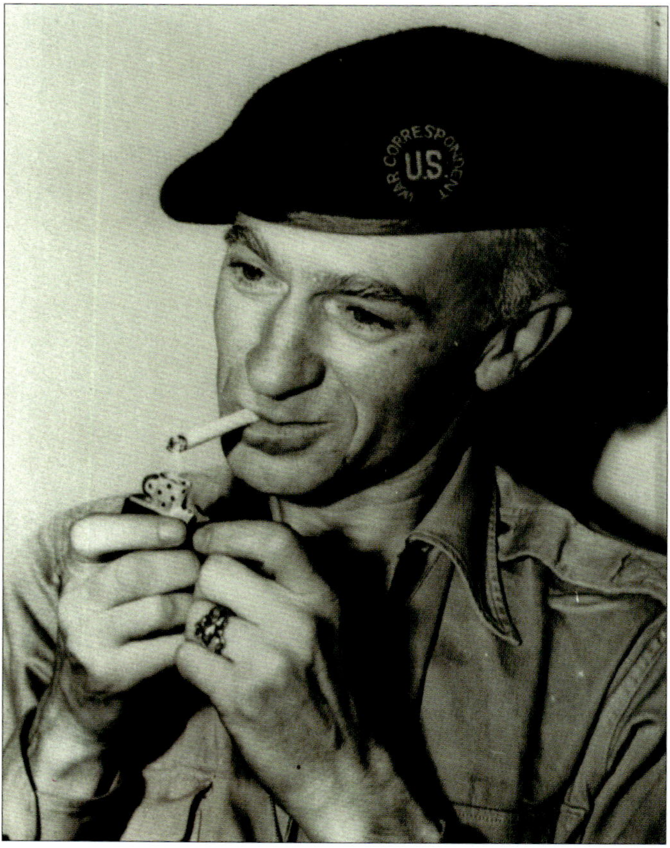

Ernie Pyle, famous wartime correspondent, who wrote about the Zippo lighter in many of his columns. Indeed, the title 'Mr. Zippo' — synonymous with George Blaisdell — was coined by Pyle. Here he is pictured with his faithful Zippo.

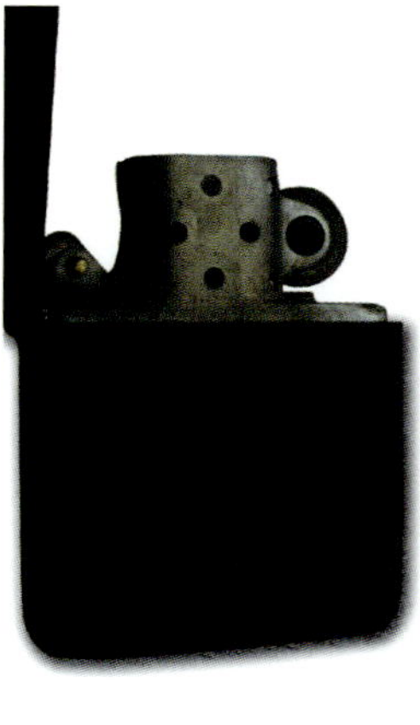

World War II black 'Crackle' lighter.

ERNIE PYLE

Ernie Pyle was the 'GI's correspondent,' he wrote of the daily lives of the ordinary troops in their own language, and he accompanied them in action, so his despatches were trusted for their authenticity. The novelist John Steinbeck (also a correspondent in World War II) had this to say of him during the Tunisian campaign:

'There are really two wars and they haven't much to do with each other. There is a war of maps and logistics, of campaigns, of ballistics, armies, divisions and regiments — and that is General [George C.] Marshall's war. Then there is the war of the homesick, weary, funny, violent, common men who wash their socks in their helmets, complain about the food, whistle at the Arab girls, or any girls for that matter, and bring themselves through as dirty a business as the world has ever seen and do it with humor and dignity and courage – and that is Ernie Pyle's war.'

When Ernie Pyle received a fan letter from George Blaisdell it represented the start of a long and close association by correspondence. The title 'Mr. Zippo' was coined by Pyle in his daily column — a name that has become synonymous with George Blaisdell. Between April and May of 1944 Pyle was in Great Britain, and in his despatch entitled This England he wrote:

'The Zippo Manufacturing Company, of Bradford, Pennsylvania, makes Zippo cigarette lighters. In peacetime they are nickel-plated and shiny. In wartime they are black, with a rough finish. Zippos are not available at all to civilians. In army PXs all around the world, where a batch comes in occasionally, there are long waiting lists.

While I was in Italy I had a letter from the president of the Zippo Company. It seems he is devoted to my column. It seems further that he'd had an idea. He had sent to our headquarters in Washington to get my signature, and then he was having the signature engraved on a special nickel-plated lighter and was going to send it to me as a gift.

Pretty soon there was another letter. The president of the

Zippo Company had had another brainstorm. In addition to my superheterodyne lighter he was going to send 50 of the regular ones for me to give to friends. I was amused by the modesty of the president's letter. He said, 'You probably know nothing about the Zippo lighter.' If he only knew how the soldiers coveted them! They'll burn in the wind, and pilots say they are the only kind that will light at extreme altitudes. Why, they're so popular I had three of them stolen from me in one year.

Well, at last the lighters came, forwarded all the way from Italy. My own lighter was a beauty, with my name on

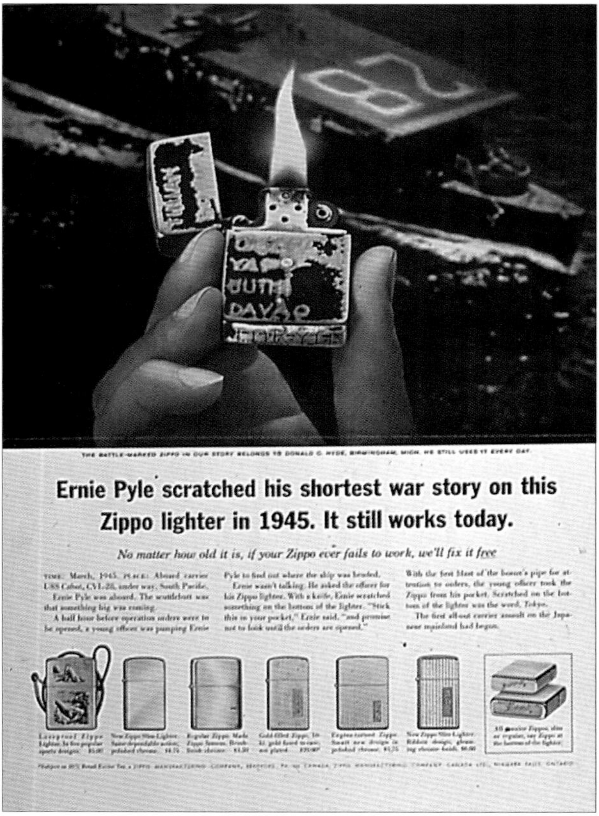

Zippo made use of Ernie Pyle's 'Tokyo' story in advertising.

one side and a little American flag on the other. I began smoking twice as much just because I enjoyed lighting the thing. The 50 others went like hot cakes. I found myself equipped with a wonderful weapon for winning friends and influencing people. All 51 of us are grateful to Mr.Zippo.'

Perhaps Pyle's shortest and best-known story was written on board the aircraft carrier U.S.S. *Cabot* in the South Pacific. So engaging was this story that Zippo decided to use it in an advertisement in 1961; the text read as follows:

'Time: March, 1945. Place: Aboard carrier U.S.S. *Cabot*, CVL-28, under way South Pacific. Ernie Pyle was aboard. The scuttlebutt from galley to bridge was that something big was coming. A half hour before the operation orders were to be opened, a young lieutenant was pumping Ernie Pyle to find out where the ship was headed. Ernie wasn't talking. He asked the officer for his Zippo lighter. With a knife, Ernie scratched something on the bottom of the lighter. "Stick this in your pocket," Ernie said, "and promise not to look until the orders are opened." With the first blast of the bosun's pipe for attention to orders, the young officer took the Zippo from his pocket. Scratched on the bottom of the lighter was the word TOKYO. The first all-out carrier assault on the Japanese mainland had begun.'

Ernie Pyle was killed by Japanese machine gun fire on

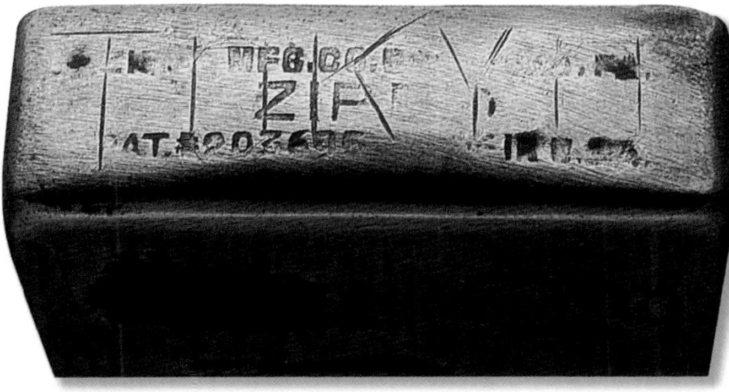

The lighter on which war correspondent Ernie Pyle scratched 'TOKYO' while aboard the carrier U.S.S. *Cabot* in the Pacific, March 1945.

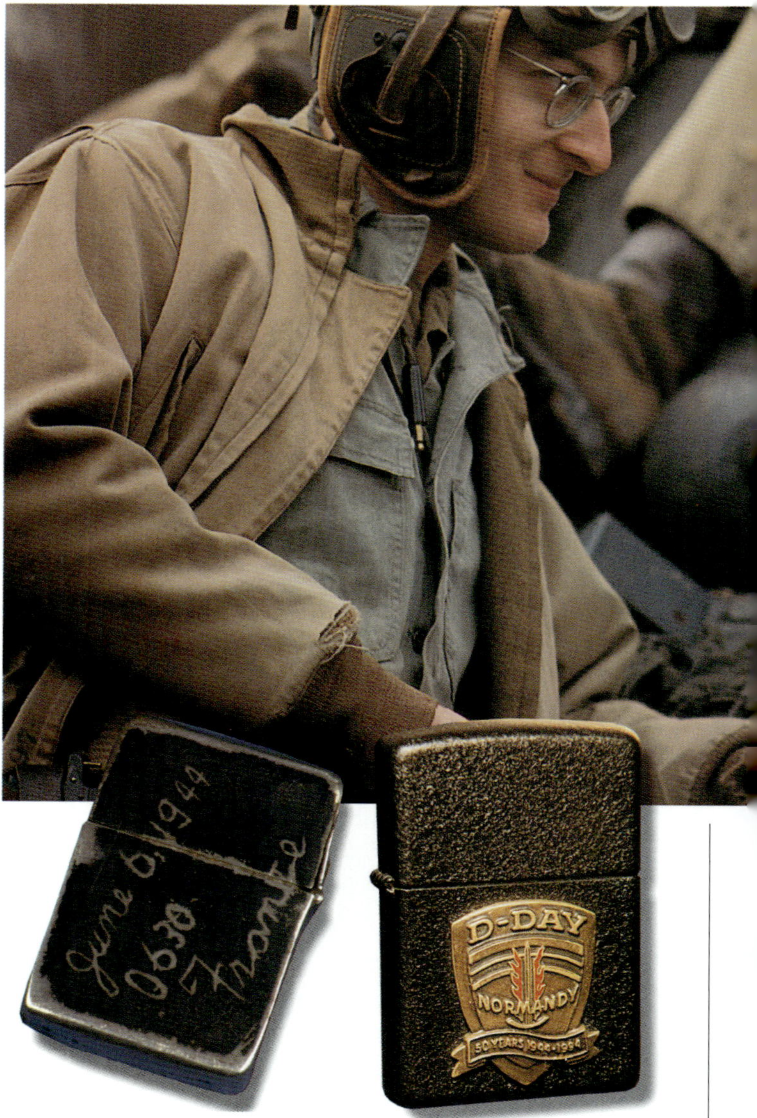

With the time, date and location — 'June 6, 1944, 0630, France' — scratched into its black crackle covering, this Zippo is a real D-Day memento.

50 years later, in 1994, Zippo produced an excellent D-Day anniversary lighter.
Photo A. R. Baer

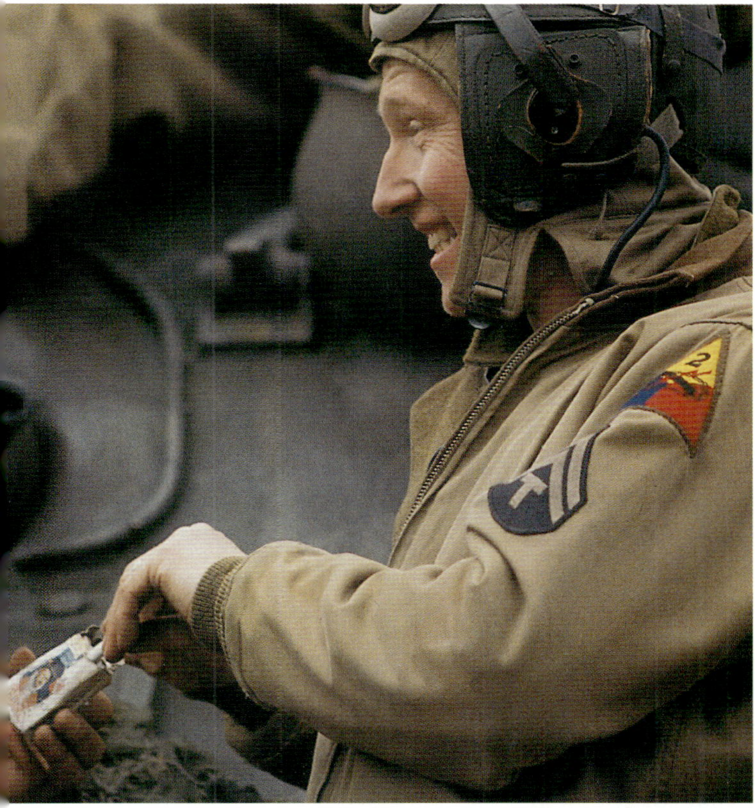

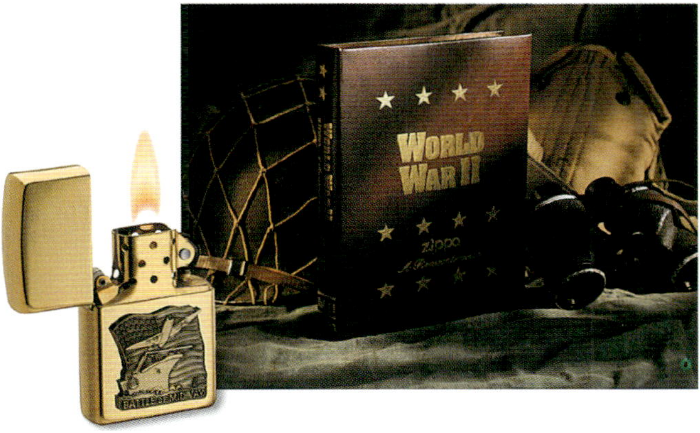

World War II commemorative presentation pack.

Ie-jima while covering the battle for Okinawa the following month. The soldiers erected a plaque reading: 'At this spot the 77th Infantry Division lost a Buddy, Ernie Pyle, 18 April 1945.' George Blaisdell arranged for engraved Zippos to be given as gifts in his memory to the crew of the U.S.S. *Cabot.*

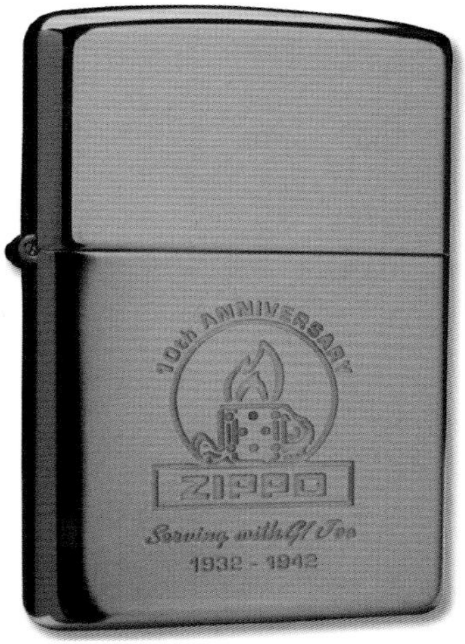

Replica of the 10th Anniversary issue – 'Serving with GI Joe'.

Soldiers, sailors, and airmen discovered new uses for their Zippos depending upon the situations in which they found themselves. There are stories of Zippos being used to heat soup in GI helmets, to warm freezing hands in winter, as beacons to attract rescuers to rafts adrift on the ocean at night, and to throw light on a pilot's damaged instrument panel as he struggled to return to base after dark. Among George Blaisdell's most treasured mementoes were three badly damaged Zippos given to him by war veterans who claimed that their lives had been saved when bullets which would have killed them struck the steel-cased lighters in their pockets.

World War II was undoubtedly the moment in history which saw the Zippo's popularity spread all over the world. The fact that Blaisdell was far-sighted enough to make sure that his lighters got into the PXs would not alone have been sufficient reason for their popularity. The soldiers loved them and looked after them as carefully as they did their guns, because the Zippo worked; it never let them down, and even when it ran out of fuel a few drops of gasoline would rekindle the flame. A soldier's Zippo was part of his life.

CHAPTER 5

ZIPPO GAINS MOMENTUM

In the post-war years, Zippo took off like the proverbial rocket. Fuelled by demand in Europe and a Zippo-starved USA, this was a period of innovation and expansion.

A major change took place in 1946 when all shipments of the Zippo lighter were put on hold, after George Blaisdell decided that the striking wheel in the Zippo lighter — manufactured by an outside source — was not up to his exacting standards. After consultation with metallurgists, experimentation with numerous types of steel, and many and various manufacturing operations, a new striking wheel was developed. It was and still is, arguably the best striking wheel in the world, and is manufactured in-house to specifications that are a company secret.

After the war brass became available again and the black crackle finish of the wartime lighter was replaced with nickel silver. The bottom of the case, previously flat, was now indented in a can style.

The year 1947 saw another milestone in Zippo's advance in the market. The ten millionth Zippo was produced, only nine years after the first million in 1942. 1949 also saw the introduction of the 'Town and Country' series of designs, featuring a pheasant, mallard, geese, sailboat, lily pond, trout, setter, and horse, using a new process consisting of

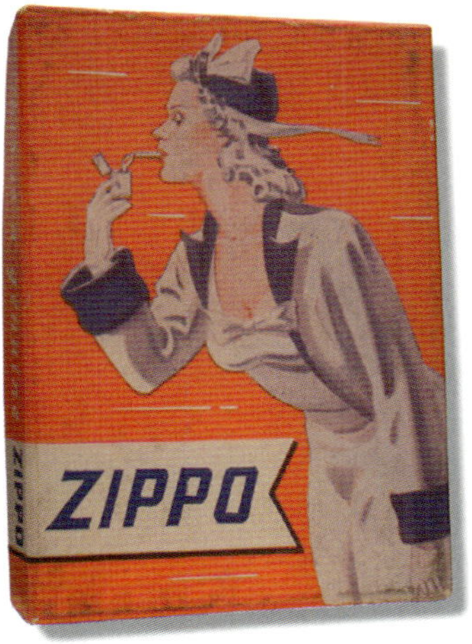

Zippo boxes were used only for a very short time, and hence are very rare. This one dates back to 1946.

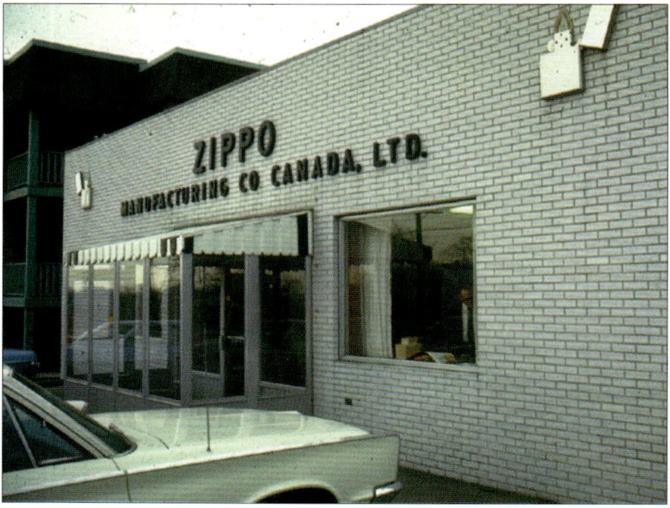

The Zippo plant in Niagara Falls, Ontario, Canada,
as it used to look.

engraving, airbrushing, and other special techniques.

In 1949 Zippo established a manufacturing plant outside the United States — Zippo Manufacturing Company, Canada, Ltd. It operated from Niagara Falls, Ontario, under the leadership of Richard Barber, a vice president of the company. The subsidiary was started for tax avoidance reasons — by manufacturing in Canada, high import duties could be avoided. Many first-time collectors of Zippos become

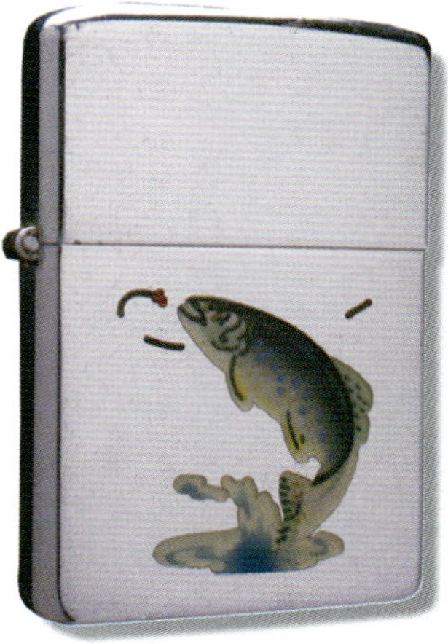

Town and Country series Zippo
with Trout design. This lighter was
introduced in 1949.

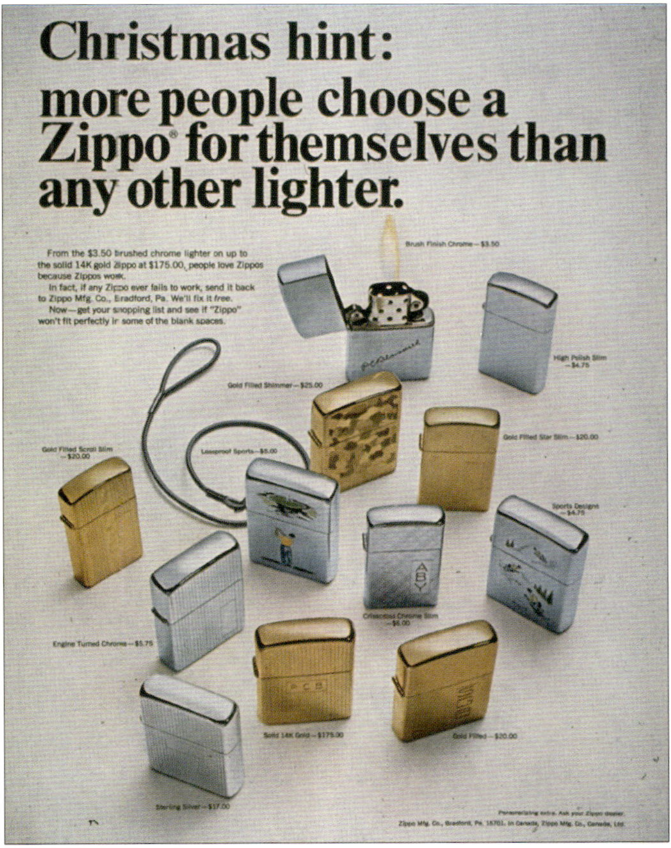

Christmas was a main sales period for Zippo as these two advertisments show. Here (Below) the original Christmas leaflet introduced in 1936: it was used until 1940. A later advertisement (Above) shows an assortment of lighters including a 'Loss-Proof' model with a lanyard.

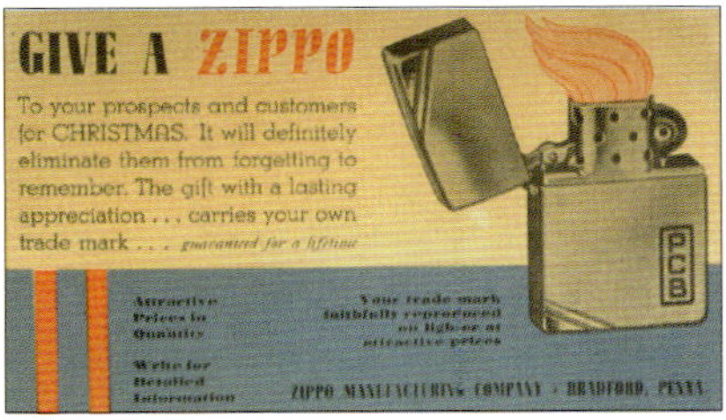

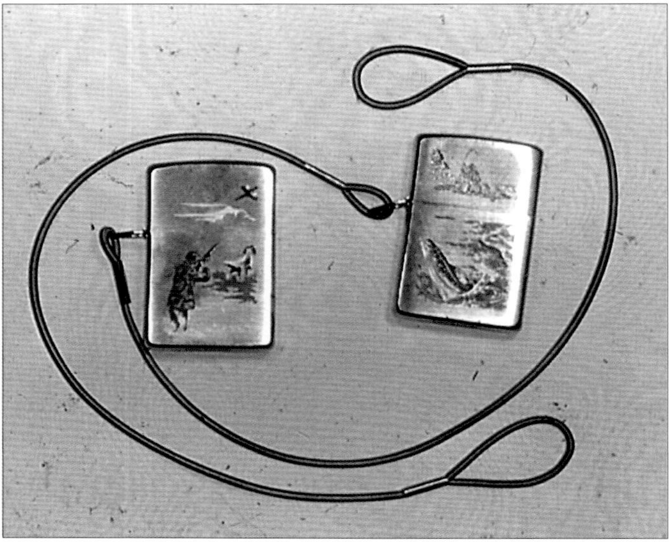

Two early examples of the Loss-Proof lighter
with Town and Country designs.

very confused when they see a Zippo with 'Niagara Falls Ontario Canada' etched into the base. In comparison to the output of the Bradford plant, few are made in Canada, but these lighters do exist.

The following year, 1950, ushered in changes to the Zippo sales force, taking it from a two-man cigar salesmen operation, to a true sales force. Directed by Blaisdell, there were managers for designated districts appointed around the US.

The Loss-Proof Lighter made its first appearance in 1948, under the name 'Loop Lighter.' It had a U-ring attached to the hinge pin which permitted users to attach chains or leather thongs to the lighter, so that it could be threaded on to a belt loop, or worn like a necklace pendant. The lighter was renamed 'Tach-A-Loop' in 1949, and the U-loop was replaced by a V-loop all-in-one with the hinge pin.

In 1955 there was another renaming, and the lighter appeared as the 'Loss-Proof Zippo,' and had a lanyard attached

A fine example of the leather-bound Zippo (priced at $6.00) manufactured only in 1950 and early 1951.

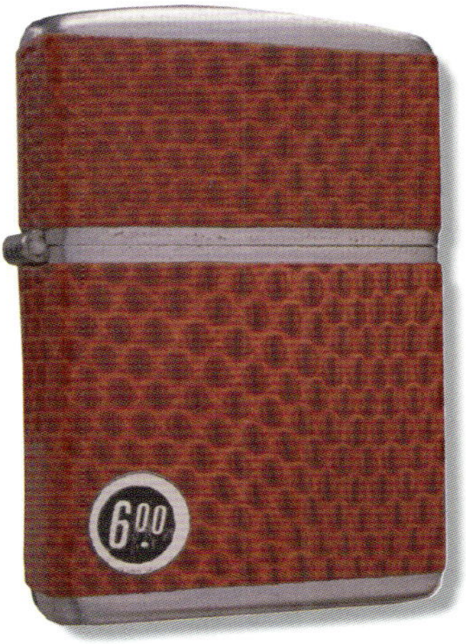

to the ring. This lanyard was replaced by an elastic one in 1957, and became the 'New' Loss-Proof Lighter.' Small changes were made in 1962 to the size of the ring (smaller), and the color of the lanyard (gray), and again in 1991 when the lanyard was made black. Many Loss-Proof lighters are decorated with sports series designs, and are much sought after collectibles.

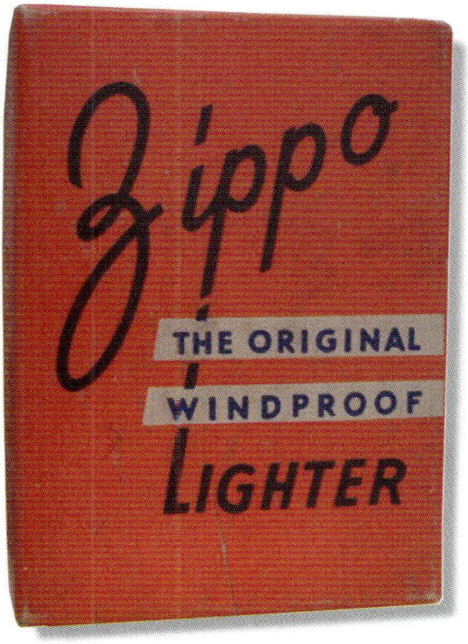

From 1947 through 1951, Zippos came in a box like this one.

1950 saw the introduction of the leather-bound Zippo with gold foiling. This lighter was only made in 1950 and early 1951, and used inside units manufactured in 1947. They were made of calfskin or Moroccan grain leather and are highly sought after by Zippo collectors worldwide. Two styles were available. The first had leather all around the lighter including the base, with the Zippo logo set in gold foil on the base of the

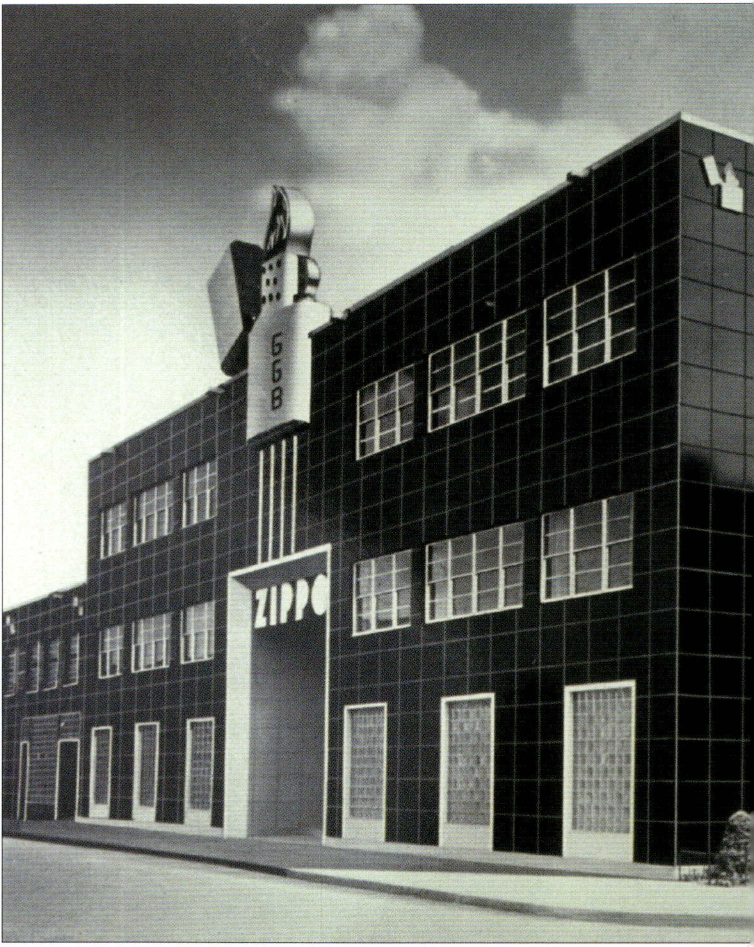

lighter. Gold foiling was also used to create a decorative border on the face of the lighter. The later style, the leather wrap lighter, only had the leather going around the bottom and the top of the lighter like a loop. As these lighters had their bases exposed, it was very easy to determine their date of manufacture.

While Zippo may have started in a $10 a month room over a service station in the early 1930s, it certainly expanded

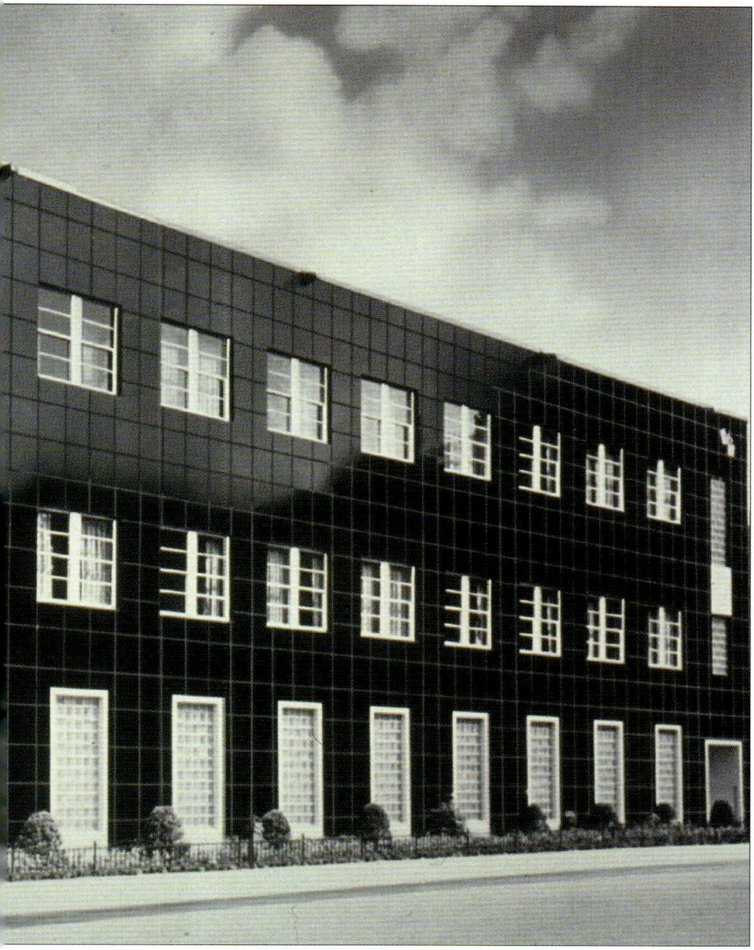

Zippo headquarters photographed in 1955. The impressive half-block long building on Barbour Street was finished in black Carrara glass. This building, although modernized, today still attracts hundreds of visitors every year.

all over Bradford in the years to come. In 1938 Blaisdell purchased an automobile shop at 36 Barbour Street. This was the first property owned by Zippo and was to become —

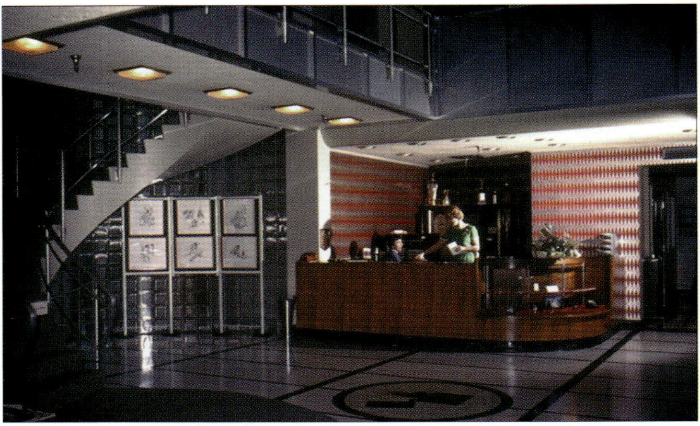
The lobby of the newly erected Zippo headquarters in 1955.

until 1955—Zippo's corporate office and production facility as well as administration office. Ongoing success into the 1950s allowed Zippo to build a new headquarters across the street from this facility in 1955.

The new, ultramodern, building became the talk of Bradford – it was furnished and decorated at a cost in excess of $800,000 and was truly a showpiece A huge Zippo lighter dominated the entrance of the building and the lobby with its curvaceous staircase, was more than two stories high. The entire building was airy and boasted a unique design in the cement beneath the staircase – the hand prints of the founder and his immediate family cast in an oval around the date (also inlaid) of 1955. Also around this time the company erected the famous neon sign that can be seen at night for miles around Bradford. It shows a flaming Zippo and the words 'They Work' – symbols that are still the basis of Zippo's marketing image today.

At the same time as Zippo moved into its new headquarters, the Fuel Products Division moved into the newly vacated old building.

Zippo has always tried to ensure that the presentation of their lighters was to the highest standards and because of this

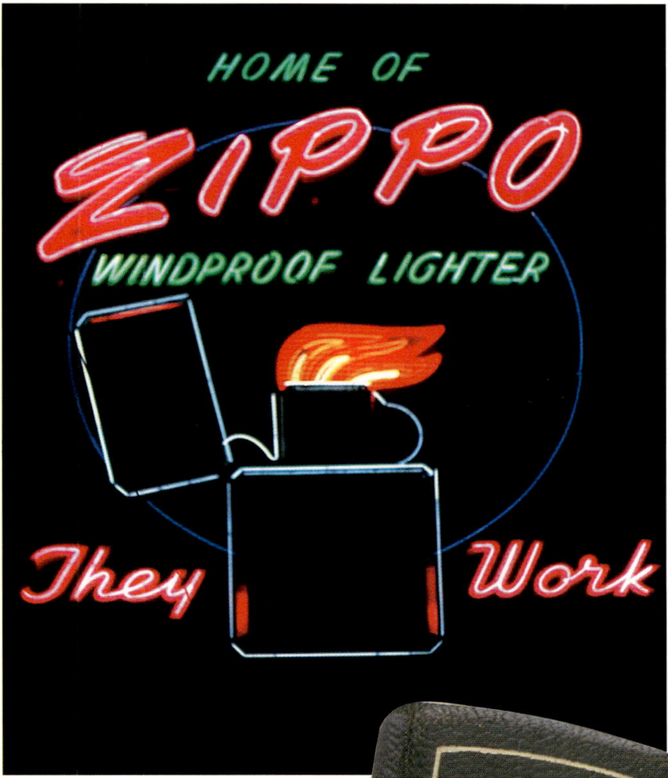

The famous neon Zippo sign which stands on the roof of Zippo's headquarters on Barbour Street in Bradford, PA. The sign at night is a fixture of Main Street.

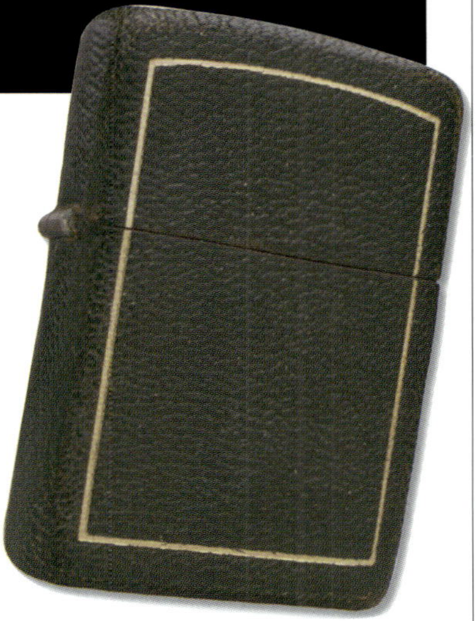

Original leather-bound Zippo from 1950. Note that the leather goes over the top and base of the lighter.

Zippos are beautifully packaged. The gift boxes that became popular in the late 1930s are a Zippo tradition that has lasted until today, and you can still be assured of a nice presentation box, tin, or package, when you buy a Zippo. In the 1950s the 'Town and Country' lighters were presented in a natural finished cardboard box, and the Christmas stock was always sold with a festive Christmas ribbon. All lighters are still sold with detailed instructions on use and care, along with the lifetime guarantee.

TABLE LIGHTERS

The Barcroft 10 table lighter, introduced in 1938 was discontinued in 1941. A slightly shorter version was introduced in 1947 Originally called the Number 10, the lighter was renamed the Deluxe All-Purpose Table Lighter and priced at $10.

The second Barcroft table lighter was introduced in 1950. This model had a two-tier base and its overall height was reduced by a quarter of an inch. While it still had a very large fuel capacity, it also had a storage area in the bottom of the lighter for an extra wick. The top of the lighter was very

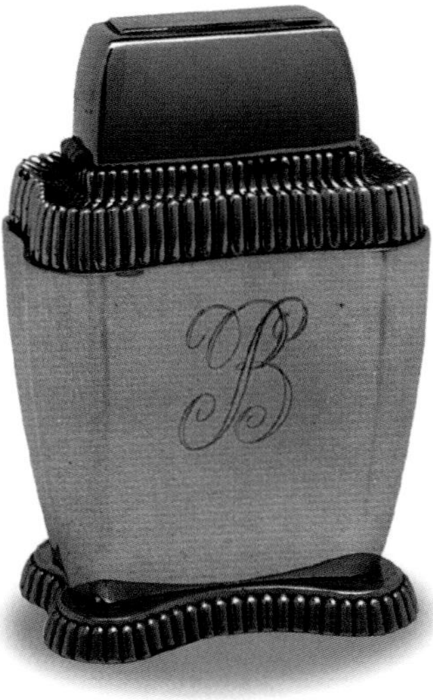

The Lady Bradford Table Lighter. This was George G. Blaisdell's personal lighter; it remained on his desk since its introduction in 1949.

Promotional photograph of the first Lady Bradford, without a base.

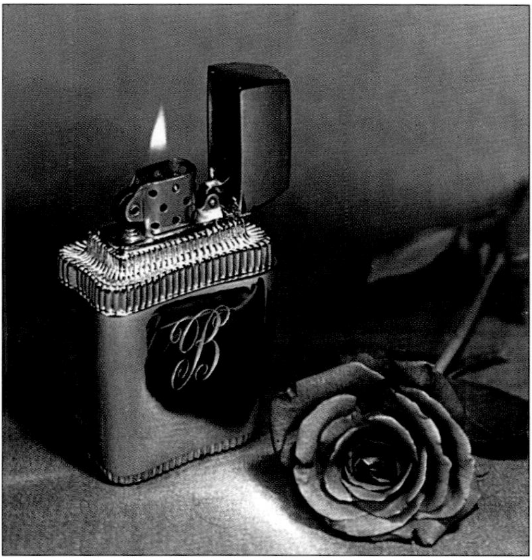

wide (almost twice the size of a regular Zippo), and used one large hinge. The name Zippo was placed on the felt on the bottom of the table lighters.

In 1949 Blaisdell introduced a new, elegant, table lighter, the Lady Bradford. Zippo declared it 'A triumph in design.' Zippo's advertising leaflet at the time stated:

'Different from any other table lighter on the market! It was created by one of America's foremost industrial designers, and executed in shimmering rhodium plate by expert craftsmen. A perfect combination of classic grace and modern efficiency! It's designed for quick, easy, operation . . . easy to light . . . easy to refuel! The perfect gift for a lovely home or well appointed office.'

From the date of its introduction, this table lighter, the Lady Bradford, was always to be seen on Blaisdell's desk.

In 1953 the fourth Barcroft was introduced. While it had the same look and feel as the third table lighter, it was manufactured to use the same inside unit as the pocket lighter. It came out in two variations, a chrome model and a gold plate

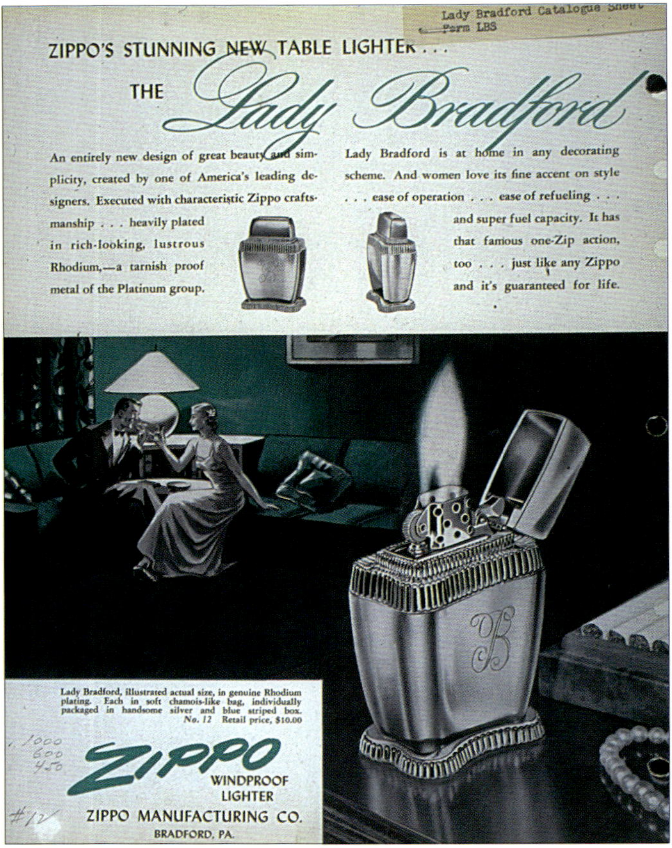

Advertising leaflet used in 1950 to introduce and promote the Lady Bradford.

model. A leaflet produced in 1953 detailed how the lighter worked.

'The cotton insert is kept saturated by the capillary action of the U-shaped lamp wick, supplied from the fluid-saturated cotton reservoir in the base, and sides.'

A neoprene seal was also introduced to prevent fuel evaporation from the cotton filled reservoir and the inside unit's mechanism.

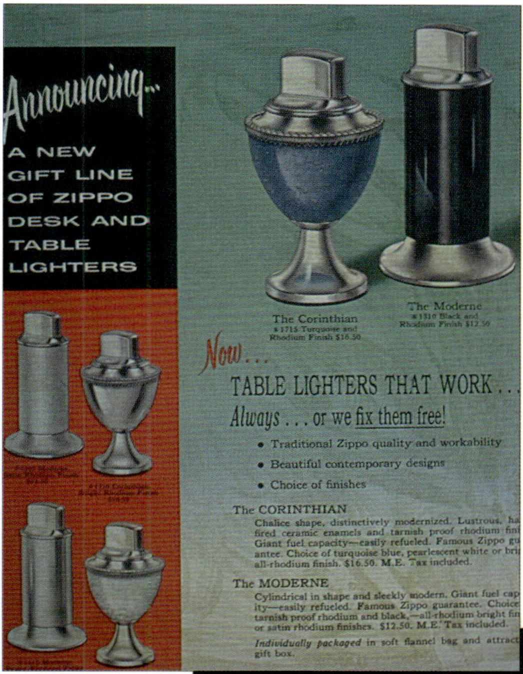

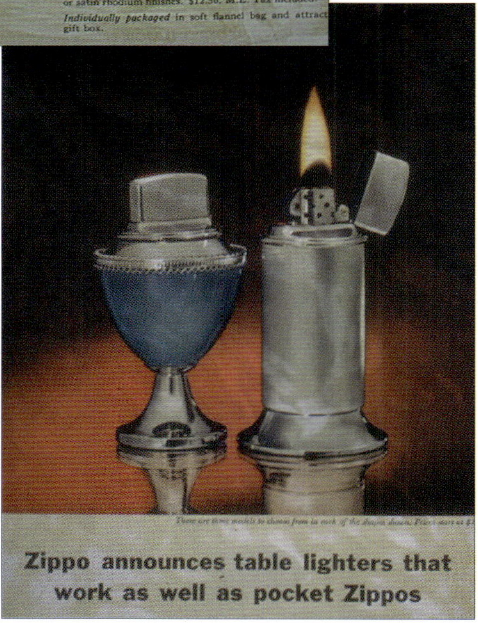

In 1960 Zippo introduced the Moderne and the Corinthian, both stylish table lighters. Neither proved successful and manufacture was discontinued in 1966. The eggcup-shaped Corinthian sold for $16.50, the Moderne for $12.50.

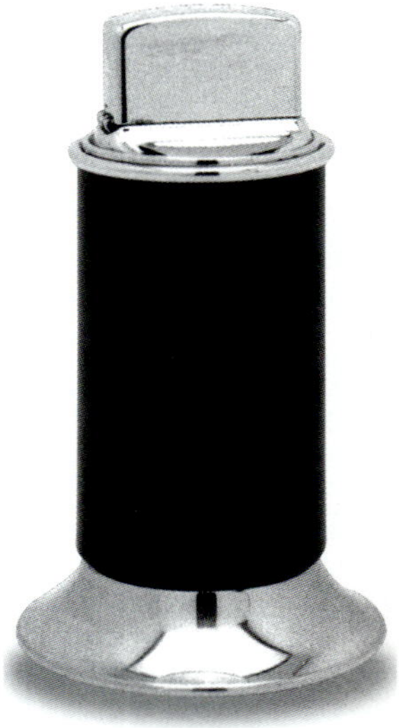

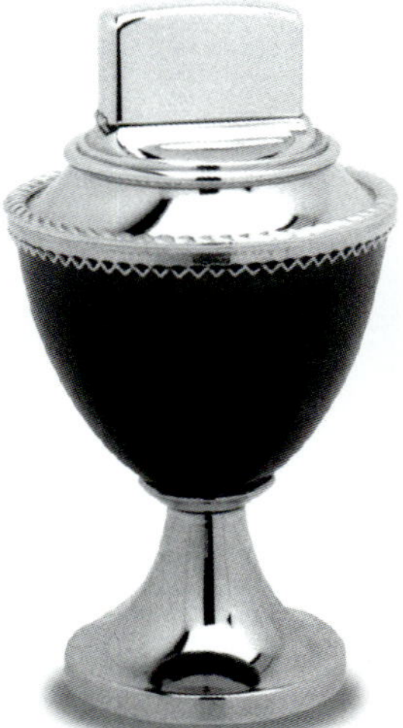

The Moderne (Top) and Corinthian (Above) both used a slim line lighter unit.

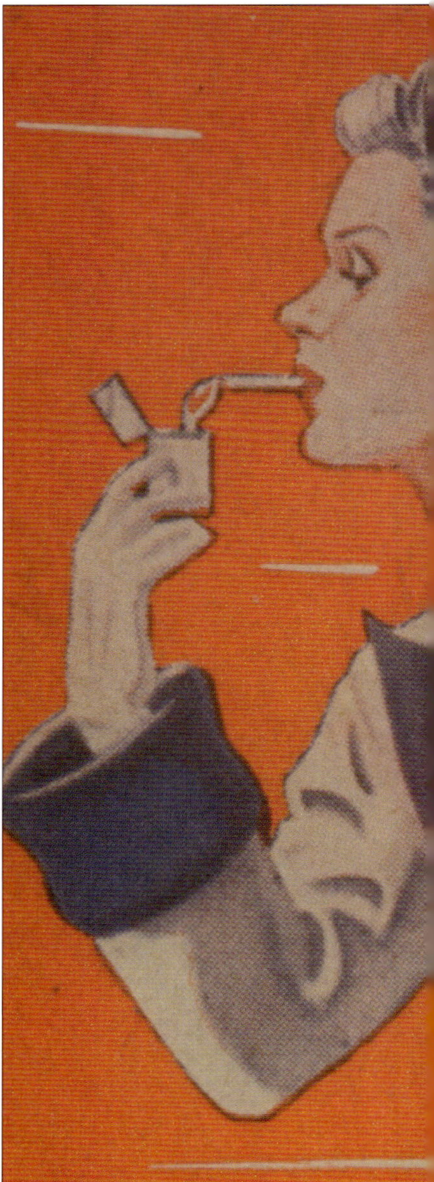

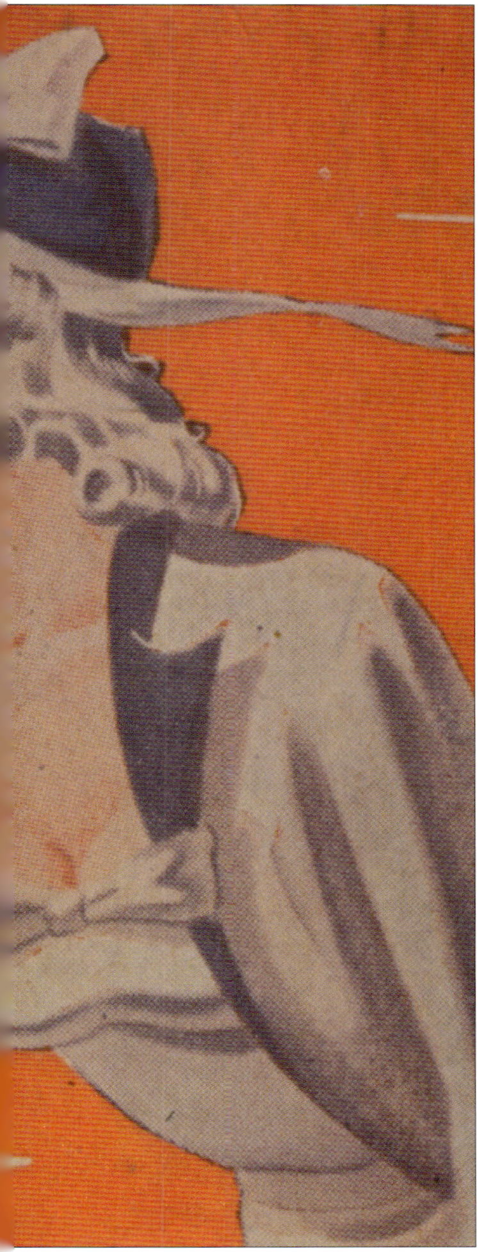

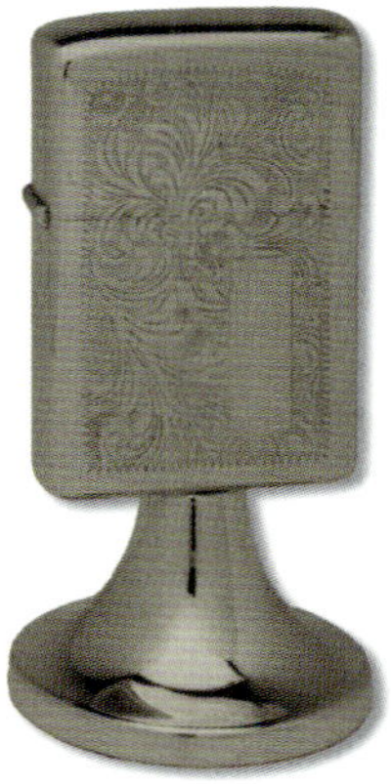

The Handilite replaced the Barcroft in 1979. Using a similar base to that of the Corinthian, ordinary hand-held Zippos could be attached.

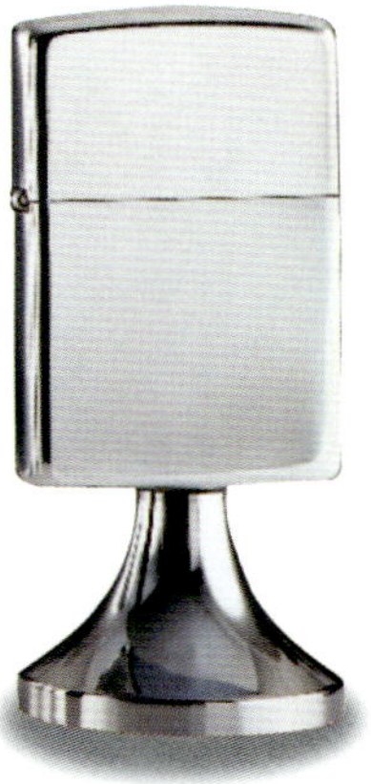

Today's Handilites include gold electroplate and high polished chrome pedestals.

ZIPPO GROWTH IN THE 1950s AND 1960s

The year 1950 once again saw American GIs in action – this time in Korea, as part of the United Nations contingent – and a Zippo was a soldier's invaluable companion. During the Korean War (due to the shortage of brass) the cases of the Zippo lighter were manufactured from steel, only reverting to chrome-plated brass towards the end of 1953.

The Zippo Slim lighter was launched in 1956, with a highly polished drawn brass case, especially designed to woo the female market. These lighters also introduced a change in the identification coding on the bottom of the lighters; the markings now showed four dots on each side of the Zippo logo; a change which was applied to the standard Zippo lighter marketed in 1958. (See lighter identification codes in Chapter 16.)

The Slim Zippo weighed 1.5oz against the 2.05oz weight of the standard Zippo. When introduced they were available in high polish chrome and came in three different styles. All three variations had an engraved plaque in the design where owners of the lighter could engrave either their name or initials, (as was popular at the time). It was also around the time

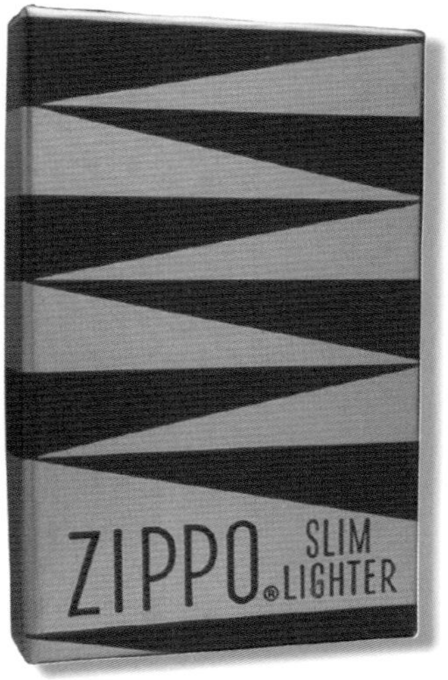

The first Zippo presentation box manufactured by Dennison packaging was for the introduction of the slim lighter in 1956.

of the launch of the Slim lighter that Zippo started using bright colors in their leaflets as well as the displays that were put into tobacconists. Many of these advertisements and point of sale materials were so popular that Zippo relaunched them in the 1980s, when period art of the 1950s came back into fashion.

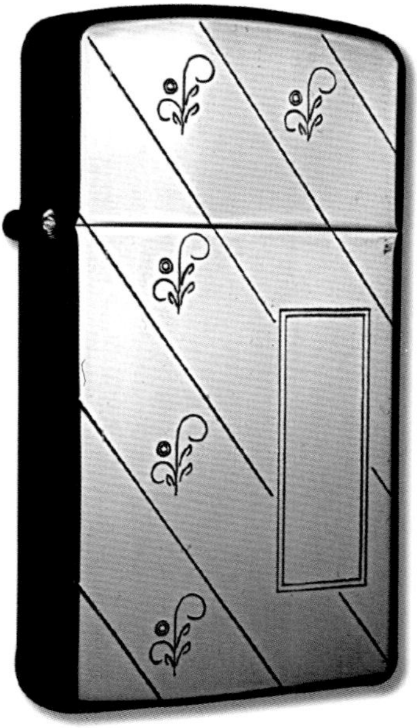

An original 1956 Diagonal Design (No. 1625) Slim Zippo.

It was not long before the slim lighter became a success and in 1938 Zippo introduced an upmarket 14-carat gold version.

Lighters with cases patterned with silver or gold were introduced in 1955, and the same technique was used for the Slim lighter, circa 1957. The refinements to the chemical etching and color filling process were completed in that year, making complicated designs available in an almost infinite number of colors.

This meant that companies were now able to fully promote themselves and their products on Zippo's portable billboard and – as this added considerably to Zippo's product range – sales started to climb. By 1960, Zippo sales had hit the 50 million mark.

Zippo's famous car made its first appearance in 1948, and was often seen in parades across the nation. The car, a converted 1947 Chrysler Saratoga-New Yorker coupe, featured twin Zippo lighters in the cab section of the car, with open lids revealing simulated flames. The name Zippo appeared in gold on the hub caps, and front grille above the

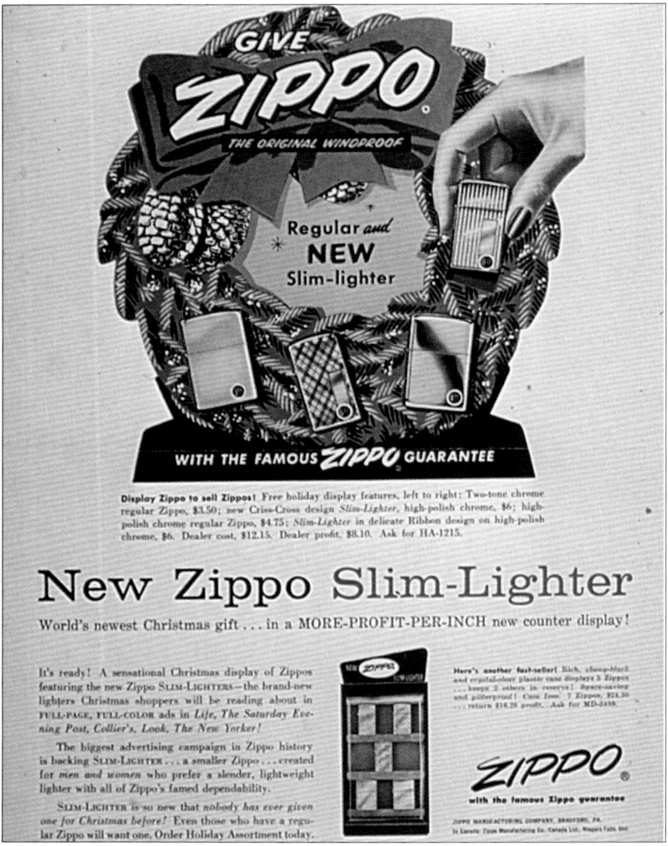

ABOVE: This point of sale display panel was specially designed to show off the new range of Zippo slim lighters.

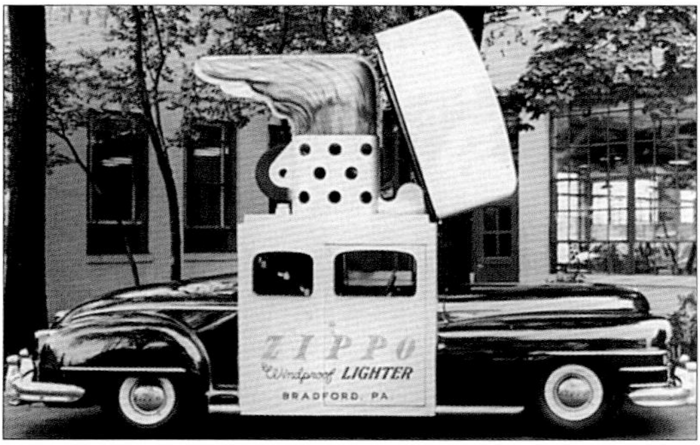

LEFT: The famous Zippo car was used in parades and special events from 1948 to the 1960s.

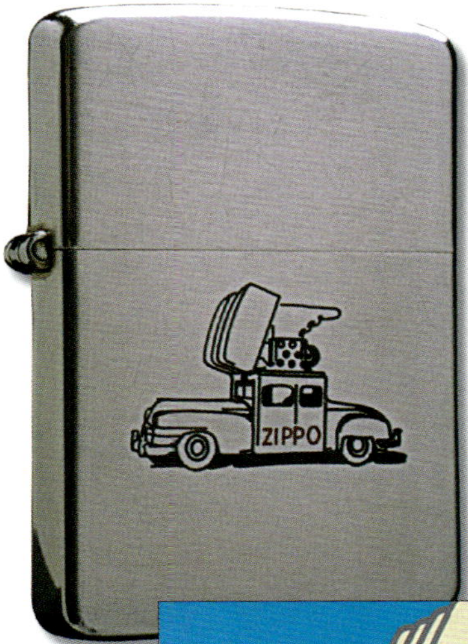

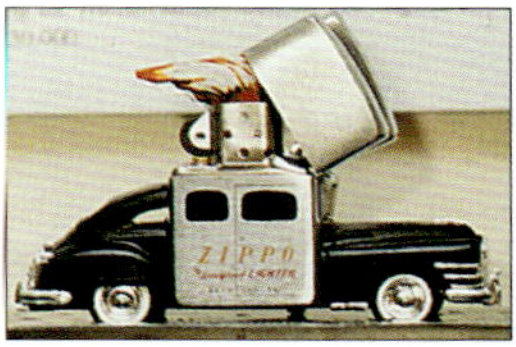

ABOVE: Handmade desk-top model, 1996.

LEFT: Zippo with car insignia.

BELOW: An enamel (metallique) plaque of the car.

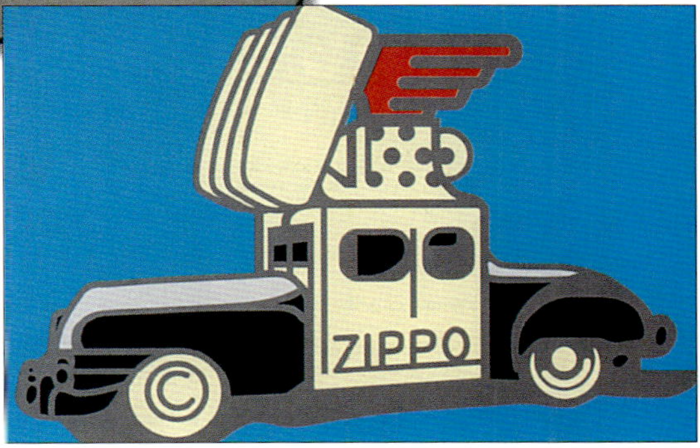

Pennsylvania number plate 7268C. Mystery surrounds the disappearance of this advertising icon – is it hiding in some collector's garage?

By the early 1960s, the United States was becoming more and more embroiled in Vietnam, an involvement started by President Eisenhower, inherited by President J. F. Kennedy, and which would only end in 1975 during President Gerald Ford's term of office. As in World War II and Korea before it, Zippo would go to war with the U.S. troops.

CHAPTER 6

ZIPPO IN VIETNAM

As in World War II, and Korea, Zippo was again an indispensable tool for members of the armed forces. It is estimated that a staggering 200,000 Zippo lighters were in use by troops in Korea. These Zippos performed a multiplicity of tasks for the soldiers, including that of a mirror, a hammer, a signaling device, and a portable source of heat.

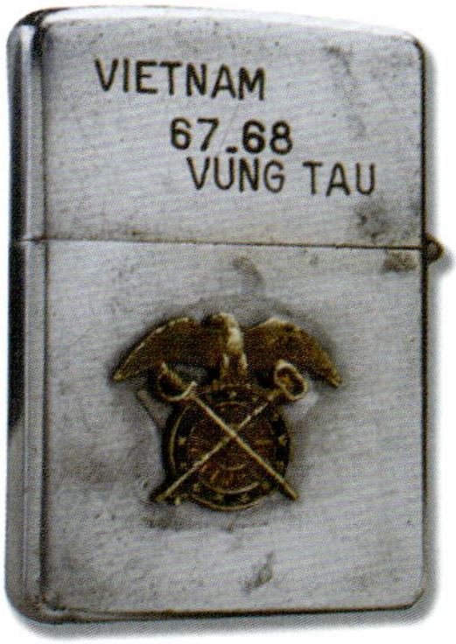

Lighter depicting the years its owner spent in Vung Tau.

Zippos were variously carried in breast-pockets, strapped on to helmets, and in ammunition pouches. Because of the difficulty in obtaining lighter fluid, the lighters were often refilled with gasoline, alcohol, and even diesel fuel.

Zippos were personalized and embellished in Vietnam to a far greater extent than in previous wars. Much of the credit for the inscriptions and engravings must go to the local Vietnamese craftsmen, who would artistically engrave the additions requested, while the owner waited.

The Zippo lighter carried by a GI would often serve as a means of unofficial ID as he often inscribed his name, unit, base address, or unit emblem. His Zippo became the GI's canvas, describing and picturing particular events, emotions, poems,

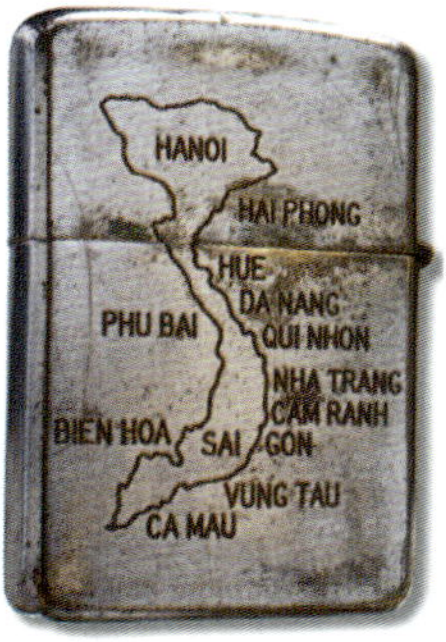

The map of Vietnam was one of the most popular motifs to be engraved on a soldier's Zippo in Vietnam.

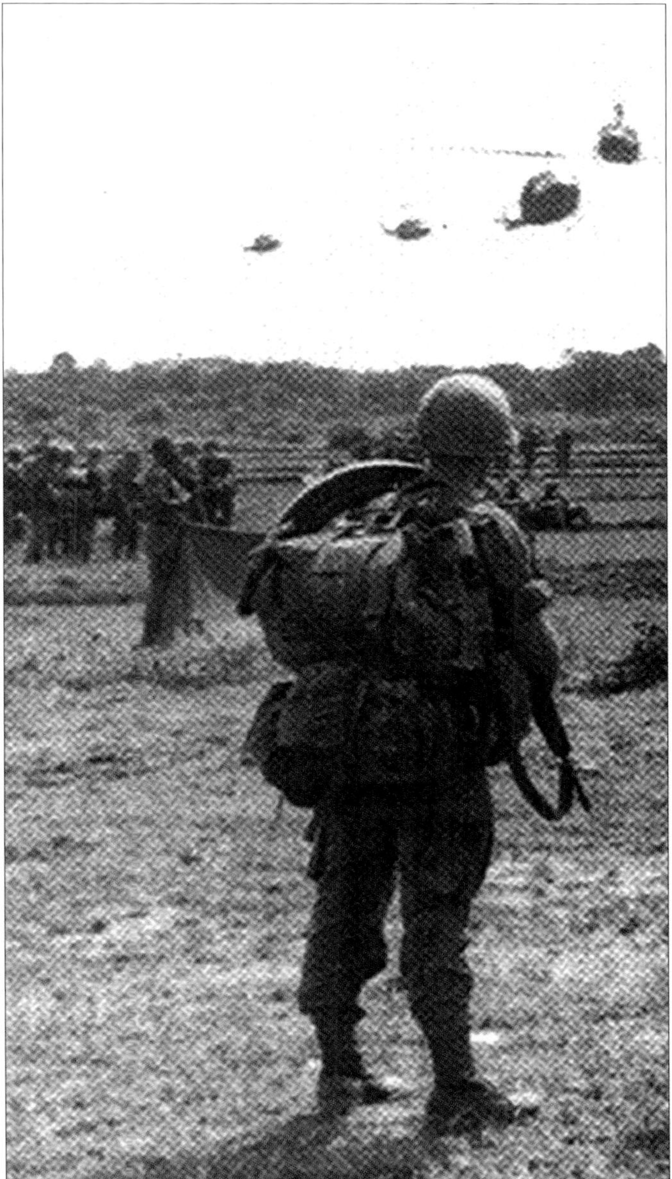

historic dates and places, alternatively they were often engraved with cartoons.

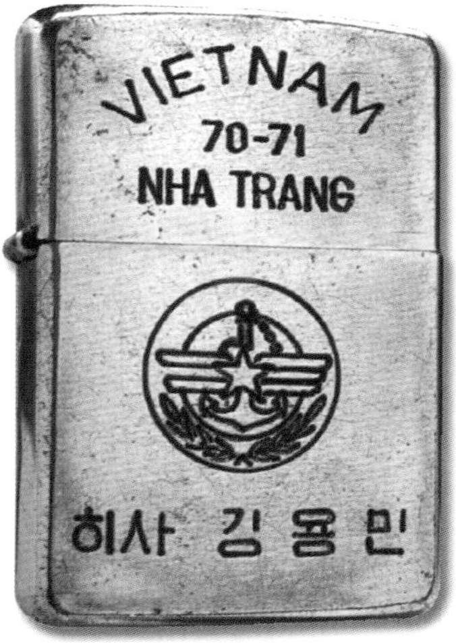

Zippo used in Vietnam 1970-71.

ZIPPO STORIES

Stories from Vietnam War Veterans abound, telling of their relationships and experiences with their Zippos. A particularly good selection was printed in *The Orange County Register*, of February 27, 1997, under the headings: 'Vets Still Carry a Torch for an Old Friend,' and 'Rekindling an Old Flame.'

VETS STILL CARRY A TORCH FOR AN OLD FLAME

HISTORY: Local former servicemen reminisce about a piece of equipment that wasn't standard-issue in Vietnam: the Zippo lighter.

If there were six GIs sitting around in a poker circle, there were six Zippo lighters on the table. Good-luck tokens. In Vietnam, many carried their Zippos in their breast pockets. There was always the rumor about the Zippo that stopped a bullet meant for some soldier's heart.

There were about 200,000 Zippos used by Americans during the Vietnam War, according to the Zippo Manufacturing Co.

Whether purchased before they left the world to carry during their tours of duty, or souvenirs bought in country, these Zippos were often the only things that accompanied the young men and their memories back from the war they would never forget.

In a country where the rain, mud and general wet were inescapable, Zippos were most popular because they always worked, said Michael Johnson of Anaheim.

With no shortage of lighter fluid, and disposable lighters not on the scene yet, Zippos were the thing to have.

We recently asked Orange County veterans to share their memories of Zippo lighters. Here are some of their stories:

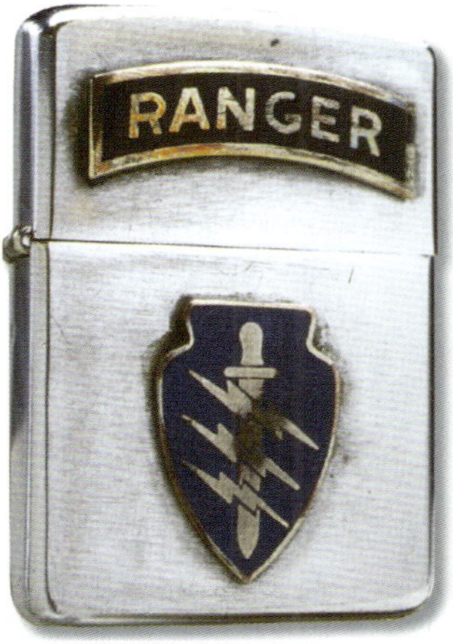

Zippo depicting the insignia of the U.S. Special Forces.

ZIPPO DID IT ALL

GIs learned to use their Zippos to cook and heat with, often lighting C-4 plastic explosives that would burn hot but not detonate. Under a helmet, this method was convenient for boiling water. Besides this kind of improvisation, there was also Zippo entertainment:

'You had to be able to do all the tricks,' said Jim Collins of La Habra Heights, who was stationed in Bien Hoa in 1967-68.

'You could open the Zippo with one hand by pinching it and you could take your thumb and rub the top over and get it to open. You could snap your fingers and make it light. You could inhale the flame, or make 5-foot flames with the darn thing. There were a lot of fun things you could do that were entertaining between some of the more memorable moments.'

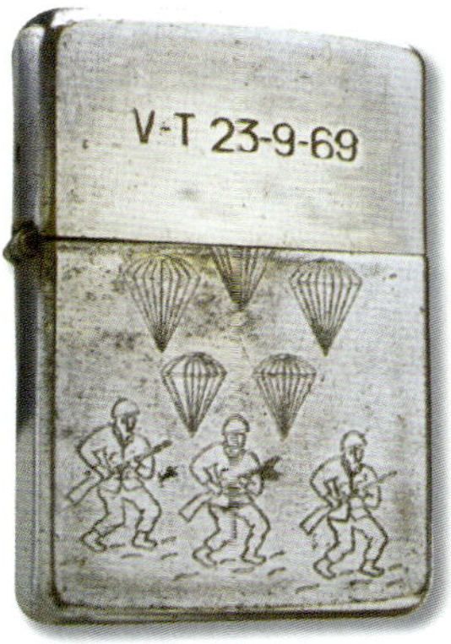

Well-used Zippo from the Vietnam War.

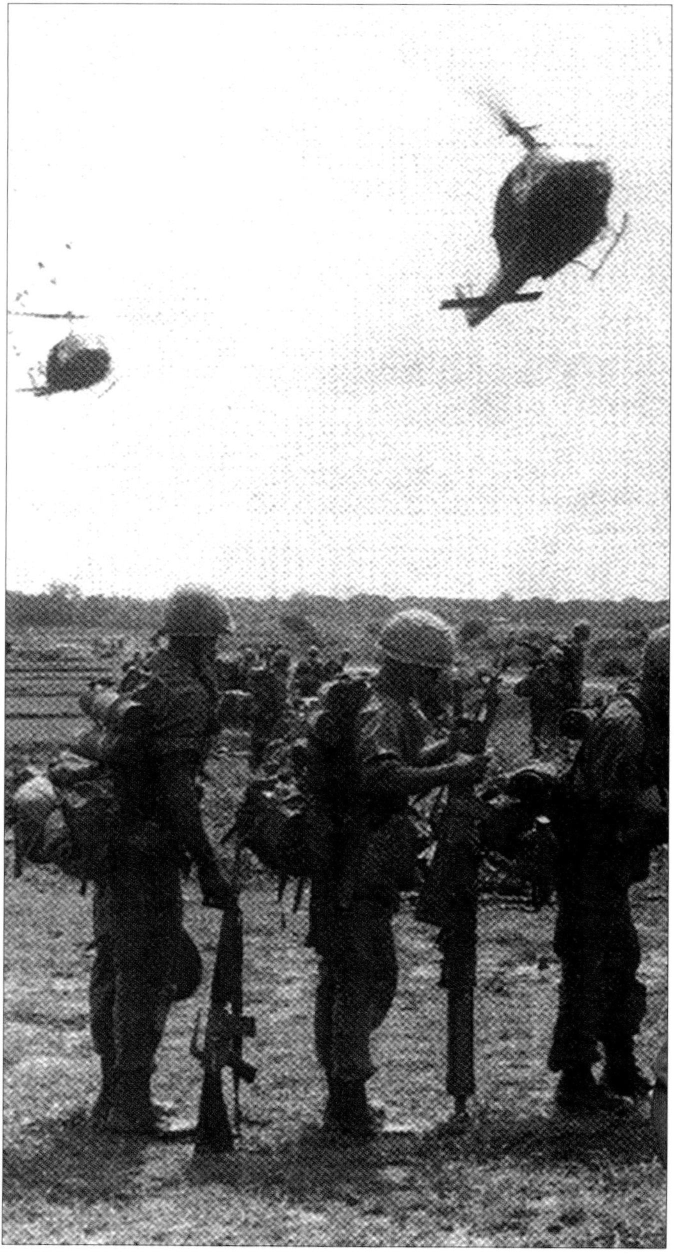

A LIGHT FOR A LEECH

'It was one of the very few things I came back with,' said Joe Matyasik of Lake Forest.

Matyasik, 21 at the time, purchased his Zippo about 10 miles outside Da Nang, in September 1965.

'It was one of those things you cling on to,' said Matyasik, a lance corporal in the Marine Corps, Bravo company. 'I keep it in a jewelry box now with my service ribbons.

'We also bought berets that said "Vietnam" on them. I don't even know where that is, but I still have my lighter.'

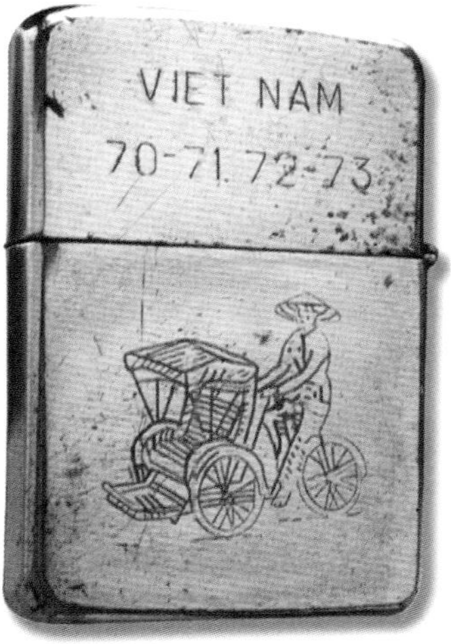

Zippo used in Vietnam, showing this soldier spent two terms in South East Asia 1970-71 and 1972-73

Matyasik's lighter turned out to be a Zenith, an imitation of the famous Zippo, but he found it useful nonetheless. The lighter was even used in ways he could never have imagined:

'I'll never forget one story on this lighter. Our company commander wanted myself and Lance Cpl. Tate to place communication wire in the valley below our position on hill 327, overlooking the Da Nang airport.

'Tate said he would lay the wire, and I was shotgun. Most of the area was rice paddies, and he went under a little bridge that was built by the Seabees. When he came out of the other side he was screaming for help and covered with bloodsucking leeches.

'I quickly lit a cigarette and handed it to him so he could apply it to the leeches. I took my lighter and began burning the leeches off his body. It seemed to take forever at the time, but it worked. We were deep in enemy territory to boot.'

THE ZIPPO AS HISTORY

John Dahlem, now 53 and principal of Loara High School in Anaheim, never smoked but carried his Zippo at all times.

'I bought it off the street and had it engraved,' said Dahlem, a company commander with the Army in 1968. 'I was proud of it because it was, like, macho time.'

Dahlem estimated that he paid about $1.50 for the lighter and 25c for the engraving done on a foot pedal-operated etching machine. He had two lighters: one with his name engraved on it and one with his wife's.

'It was the cool thing to do to carry around those lighters, because they make that unique snap,' Dahlem said. 'But you had to be careful not to fire up or make that noise when the V.C. were around and could spot you in the dark.' In 1996 Dahlem visited the Vietnam Veterans Memorial in Washington D.C., for the first time. When he tells his history classes today about Vietnam and the memorial wall, he mentions the Zippo lighters many veterans leave as tributes to the rows and rows of names.

'The Zippos were like a lucky source,' Dahlem said. 'The funny thing is, I don't think I ever lit the thing up, but I always carried it around.'

AN EASY MEMENTO

Many veterans traded or misplaced their Zippos. Some have long since quit smoking and have given their little metal good-luck charm a place in a curio closet. But others are still using their trusty, rusty lighters three decades after their tour of duty.

Michael Johnson said he continues to carry the Zippo his squadron gave him after he worked as a gun ship pilot with the Green Berets in 1971. He smokes, and says he has to light cigarettes with something but there is more to his old lighter, which has been sent back to the manufacturer for several repairs under its lifetime guarantee.

Maybe it serves as a reminder of surviving 343 flight missions at ages 20 and 21. Or of his 137-member flight class,

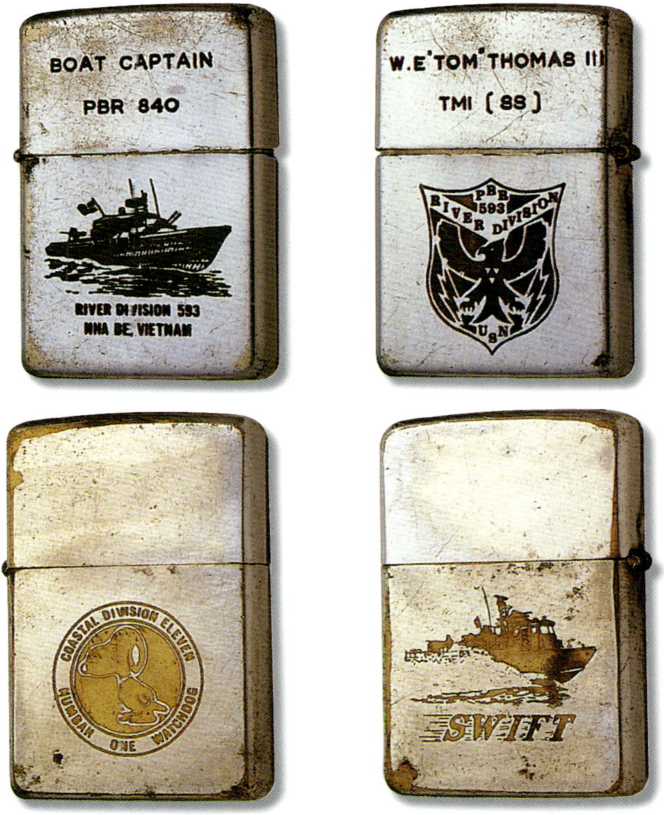

Examples of military Zippos from the Vietnam war.

of which 33 pilots returned home alive, 11 permanently disabled. Instead of the Zippo the Army gave him, or the one from the Korean army, Johnson carries the beat-up gift from friends in combat.

'I have uniforms, pictures, medals and decorations, but they don't mean much to me,' Johnson said. 'The Zippo is an easy memento. You pull it out, and for a moment you can remember people that aren't here.'

'That was a defining moment in a young man's life. We were old men with young shoulders when we got off the plane.'

REKINDLING AN OLD FLAME

'My Zippo came to me in a little Christmas gift from a protestor back in the states, and it was all beat up and didn't work. It was one in a big pile of presents for an exchange, and I just grabbed that particular package. It had a picture of a life-insurance company on it and came with a letter that said, "I hope they find this on your dead body." So I found a way to make it work. Then I had it engraved with "Crash Collings, Vietnam '68" and a neat saying, "Fighters by day, lovers by night. Drunkards by choice." United States Airforce was on the back with Snoopy on a doghouse with an unprintable saying. I carried it not as something to be angry at a protestor but as something for good luck. Some mean-spirited human being sent that over there, but it turned out to be the best thing for me. I wish I could thank them.'

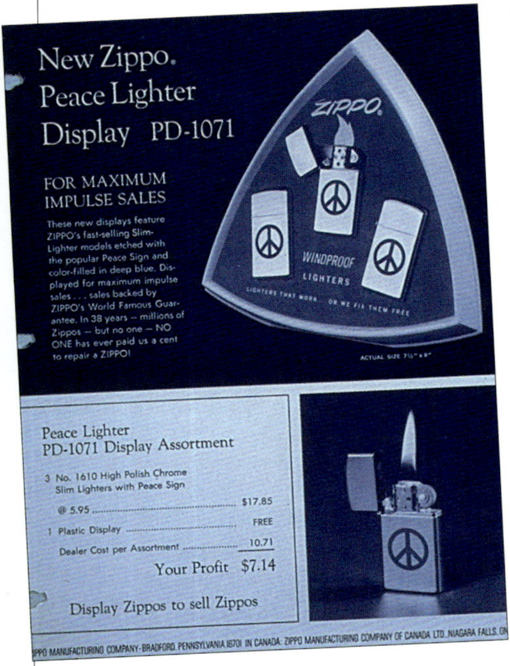

Jim Collings, 49. Yorba Linda

'I carried a Zippo lighter in Vietnam in 1967. I got it from a childhood friend named Frank Jakubaitis. He carried it in his tour of Vietnam prior to my going there, and he gave

While a much-used symbol at the time of the Vietnam War, it would not be until the 1990s that Zippo introduced the Peace Lighter.

it to me as a good-luck token. I think he was more worried than I was because he knew what I was in for. But when I got back, I gave it back to him. It had a takeoff of the 23rd Psalm engraved on it. It said, "Though I walk through the valley of the shadow of death, I will fear no evil, because I am the biggest S.O.B. in the valley."

John Venti, 49, Fountain Valley
'I was with the First Air Cavalry in Vietnam in '65 and '66. I was a crew member on a Ch-47 Chinook helicopter. We got shot down a couple of times together. I had the lighters made for our crew in Saigon in '66 and had our names engraved on them. We were a close group, and I thought it was something to keep us together. I don't have it anymore because some girls in Niagara Falls liked it better than I did, I guess. But I still carry a Zippo because they're always dependable. I don't think anyone would ever throw them away.'

Gary O'Neill, 51, Westminster
'I served in Vietnam '67-'68. I had my Zippo lighter engraved with the names of all the places that I visited in Vietnam. When I got back, I was going to Santa Ana College and went to a party and took my lighter with me. I was showing it to some people and this kid came up to me. He looked at me like I was dead. He said, "Why did you come home and my brother didn't?" I still don't have that answer today. We had gone to high school together. After that, I put my lighter away in a box, and it's been there ever since. My dad also had his from serving in India in World War II. When I go my lighter goes with me. I didn't carry that thing 10,000 miles to leave it to someone else.'

John Sawmill, 49, Westminster
'I have a lighter that I had when I went in the army in 1960. I was stationed in Hawaii. I was there from 1960-62, and my unit, the 25th Infantry Division, was the first unit sent to Vietnam just after I got out of the service. I missed it by

maybe 90 days. It was really scary. I kept that lighter all of these years, and I haven't smoked a cigarette in 30 years. The great thing about Zippos was that they guaranteed them for life. If you sent it in, they would fix it and give it new guts. I got married in 1990, and my wife and I went back to Hawaii for our honeymoon. I brought the lighter with me, and I went back to the military base where I was stationed up at Scoffield Barracks. We went into Kimo's, that club in From Here to Eternity, where we used to hang out as soldiers. I just wanted to show them I had been there, all those years ago.'

Chuck McDonald, 55, Laguna Niguel

'I was in the Navy in the Vietnam War on the USS *Alamo* in Subic Bay, Phillipines, in 1971. This drunk Australian sailor came walking up to me, and he said he wanted my Zippo lighter. I said "Well, I don't want to sell it."

'He said, "I'll give you anything you want, even the shirt off my back." And I thought, "Well, yeah, that'd be a nice souvenir, to have an Australian Navy shirt." So he pulled his shirt off, and I gave him my Zippo lighter, and I don't know how he got back to his ship. One of the rules of the military is that you've got to go on the ship fully clothed. I still have that shirt. And I just went to the ship store and got a new Zippo. I still have that, too.'

Jeff Benefiel, 45, Trabuco Canyon

'A large number of imitation Zippos were produced, in Korea and Japan, some bearing the name "ZIPPU," or "ZPPO," and one model was blatantly marked "ZIPPO, Bradford PA."

'These sometimes shoddy rip-offs were generally cheaper than the real thing, and many greenhorns fell for the scam. When these imitations broke, as they often did, and needed repair, the soldiers who owned them soon found out that they had been had.

'There was neither a lifetime guarantee, or any sort of guarantee covering them. The weight was wrong, the metal and finish were wrong, and the "click" was a damp squib.'

CHAPTER 7

ZIPPO IN SPACE

While the war was raging in Vietnam, the United States, which had founded the National Aeronautics and Space Administration – NASA – in 1958, was aggressively pursuing the conquest of space.

The first American in space, Alan Shepard, on the inaugural Mercury flight on May 5, 1961, was celebrated some three weeks after the USSR's Yuri Gagarin had become the first man in space. Spurred on by the Soviet competition, and with the enthusiastic blessing of President J. F. Kennedy, the Apollo Moon Project was launched to land a man on the moon.

In spite of the tragedy that befell Apollo I in 1967 when all three astronauts on board died in flames, the project continued.

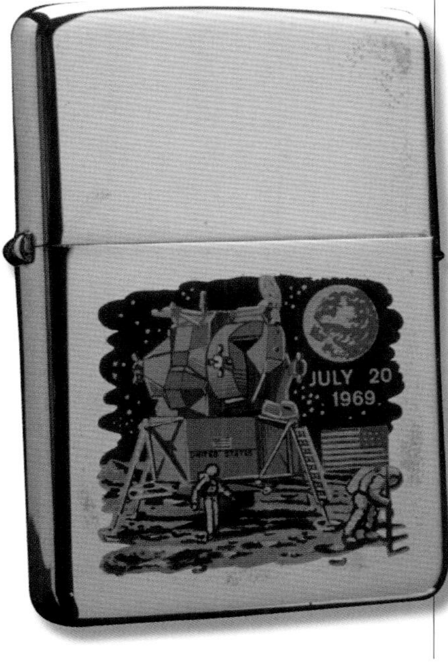

Apollo XI moon landing commemorative lighter depicting the date July 20, 1969. At a mission time of 100hr 15min after the departure of the Saturn V rocket from Kennedy Space Center, the lunar module *Eagle* separated from the command ship *Columbia*, to land two astronauts, Neil Armstrong and Buzz Aldrin, on the moon. Mike Collins remained on Columbia as the Eagle reached the surface of the moon. Just over eight hours later Neil Armsrong became the first man to set foot on the moon.

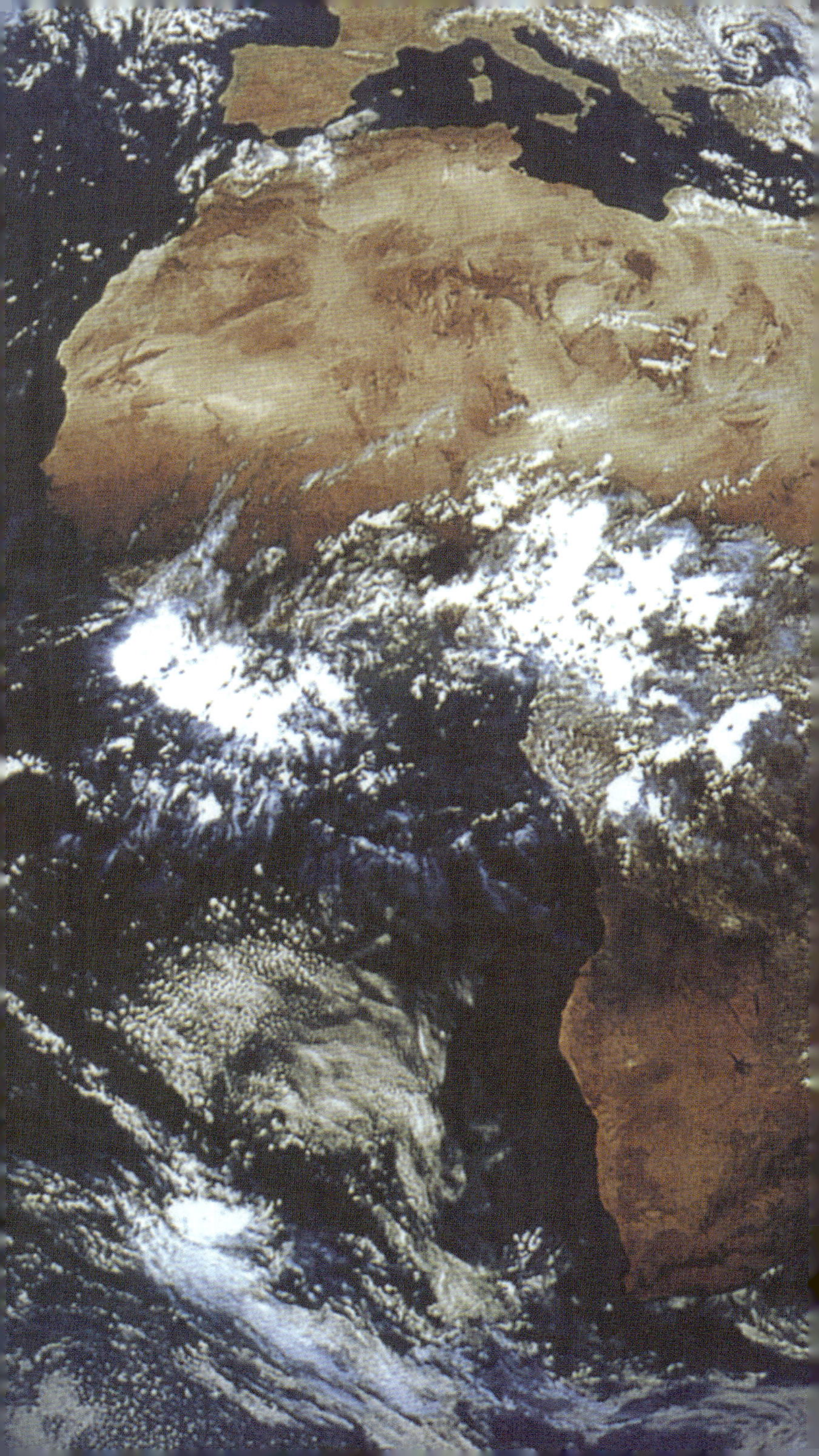

Apollo VIII, on December 24, 1968, with Colonel Frank Borman, Captain James A. Lovell Jr., and Major William A. Anders, became the first manned space vehicle to orbit the moon. Seven months later, July 20, 1969, man landed on the moon. Nobody will ever forget the two announcements relayed from the moon to mission control in Houston, Texas:

'Houston, Tranquillity base here. The *Eagle* has landed.'

While Lieutenant-Colonel Michael Collins remained in the Apollo capsule, Neil A. Armstrong and Colonel Edwin E. Aldrin Jr., descended in the four-legged lunar module (LEM), and six hours later Armstrong took his place in history as he delivered the immortal words 'That's one small step for man, one giant leap for mankind.'

Through all the years of the space program Zippo's relationship with NASA was a close one. Not only did Zippo manufacture lighters with the NASA logo, but many lighters were produced with all the different spaceships, as well as the more recent space shuttles. After every space mission Zippo produced commemorative lighters for the astronauts with varying designs that always depicted America's greatness.

Apart from all the commemorative lighters that Zippo produced, all the Apollo missions also appeared in one way or another on Zippo Lighters. Many collectors today – who have a particular interest in the space missions of NASA – concentrate solely on these lighters to build their collections. A prized collector's piece today is the Chrome Zippo produced in 1969 commemorating the Apollo XI landing on the moon. This lighter depicts the Lunar Module and the US flag with the earth in the background.

Zippo also honored and commemorated the Gemini project, crews of space modules and the naval vessels that recovered the modules, space shuttles, NASA, satellites, Skylab and the space shuttle's Endeavour and Columbia. Even companies that partnered with NASA were often commemorated on Zippo lighters. Nikon the Japanese camera company was responsible for the adaptation of the Nikon F3 SLR camera, that was used for space exploration. Astronauts on the moon had very limit-

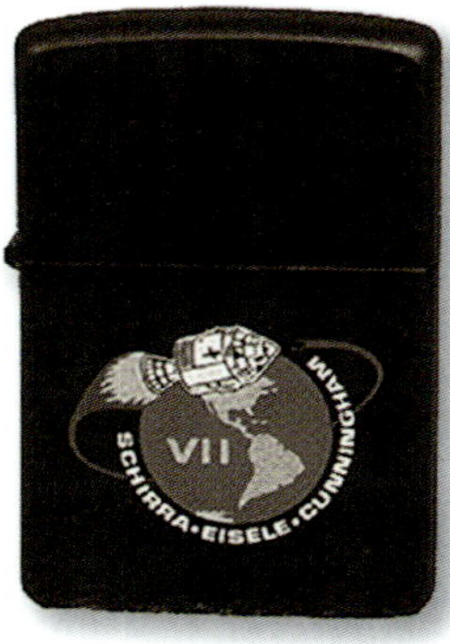

Apollo VII crew Cunningham, Schirra and Eisele were the first U.S. astronauts to launch into space following the tragic Apollo I fire in January 1967.

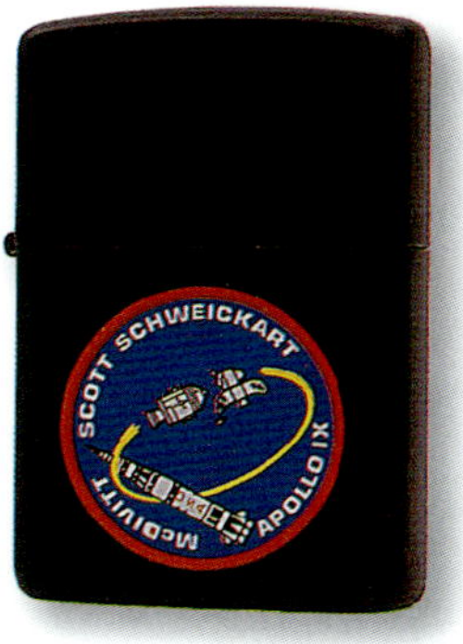

Lighter commemorating the Apollo IX mission, when astronauts Scott, Schweickart and McDivitt tested the lunar module preparatory to Apollo XI.

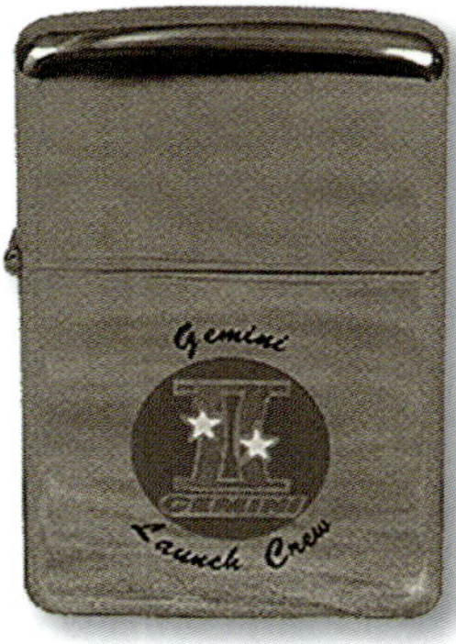

The Gemini missions followed the first U.S. manned space program – the 1960 Mercury launches. The first two Gemini missions were tests, the second carrying a 'simulated man.' This lighter was given to the launch crew.

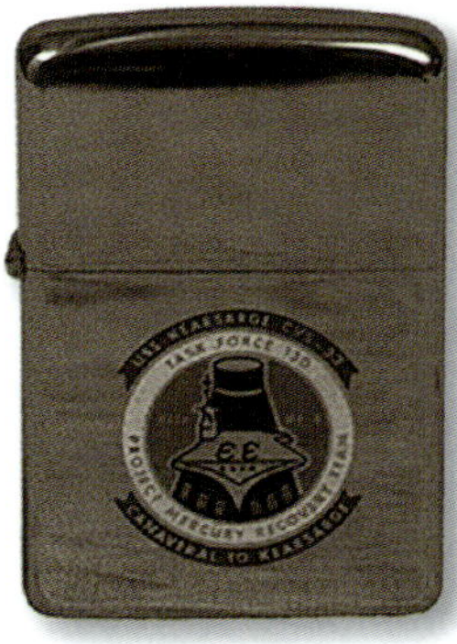

The Mercury command capsules were recovered by naval task forces as were those of the later Gemini and Apollo missions. This lighter is emblazoned with the name of USS *Kearsarge* (CVA-33) which recovered the last two Mercury astronauts – Walter Schirra in Sigma 7 and Gordon Cooper in Faith 7.

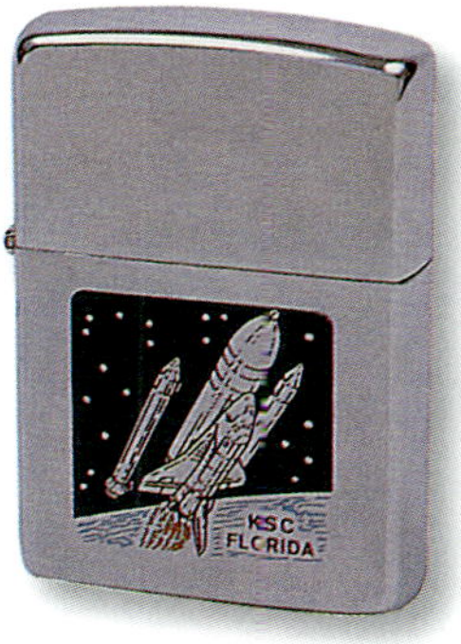

Space shuttle commemorative lighters.

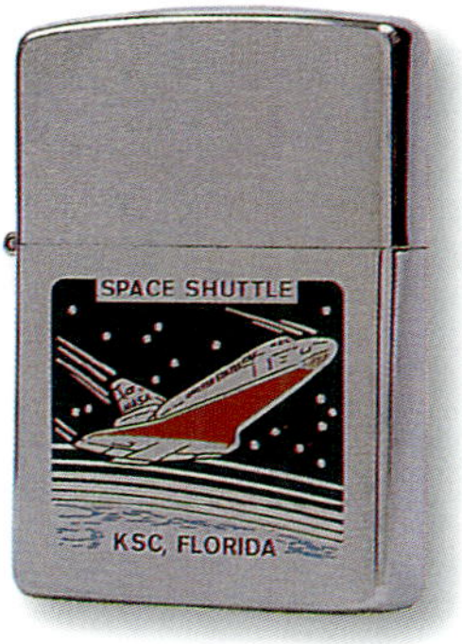

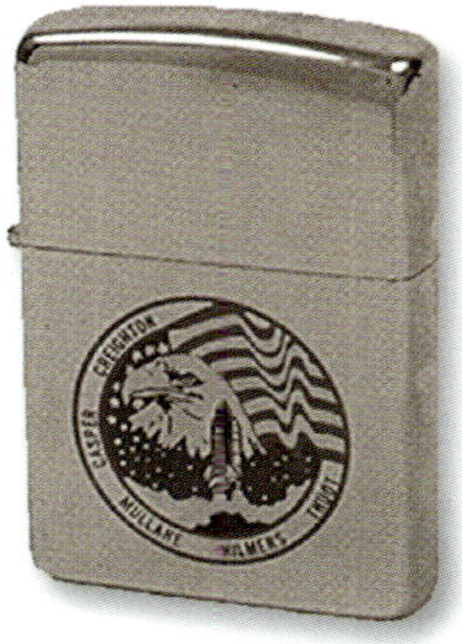

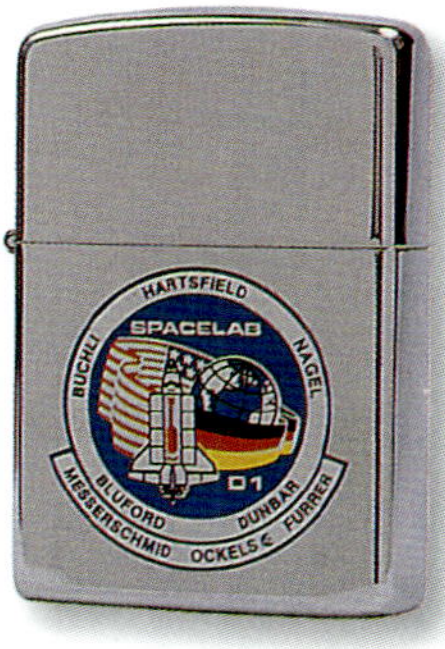

This Zippo commemorates the 34th mission of the Space Shuttle Transportation System. STS-36 was the sixth m ssion flown by the shuttle *Atlantis* crew was John O. Creighton (Commander), John H. Casper (Pilot), Richard M. Mullane (Mission Specialist 1), David C. Hilmers (Mission Specialist 2 , Pierre J. Thuot (Mission Specialist 3). The mission lasted 4 days, 10 hours, 18 minutes, 22 seconds, circled the earth 72 times – a journey of some 1,920,000 miles. Landing took place on March 4, 1990.

This Zippo commemorates the flight of mission 61-A, the 22nd shuttle mission and the ninth flown by *Challenger*. It was crewed by Henry W. Hartsfield, Jr. (Commander), Steven R. Nagel (Pilot), James F. Buchli (Mission Specialist 1), Guion S. Bluford, Jr. (Mission Specialist 2), Bonnie J. Dunbar (Mission Specialist 3), Reinhard Furrer (Payload Specialist 1), Ernst Messerschmid (Payload Specialist 2), Wubbo J. Ockels (Payload Specialist (ESA) 3). Mission 61-A carried Spacelab D1 *Glomar*, and lasted 7 days, 44 minutes and 51 seconds after launch on October 30, 1985.

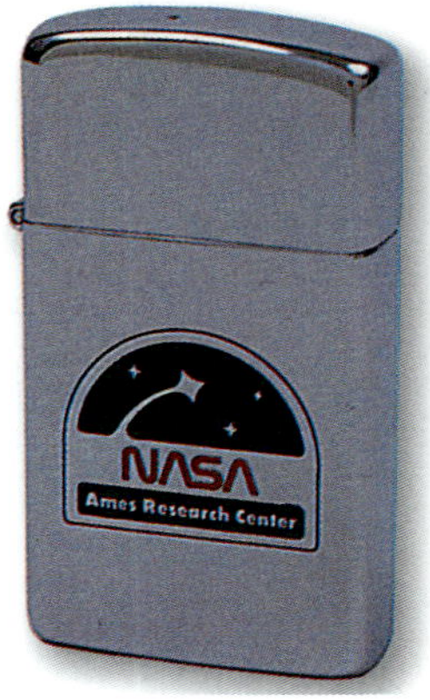

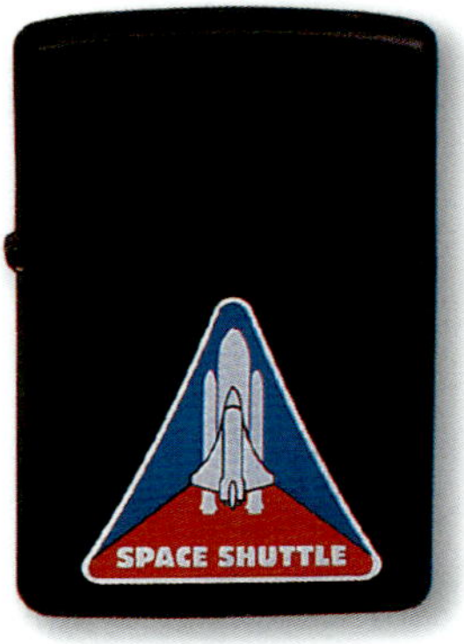

NASA and Space Shuttle commemorative lighters.

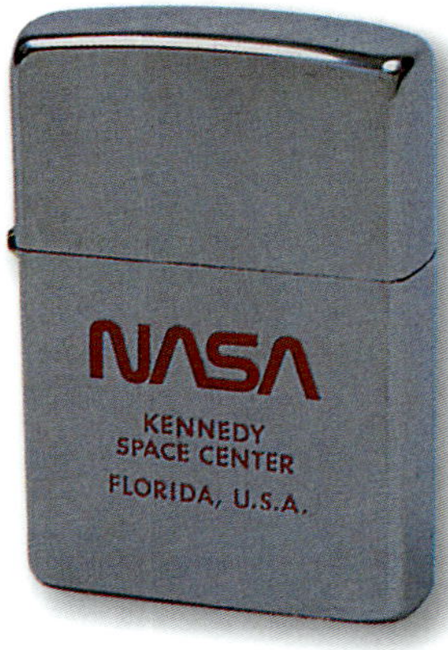

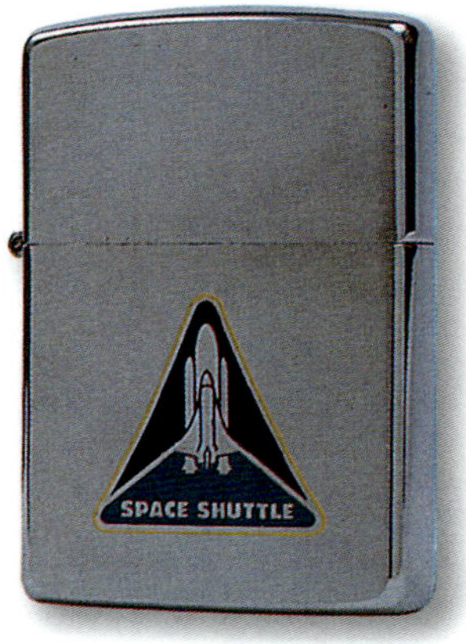

ed mobility and changing a camera spool would have been impossible while walking on the moon. The adaptation that was made to the F3 was the addition of a camera back that could carry over 250 exposures of 35mm film, thus allowing the astronauts to capture as many images as they could.

Today, with the collapse of the Soviet empire, there is a new spirit of cooperation with the Russians, resulting in pooled technologies and combined space projects – and you can be sure that Zippo will be there too.

CHAPTER 8

ZIPPO HIGHLIGHTS

With the steady introduction of new art techniques, surface treatments, collectibles, and commemorative issues, Zippo's horizons continued to expand. Like the T-shirt, the Zippo lighter had become a miniature canvas and it was up to the artists and designers to begin making this medium work, and indeed they did. The explosion of new and exciting images, advertisements, pop stars, and just simply beautiful and decorative designs that began to embellish the Zippo lighter, certainly paved the way to the creation of the collecting public and huge following Zippo has today.

The early 1970s saw the introduction of the wood grain model, in which a pressure sensitive vinyl appliqué of simulated wood, was applied to the case.

The NFL (National Football League) series, with its helmet imprints was introduced, and has become a much sought after collector's item, not only amongst Zippo lighter collectors but football fans as well. This series included, among others, helmets featuring The Miami Dolphins, The Kansas City Chiefs, The Chicago Bears, The Detroit Lions, The Pittsburgh Steelers, The New York Jets, and The Cleveland Browns. Almost every year Zippo brings out a new NFL series and very often the designs are always better than the previous year's. Today the NFL series comes complete in a tin with an 'authentic licensed product' wrapper.

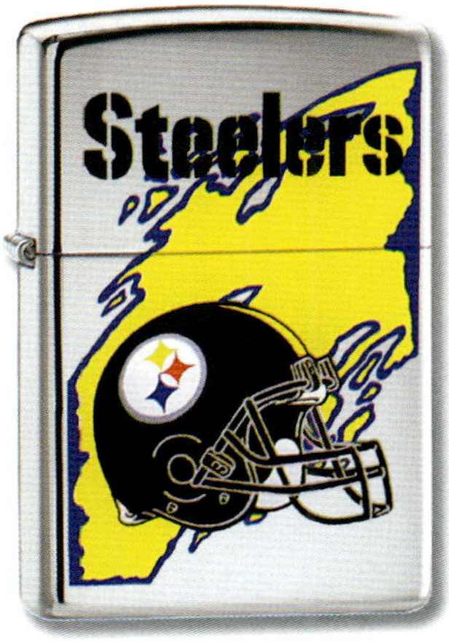

Zippo lighter with design on both lid and base depicting the NFL team the Pittsburgh Steelers.

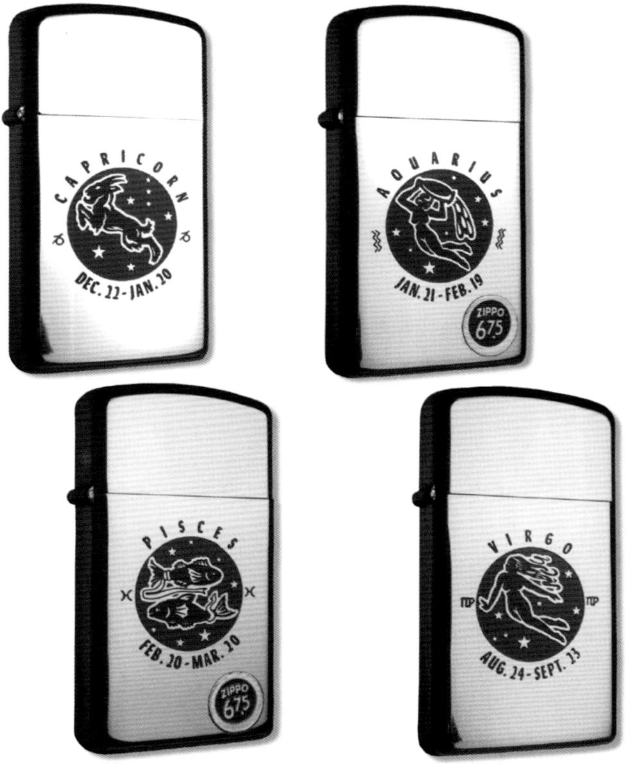

Four slim Zippo lighters from the original Zodiac series.

In 1972 a 40th anniversary commemorative was issued, featuring a lighter bearing a message from, and autograph by George G. Blaisdell. Today Zippo makes available for collectors all the anniversary lighters as a set.

In the late 1970s a Zodiac series was introduced, featuring the 12 signs of the Zodiac on slim lighters.

The 1970s certainly saw the development of the denim industry, even Volkswagen brought out a 'denim bug' in their range of cars. In keeping with the 'jeans' image of America, a denim series appeared, and Wrangler commissioned a Zippo with their logo. The football, Zodiac, and jeans lighters have become some of the most sought after of all collectors items.

The scrimshaw is a replica of designs engraved by sailors on whalebone, shells, and ivory. While there are many collectors all over the world that specialize only in the collecting of scrimshaw, you can be assured that these collectors will all have at least one of the Zippo scrimshaw lighters.

The prototype of the scrimshaw lighter was first tested in 1976, when the development of ultra light plastic made the scrimshaw process possible. In keeping with scrimshaw tradition, Zippos of this series featured etchings of whales, whalers, sailboats, and outriggers.

The intricately engraved 'Venetian' series made its debut and today is still one of the most popular of the classic series. The slim version of the 'Venetian' is very popular with the ladies. These lighters all have a rectangular space on the front of the

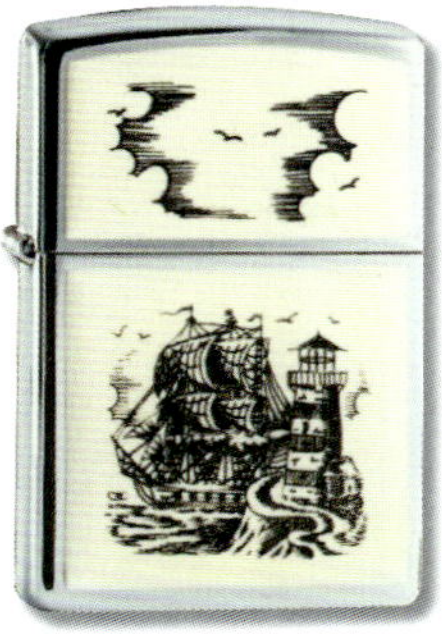

Zippo Scrimshaw lighter depicting a ship at sea. These lighters are still available today from Zippo and come in four finishes: brass, chrome, midnight chrome and black. Zippo also produces a chrome model in the pipe-lighter series. In the slim version of the lighter, the scrimshaw engraving is that of a whale.

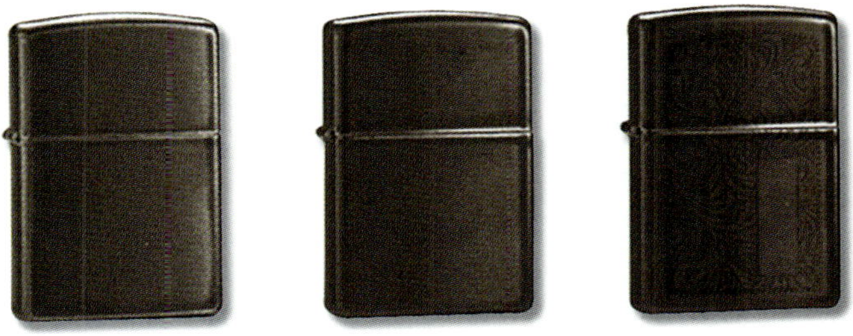

Chrome and brass Classic series.

A range of Zippo lighters showing various advertising uses.

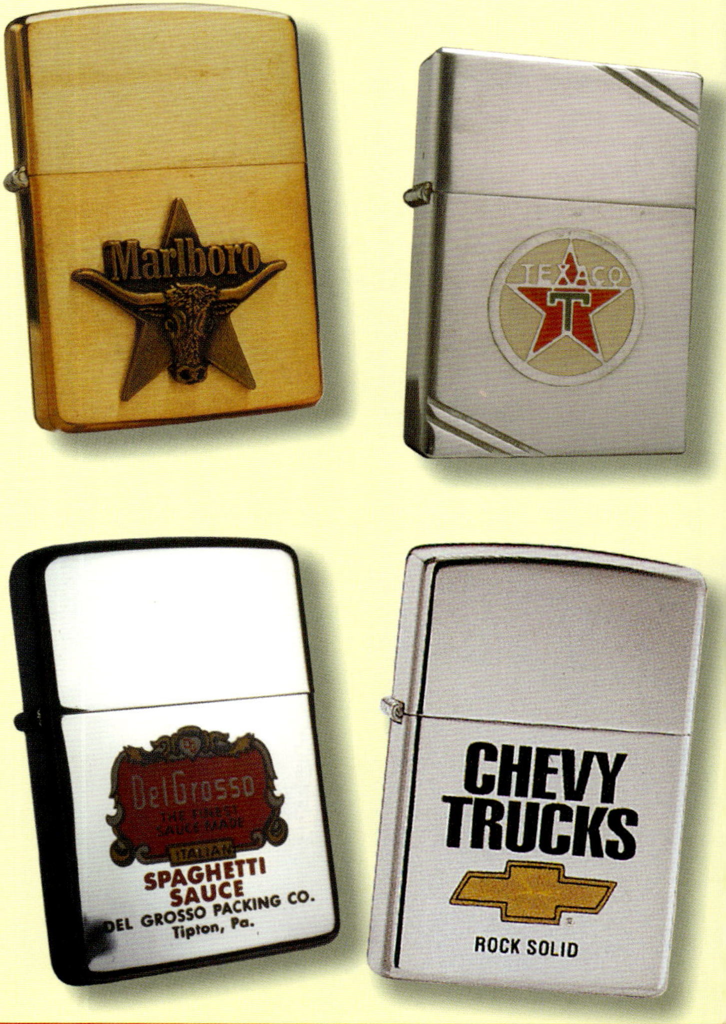

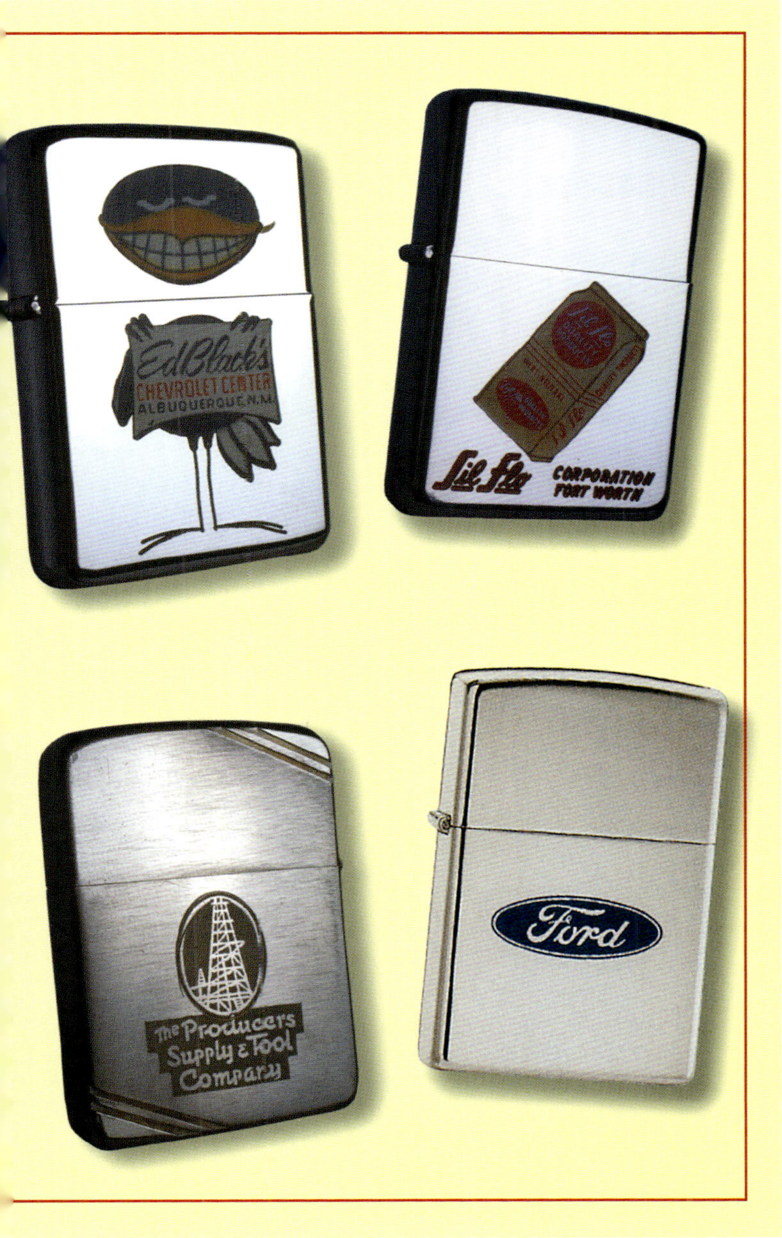
Ed Black's
CHEVROLET CENTER
ALBUQUERQUE N.M.
CORPORATION
FORT WORTH
The Producers
Supply & Tool
Company
Ford

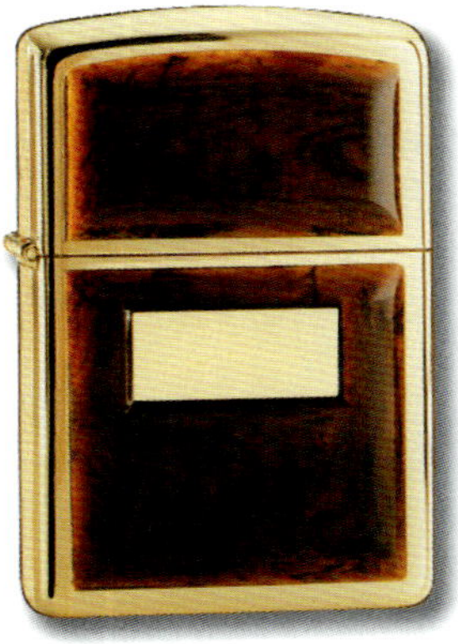

The Golden Tortoise lighter, still available today from Zippo.

lighter for owners to engrave their names or their initials. It is probably this very reason that this model is so popular as a gift item. Towards the end of the 1980s Zippo introduced another very delicately engraved Zippo, called the floral. This lighter, available in sterling silver or Gold plate, not only had the delicate design engraved on the front of the lighter but on the sides as well.

The Bicentennial lighter was manufactured in celebration of the 200th birthday of the United States, and the acrylic chip process produced the Golden Tortoise lighter.

Disney made a first appearance on Zippo lighters in 1976, on the denim series. Disney characters and Disney themes were well represented until the early 1980s. These lighters are both rare and difficult to find, as owners and collectors never let them out of their sight.

The Disney veto came at a time that Zippo – well aware of the anti-tobacco lobby and concerned with the new revelations about the effects and side-effects of smoking – was refining its image, and directing its marketing toward the Zippo lighter's use as a portable source of flame.

1978 was a year of tragedy for Zippo. Founder, president, and guiding light George G. Blaisdell died. The Blaisdell family then entrusted Robert Galey to take

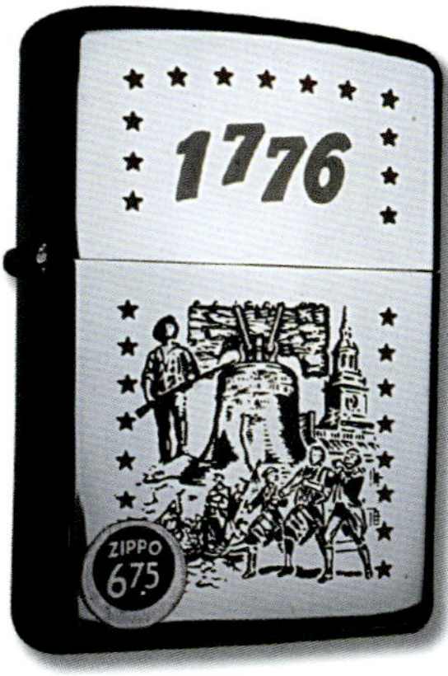

Lighter produced in 1976 to commemorate the bicentennial birthday of the United States.

over the reins, and lead Zippo for the next eight years.

The Zippo lighter was rapidly becoming a pictorial mini-view of history. Not only of history in the United States, but also of the shrinking world. This history encompassed not only the recording of small, medium, and large corporation advertising and promotions, but, also of events that shaped the world at the time.

Brand names appearing on Zippo lighters that are still known today, included, Chevron Oil Company, Coca Cola, Goodyear, McDonnell Douglas, General Electric, Sears, Exxon, Volvo, Citgo, Porsche, 7Up, Chevrolet, and Dr. Pepper. The list is endless and due to the fact that Zippo has produced product for so many companies all over the world, some collectors will only specialize in finding Zippo beverage lighters, or Zippo car related items, etc.

1976 saw a Jimmy Carter lighter, acknowledging his election as President of the United States. While many lighters have surfaced honoring presidents as well as presidential campaigns. Zippo has over the years produced many different series of American presidents. Some of the rarest Zippo lighters are those in which their owners have actually affixed photographs of famous presidents. These lighters were usually adapted at the time of presidential elections.

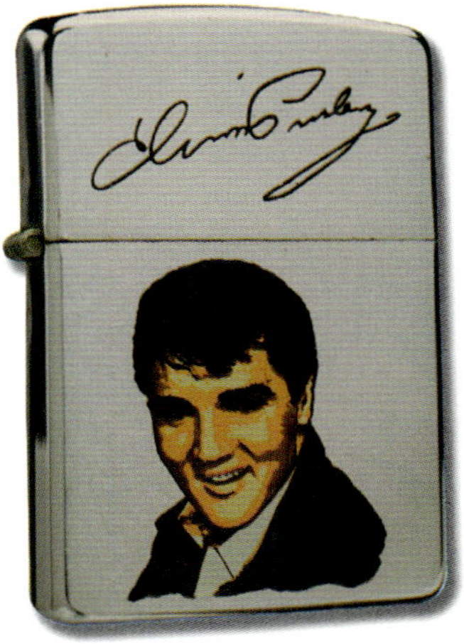

This Elvis Presley lighter with his signature debuted in 1978.

Not only did presidents find their images on Zippo lighters but famous people too; in 1978 the Elvis Presley lighter debuted and is still available today.

The GOP (Republican Party) elephant, and the Democrats' donkey were featured in cartoon format in 1979, and Alaska's 20 years as a member of the union were honored. The war in Vietnam and the conquest of space are recorded on Zippo lighters.

Although the 1980s saw little growth from Zippo, with sales hovering around the $30 million a year, and the focus almost totally production orientated, new milestones were still reached

The Pipe lighter, first conceived in 1981, was introduced to the market in 1982. In this innovative design, a hole was cut into the center of the windhood, enabling the flame to be directed downward into the pipe. It is so effective that amongst pipe smokers there is no alternative lighter that measures up to the Zippo's effectiveness, and since its invention the Pipe lighter has remained the yard stick by which all other pipe lighters are measured and assessed.

1982 was also Zippo's 50th anniversary year, and a replica of the 1937 lighter was produced. Along with all the company's major anniversaries, Zippo always produced a commemorative edition, and the 50th anniversary was no different. This was the lighter with rounded corners, and diagonal lines on the lid and lower case. The commemorative lighter announced '50 years and growing stronger,' as well as exhorting buyers to 'Try the fan test,' rekindling the old Zippo slogan from the 1930s. (The 50th anniversary also saw the production of a Kendall Oil lighter.)

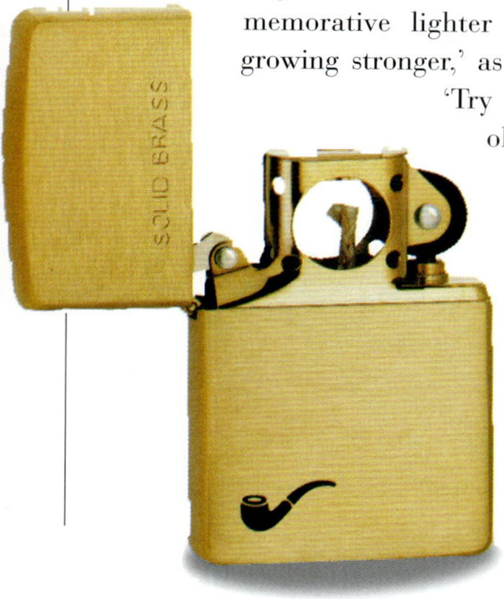

The Pipe lighter – note the hole in the windhood to allow the flame to be drawn downward.

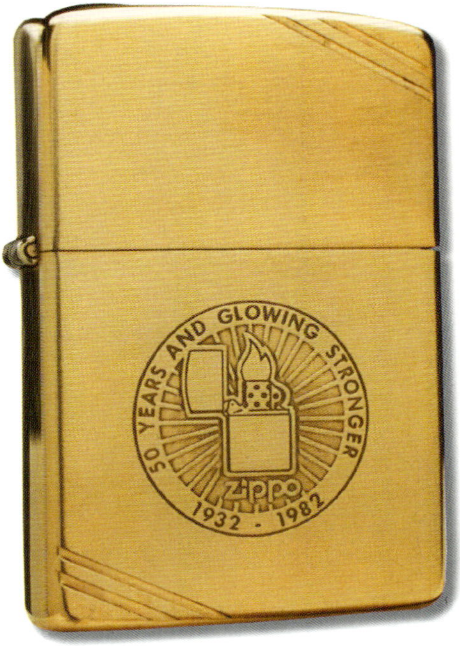

Brass 50th Anniversary commemorative lighter '50 years and glowing stronger.'

All replicas are easily distinguishable to collectors as most of them have the flat base and original markings and trademarks inscribed. The easiest way to check that you have a replica in your hand is the inscription of the patent information on the base of the 'new' lighter. When the patent on Zippo lighters expired, Zippo stopped engraving the patent number on the base of the lighter. Therefore, the replicas do not have a patent number, but the originals do.

Under Zippo President Robert Galey, the company remained strong through the end of the 1970s and mid-1980s with no significant changes. National advertising was restricted to two publications, Reader's Digest, and TV Guide, and Zippo relied almost entirely on its wartime GI image, and 'born in the USA' theme to drive its product in the

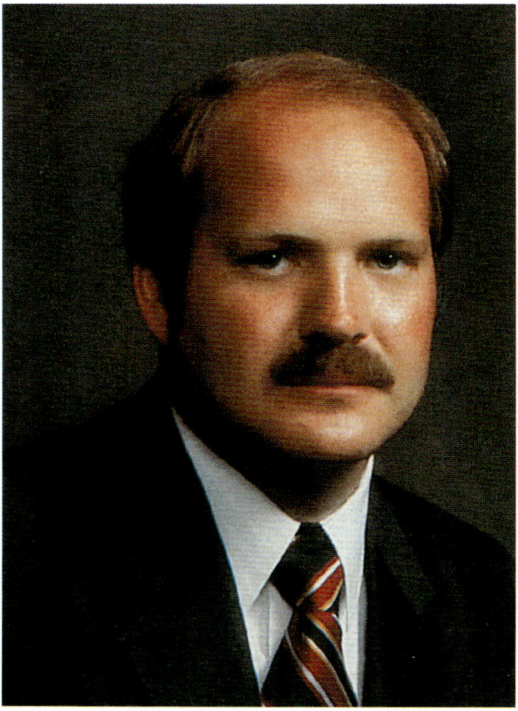

Michael A. Schuler, Zippo president.

marketplace. Robert Galey retired in 1986, and a new era began for Zippo.

Michael Schuler, previously Zippo's controller, took over as chief executive officer of Zippo Manufacturing Company, and began the introduction of far-reaching changes in market strategy. In 1991 he appointed James Baldo, to head sales and marketing.

Zippo advertisements now targeted the male population, in magazines like *Playboy*, *GQ*, and *Sports Illustrated*.

James Baldo commissioned new market surveys, which revealed that a huge number of Zippo owners bought the lighters as 'collector's items.' With this in mind, the Schuler/Baldo team started to produce lighters specifically aimed at the collectors' market. The first lighters featured

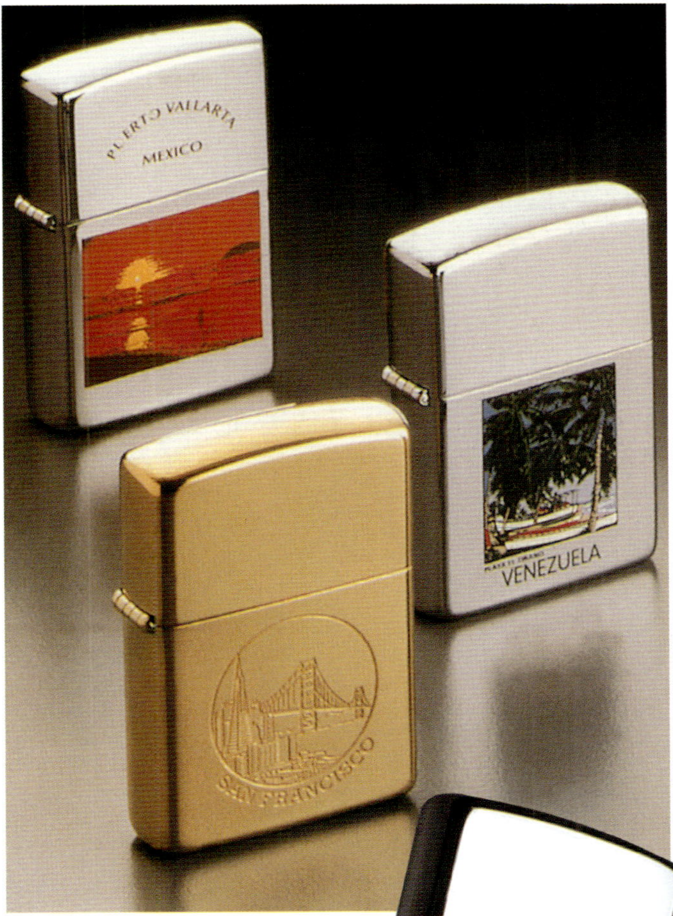

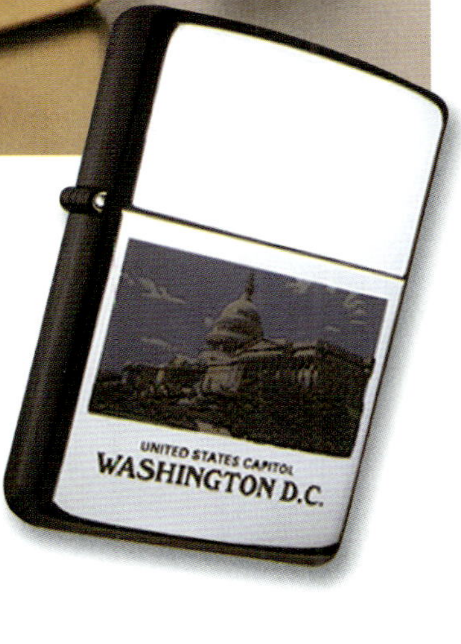

Souvenir lighters from around the world – 1: many Zippos depict locations or tourist destinations, such as Washington DC.

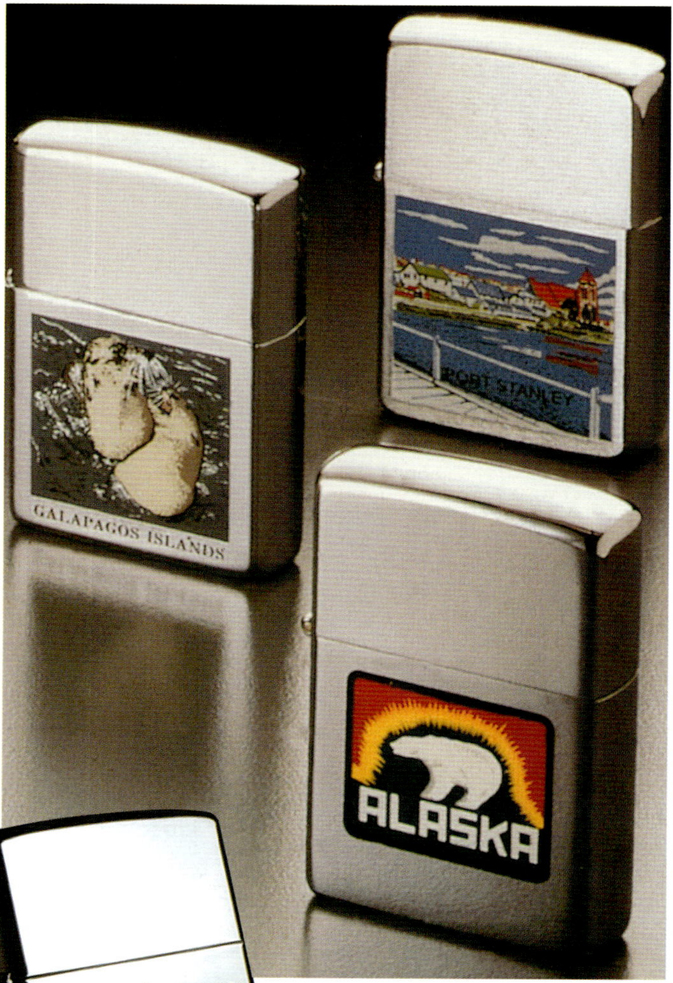

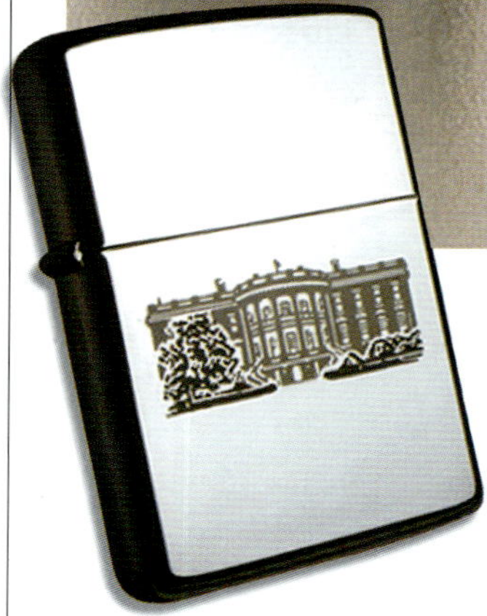

Souvenir lighters from around the world – Zippos can depict locations as far afield as Alaska and the Falkland Islands. Many US tourist destinations, such as the White House, are also covered.

were souvenir oriented, and depicted such well known tourist sites as Niagara Falls and the Empire State Building.

They issued, among others, a Barcelona Olympics series, a Harley-Davidson collection, with the 'Born To Ride' theme, Pinups, and an Aircraft Nose Art group, to mention a few. Not only did this dynamic team recognize the need for exciting and new art on the Zippo itself, but they recognized the need for a whole new way to market and package the product. Through this recognition the classic tin was revitalized. From here on Zippo offered their collectors not only the lighter, but classic tins and on some occasions hand crafted wooden boxes as well.

The Harley-Davidson limited edition lighter produced in 1993, (only 1,000 numbered lighters were made) commemorating 90 years of Harley-Davidson, was not only produced in silver plate but presented in a handsomely engraved wooden box. Now, collectors were not only buying Zippos for themselves, they were also purchasing them as gifts.

The addition of Patrick Grandy to the Zippo marketing division fortified the new era in consumer communication and advertising. To such an extent that today Zippo's largest market is in Europe, followed by Japan, and in third place, the US.

World leaders featured on Zippo lighters in 1991, include Winston Churchull, and Mao Tse Tung,

1992 saw a series of lighters devoted to Chinese year symbols. These lighters depicted the year of the Dog, Rabbit, Dragon, Boar, Monkey, Rooster, Snake, Ox, Tiger, Horse, Sheep, and Rat.

Zippo's 60th anniversary was the occasion for the unveiling of a limited edition lighter, bearing a pewter anniversary emblem mounted on Midnight chrome. The lighter was packed in a decorated presentation tin. This was the first year Zippo used the new midnight chrome finish.

The purchase of Bradford neighbor W. R. Case & Sons Cutlery Co. in 1993 added knife and lighter sets to collectors. Case itself was a manufacturer of strongly sought after collectors' items, and it was a natural choice for Zippo, in their quest for expansion. At the time of the purchase W. R. Case & Sons was a $15 Million (Sales) company. With the involvement of Zippo's proven marketing and sales genius who knows where this will go.

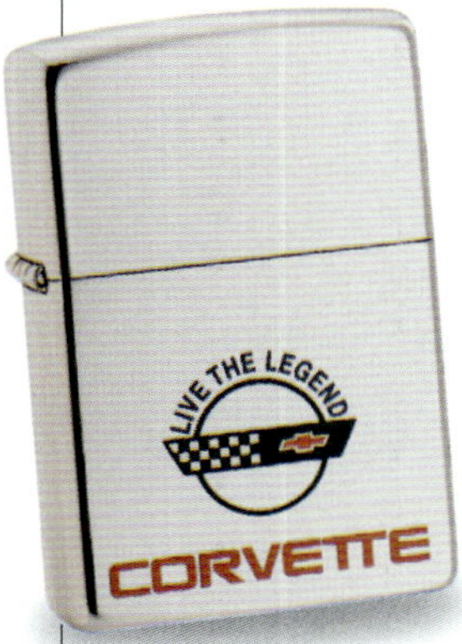

Zippo having recognized that 30 percent of its market was collectors, decided to encourage this by bringing out an annual collection of the year. Other collectors' editions produced in the years 1992-1994 also include seven different color designs on matte black lighters devoted to the Souvenir Truck Series and two different versions (etched solid brass, or full color on polished chrome) of Anheuser-Busch beer labels. Some of the other highly popular collectors editions include the Corvette

Zippo with Corvette logo from the current Chevy collection, and Chevy custom display card.

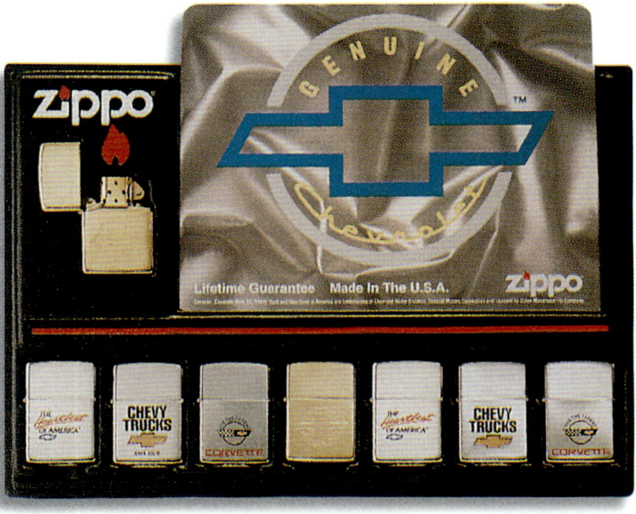

collection celebrating the 40th anniversary of this great American sports car, showing design models from 1953, 1957, 1963, 1978, 1986, and 1991.

Zippo also introduced a dinosaur series and portrayed four different views of these prehistoric reptiles, in pewter. These pewter designs were then placed on a chrome or antique brass lighter.

Zippo is currently marketing groups or collections of lighters to collectors in many different fields: the famed designs of Barett-Smythe are in a unique collection of eight different lighters, which feature Endangered Animals.

Motor sports have always been at the heart and soul of the American Sports fan. Needless to say Zippo recognized this as a huge marketing opportunity and for years all forms of motor sports have found their way onto Zippo lighters. The success of motor sport marketing to Zippo can be measured through Zippo's sponsorship of the US Vintage Grand Prix of Watkins Glen, and the Winston Cup. These two events alone gave rise to the release of the Zippo Motor Sports Collection which not only featured NASCAR drivers, but a Vintage Collection dedicated to Watkins Glen and the U.S. Vintage Grand Prix.

Today Zippo manufacturers lighters that commemorate the Daytona 500, the Indy 500, and Formula One, as well as the Indy Racing League. The Inaugural

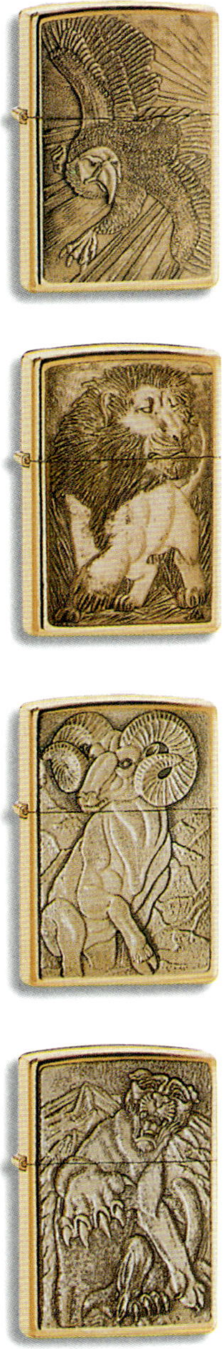

Barret-Smythe designs on Zippo lighters.

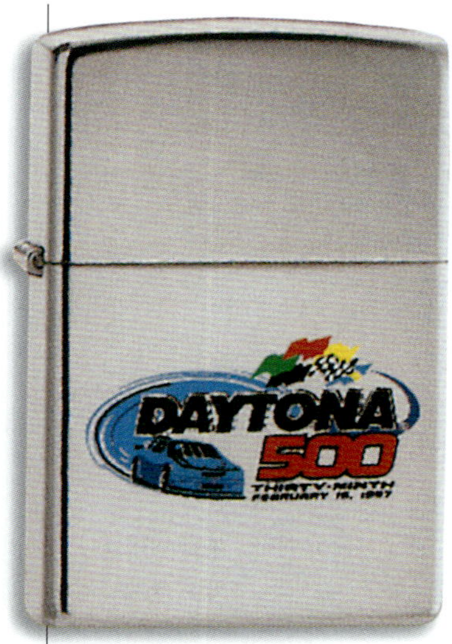

Zippo has close ties with motor sport (see Chapter 14).

Run of the Brickyard 400 at Indianapolis was accompanied by a Brickyard 400 collectable Zippo lighter. Other lighters that form part of Zippo's motor sport collections are the Smokin' Joe's racing collection, the Dale Earnhardt collection and the Jeff Gordon Collection.

The 50th anniversary of D-Day was honored by Zippo, with a black Crackle lighter, bearing an antique brass replica of the sleeve patch worn by Allied troops, and presented in a commemorative decorated tin, with General Eisenhower's D-Day message to the forces of the day reprinted inside the lid. This was the Zippo 1994 collectible of the year.

The Allied Heroes Set of four World War II Generals Eisenhower, de Gaulle, Montgomery, and Bradley also issued in 1994 were placed in a collectible decorated tin.

The combination of Zippo and Case helped to promote the swap meet concept, which was launched in Bradford on July 21, of 1995. The swap meet is quite an event in Bradford and is accompanied by live national radio broadcast, 200 collectors tables with many vary rare and hard to find Zippos. The whole of Bradford comes alive with special events all over the city. This is a very special event to collectors and enthusiasts and many come from all around the world. One of the big attractions at the swap meet is the annual "collectors only" auction in which rare collectors items and memorabilia are auctioned. The proceeds of the auction go to the Zippo/Case Museum in Bradford.

The 1996 Collectible lighter featured Pinup Girls, and Pinup of the Year, Joan, in a presentation box, and also the Four Seasons pinups in their own companion set.

Pinup Holly, reminds us of winter in December, while April welcomes Spring, Ida Redd heralds Autumn, and Sommer reveals the warmth of Summer. Collectors had the added bonus of having the opportuinity to send away for the Zippo 1996 pinup calendar through a mail in card supplied in the handsome presentation tin.

The 1996 Olympic Games held in Atlanta are remembered by the Olympic Games Centennial Series, celebrating the 100th anniversary of the modern Olympics. The Olympic lighters were available as single pieces, or in boxed sets of seven different designs. Boxed gift sets of lighter and key ring combinations were also on offer and proved to be a big success for Zippo.

1997, and the Zippo Manufacturing Company's 65th anniversary, was ushered in with the magnificent Art Deco commemorative lighter. This pewter-enhanced lighter is packed in a presentation tin that displays some of Zippo's advertisements through 65 years of their history. This year also ushered in an exciting new product line up, some of the highlights being the traditional matte black and gold Toledo Series was augmented by 10 new designs, and the relationship with Barrett-Smythe produced three trick lighters in the Surprise series

Bourbon lovers were rewarded with the Jim Beam collection,

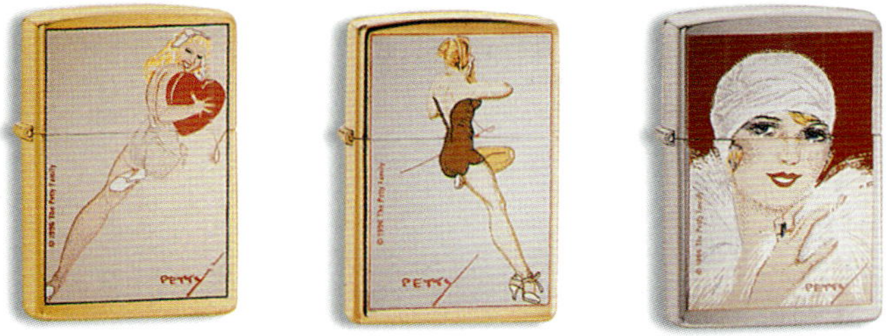

ABOVE: The 'Petty Girl' series of pinup designed by George Brown Petty IV – Heart (Left), Memphis Belle (Center), Red (Right).

OVER: 1996 Collectible of the Year was a lighter depicting Pinup of the Year, Joan.

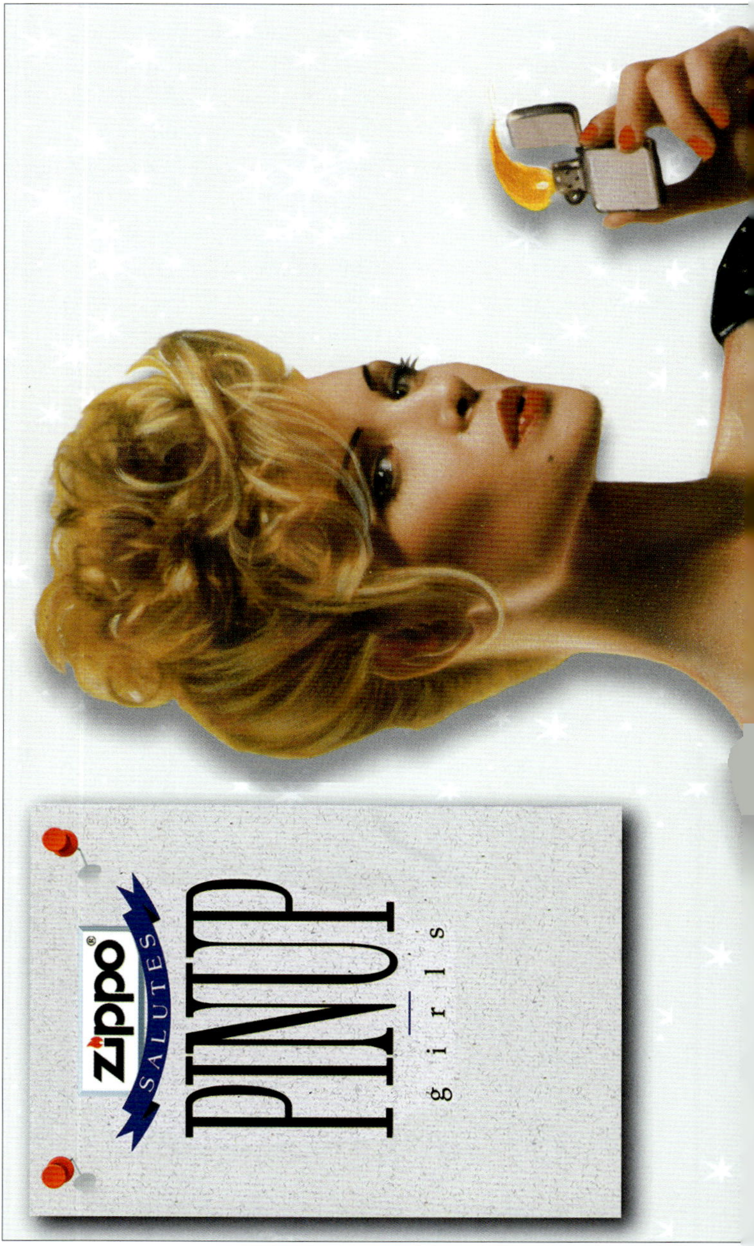
Zippo
SALUTES
PINUP
girls

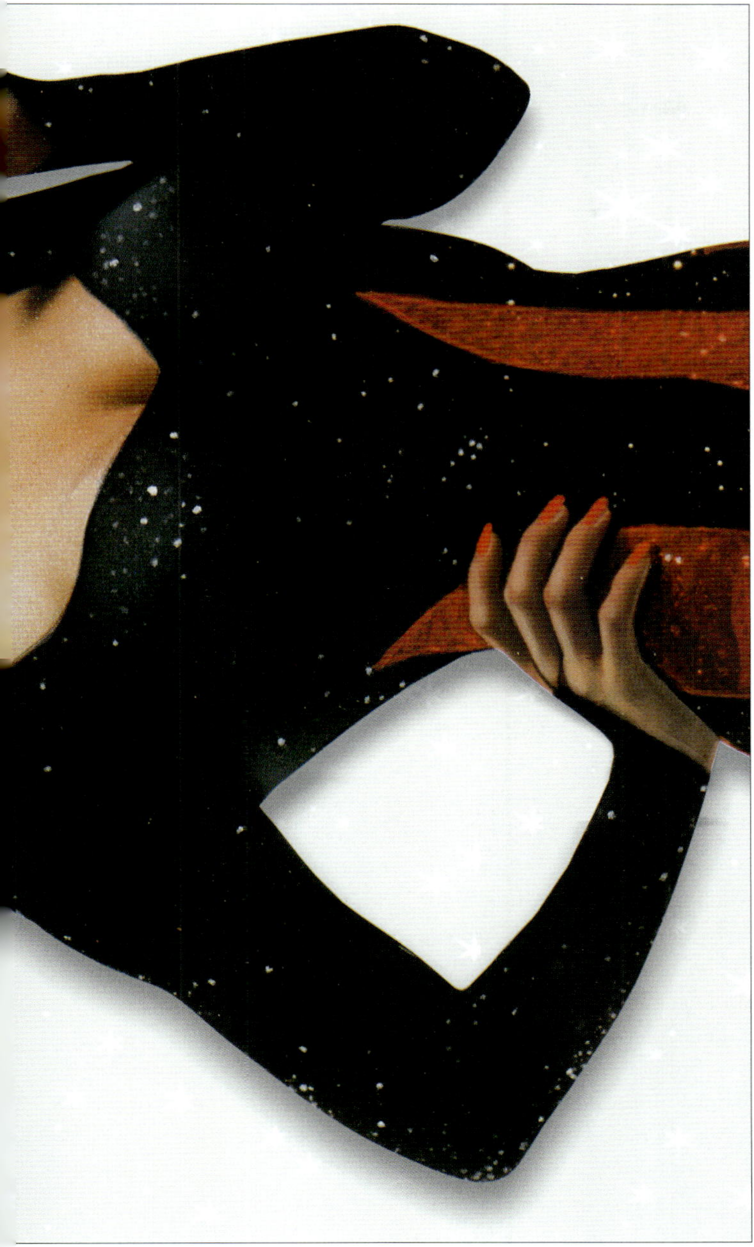

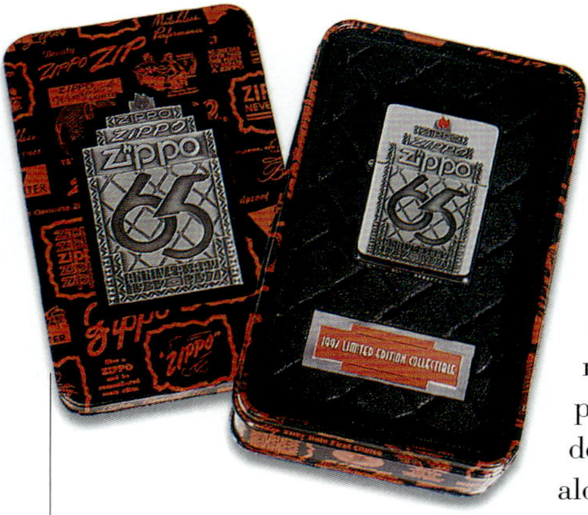

Zippo's 65th Anniversary collectible lighter and presentation tin.

and beer drinkers drank to the Red Dog, Miller, Budweiser, and Corona collections.

The legendary Colt firearm was fitted in a seven–design series, and nostalgia seekers could purchase seven different designs of Camel lighters alone!

Car racing enthusiasts were offered the six-design Dale Earnhardt series – each lighter engraved with a facsimile of Earnhardt's autograph. This Intimidator collection was available in boxed sets, or as individual lighters. Chevy and Ford had their place in the 1997 offerings along with a new NFL series.

The Zippo 65th Anniversary Personal Accessory Collection, includes a reproduction of the Lady Bradford table lighter called the Barbara Table Lighter, bearing the 65th Anniversary logo. This has a removable silver plate lighter etched with the anniversary logo.

Zippo Selects for 1997, celebrate The Beatles on eight different designs, and is offered in a set of six lighters, and individually as lighter only, or lighter with key tag sets. Seven of the lighters depict famous Beatles albums like *Abbey Road*, *Let it Be* and *Hard Day's Night*. Two lighters depict the Beatles logo and one lighter called the Beatles Anthology has numerous famous pictures of the group on the lighter.

Stanley Mouse creator of some of the finest rock art for record albums and posters and illustrations had some of his work printed on the Rock Art series of eight lighters.

Other items on offer in the 1997 Zippo catalog were Zippo's latest license, United Colors of Benetton which featured ten designs. A 'Petty Girl' series of pinups also debuted, designed by George Brown Petty IV.

1997 also saw the introduction of a new Barrett-Smythe issue, a four-lighter tribute to the Three Stooges, a Tabasco series, and a group of four lighters welcoming Zippo Jeans.

The Metallique art form from the 1930s was reintroduced in a six-lighter series. These classic reintroductions were reproduced on Vintage Series lighters, and features classic Zippo designs of the 1939 World's Fair, the Five o' Clock Club, and the Reveler, while Zippo history is recalled with Windy, A Week's Trial, and the Zippo Car,

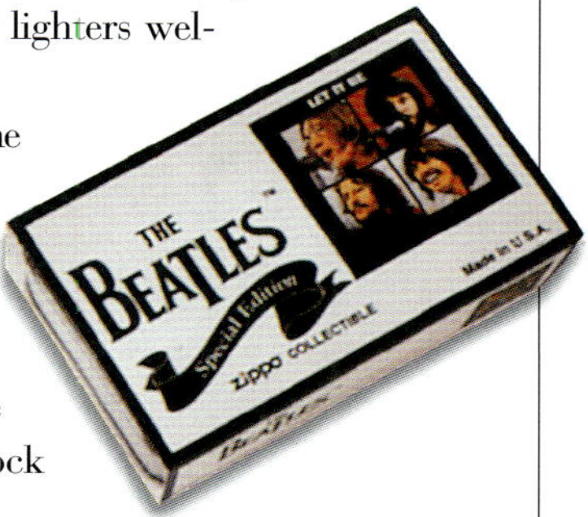

Zippo's 1997 Beatles Collection.

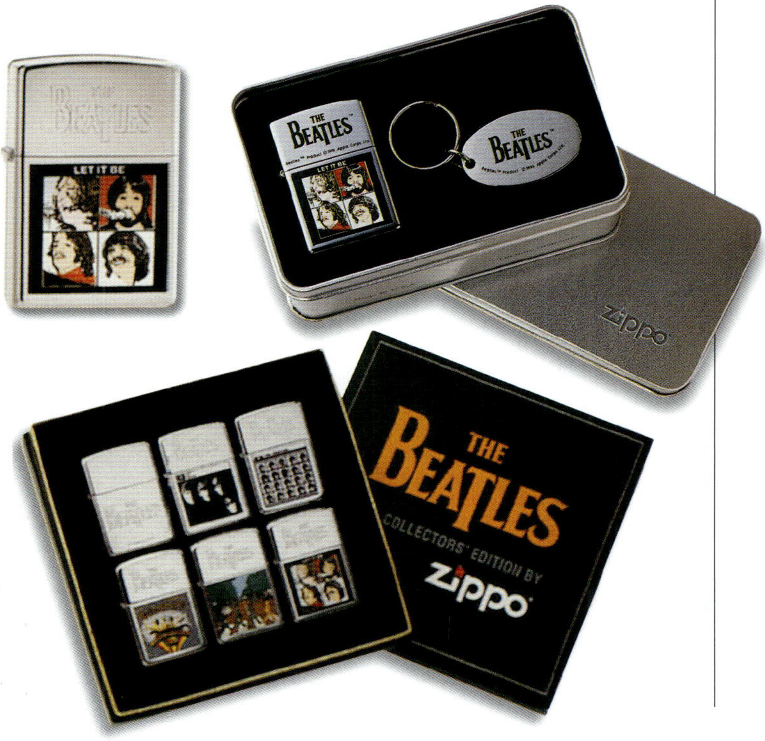

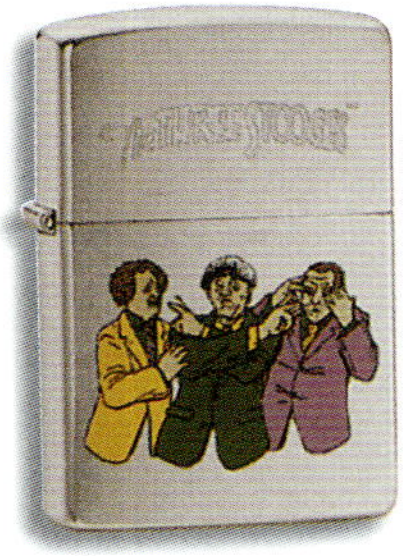

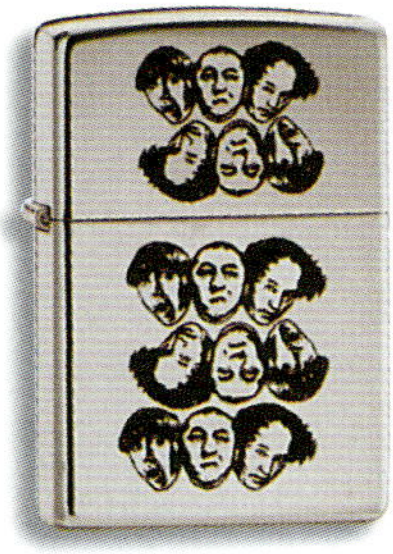

A Barrett-Smythe four-lighter tribute to the Three Stooges.

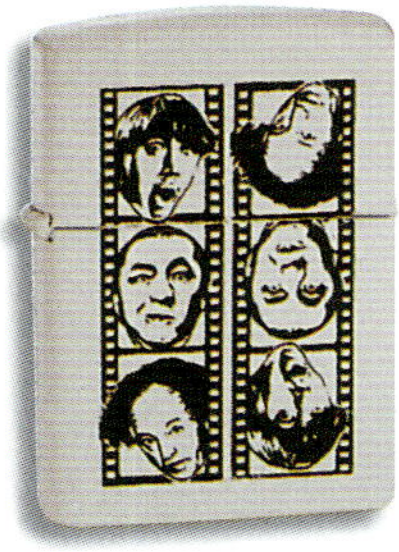

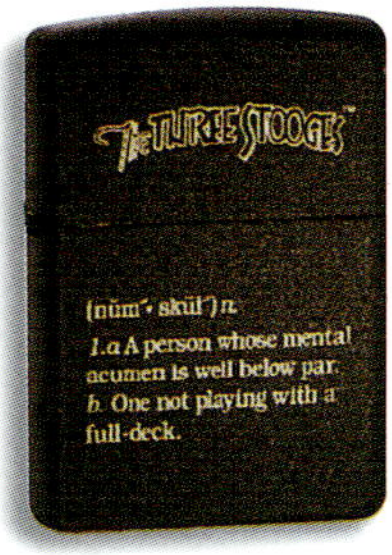

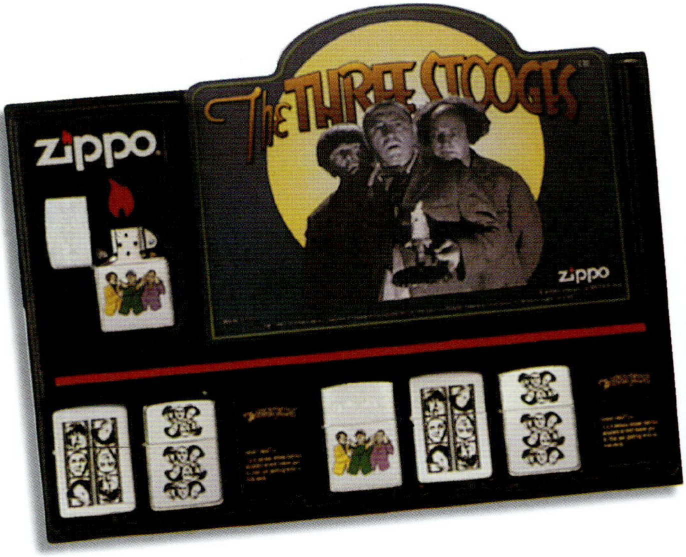

being marketing slogans and campaigns of a bygone era.

LIGHTER OF THE YEAR

To bring the story right up to date, we must mention the Millennium Edition, the eighth in the series of collectibles that started in 1992 with the first Collectible of the Year, the 60th Anniversary Commemorative Lighter in a collectible tin. In 1993 the Collectible of the Year featured Windy; in 1994 Zippo saluted the 50th anniversary of D-Day. Gen. Eisenhower's inspirational June 6, 1944 message to the troops was reprinted inside the lid of the round collectible tin.

The 1995 collectible was 'Jaguar and Cub at Turtle Falls,' sharing a graphic connection with the four-lighter Mysteries of the Forest set. In 1996 Zippo's pinup of the year, Joan, was the 1996 Collectible. In 1997 the 65th Anniversary was highlighted; the 1998 Limited Edition featured a detailed pewter rendering of the Zippo Car and the Zippo Pennsylvania license plate. The commemorative tin visually chronicled the car's colorful history.

In 1999 Zippo featured the Zippo Millennium Edition, the first-ever computer-engraved Zippo collectible. Its message is 'One World . . . One Future' and Zippo says of this message that it:

> 'expresses our belief that the challenges of a new millennium are best faced united . . . reaffirmed in our commitment to quality, utility and value, and striving to ensure a future of infinite possibilities for everyone.'

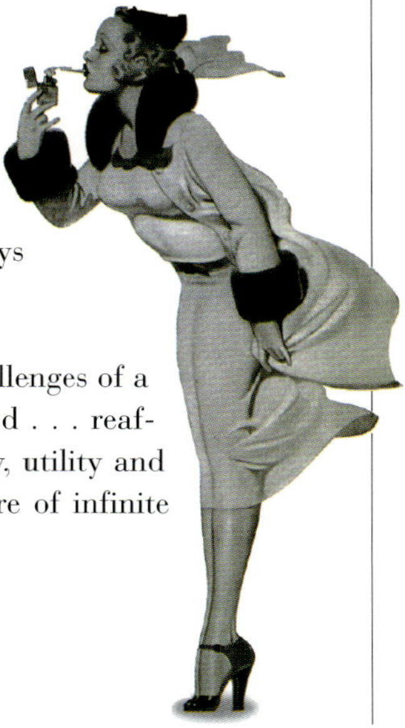

'Windy' was celebrated as part of the Vintage Series.

CHAPTER 9

ZIPPO ADVERTISING

While Blaisdell was convinced that his lighter was perfect, and it was indeed windproof, he needed to share this information with the world. The economy in 1933 was not what you would call booming, in fact few shops would even contemplate taking on new products. Blaisdell gained much experience peddling his lighters from one store to another, and although he had faith in his lighter he had to spread the word. Initially he did this by giving out free lighters to those individuals who he knew would be capable of giving his lighters good exposure. One of his earliest schemes involved a childhood friend of Blaisdell, who was now the manager of a long distance bus company. Blaisdell asked if the bus drivers on the long journeys would show his lighter to their passengers at every stop. In return Blaisdell offered the bus drivers free Zippos. This scheme enabled Blaisdell to get as much exposure as he could. Blaisdell did not have the money to advertise his product in a big magazine and this alternative worked for him. Blaisdell had created some small flyers as well as advertisements all along the theme

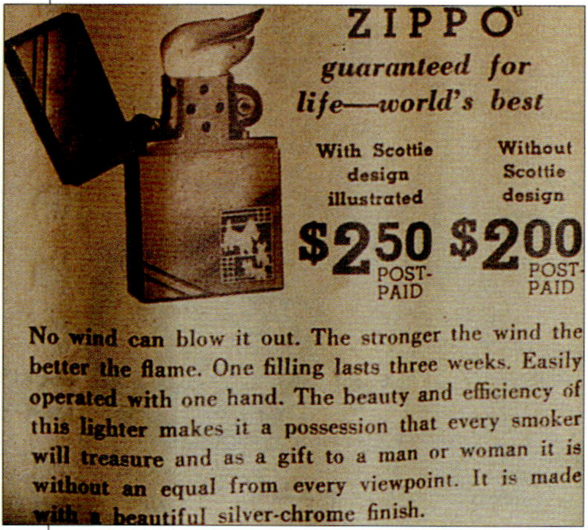

Very early winter advertisement that appeared in a catalog called 'The House of Westminster.' According to the penned inscription on the ad, it appeared in the catalog both in 1938 and 1939.
Photo A. R. Baer

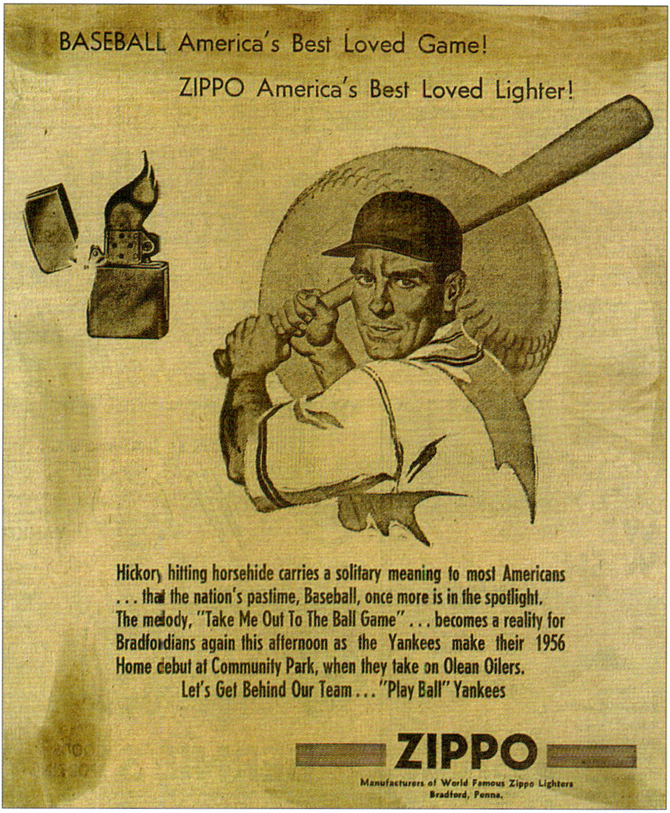

1950s advertisement, depicting baseball as America's favorite game, and Zippo as America's best-loved lighter! Advertising through the years has been a creative medium for the promotion of both Zippo and its lighters.

of sports and recreation. His main theme throughout this early period was the slogan 'Wind Proof.' In 1936 Zippo appeared in the Sports Wholesale Catalog – No 47. and this was very favorable to Blaisdell as he always felt that his lighters would appeal to the outdoor type. Already in 1936 Blaisdell had produced leaflets to the business community depicting lighters with company trademarks this was after he received an order for 500 from the Kendall Oil Company

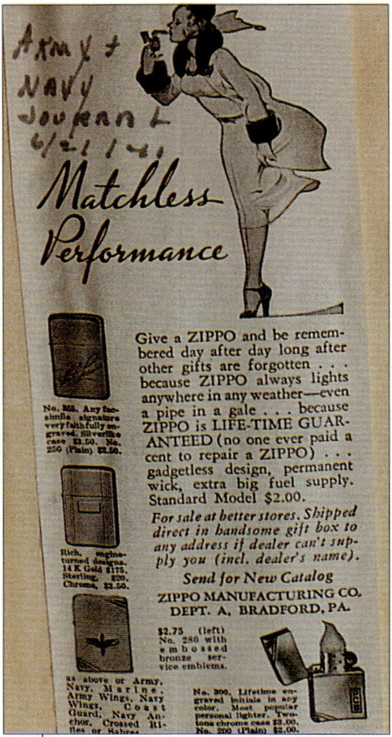

1941 advertisement placed in the *Army and Navy Journal*, making use of 'Windy,' the girl that was first used by Zippo in the 1937 Christmas campaign.
Photo A. R. Baer

a neighbor in Bradford.

While Zippo was getting a little exposure through the bus drivers as well as the few advertisements Blaisdell was placing in local publications, the growth was slow. Blaisdell realized that the time had in fact come to advertise his lighters in a national magazine. It was Christmas 1937, and Blaisdell decided to borrow $3000.00 to run what today is regarded as his most famous advertisement. the full page advertisement in the December issue of the Esquire Magazine, as noted earlier in this book, not only set the tone for the type of campaigns to come, but indeed set a standard for Zippo advertising. From this moment on all Zippo advertising was to have in essence a clear direction, and meaning, that was and still is very focused and direct. Indeed 'Windy' (as the girl was to become affectionately known), created an image for Zippo, in Zippo's advertising that was to be upheld for the next 50 years and beyond.

The advertisement in *Esquire* was not entirely a success, this was due to the lack of a broad base of retailers,

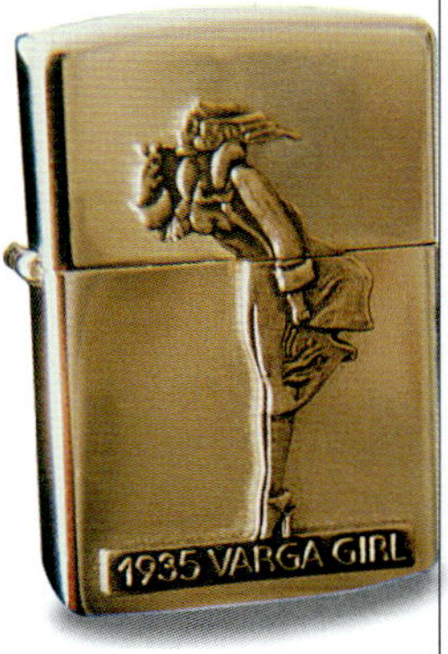

'1935 Vargas Girl' Collectible of the Year produced in 1993.
Photo A R Baer
Lighter Personal Collection of A Baer

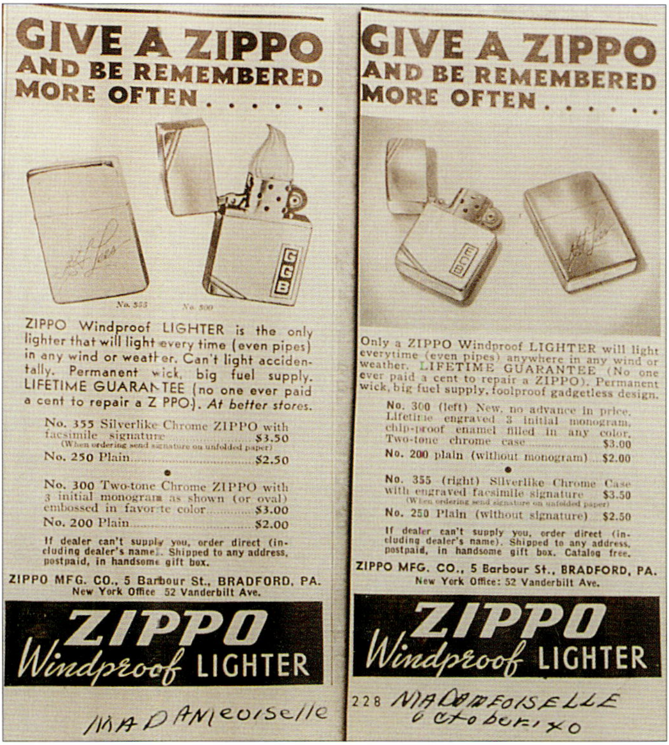

Zippo advertisements that appeared in *Madamoiselle* October 1940.
Photo A. R. Baer

across the country, hence those people who saw the advertisement did not have anywhere to go to in fact buy the lighter. But 'Windy' soon appeared on Zippo packaging as well as in other Zippo advertisements. 'Windy' became so popular an icon and synonymous with the lighter, that soon she appeared on Zippo lighters themselves.

In 1993 Zippo released a collector's edition 'Windy' lighter called the Varga Girl (See Chapter 2 Early Years, for an explanation as to why 'Windy' became erroneously know as the Varga girl). This special commemorative gift set was a standard chrome lighter with a pewter replica of 'Windy' affixed to the front of the lighter.

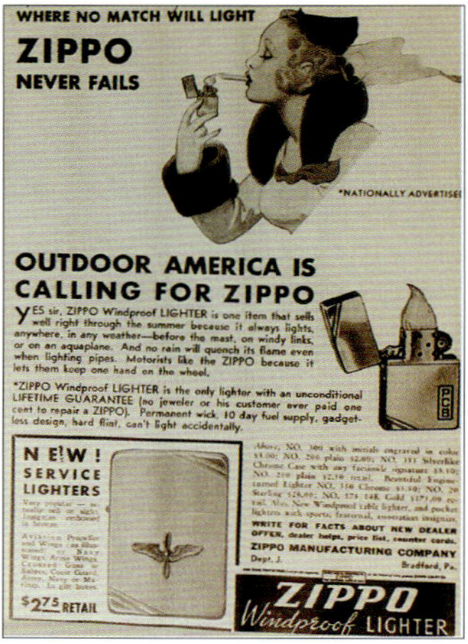

Advertisement placed in the *National Jeweler* 1941, depicting the fact that 'outdoor America' is calling for Zippo. This classic advertisement ties in many different aspects of Zippo's existence at the time of the use of 'Windy' as an advertisement feature; the focus on the fact that no lighter other than a Zippo is windproof, and the sale of service lighters reminds us that a war is in progress. *Photo A. R. Baer*

Blaisdell continued to place small advertisements in selected magazines and journals like *American Business* and *Mademoiselle*. All these advertisements were the basic design, centering their message on 'Give a Zippo and be remembered more often.' The Metallique lighter with Blaisdell's initials was the most common lighter depicted in these advertisements. It appears that Blaisdell became quite focused in terms of his ad placements in the late 1930s and 1940s as evidence exists of many small advertisements in many small journals, rather than one or two advertisements in bigger national publications. Blaisdell ran bigger advertisements in publications such as the *National Jeweler*, hoping to catch the eye of the jewelry retailer. Other more focused forms of advertisements in the late 1930s were those advertisements that Blaisdell placed in such journals as *American Business*. In fact an advertisement placed in this journal in November of 1939, centered on a

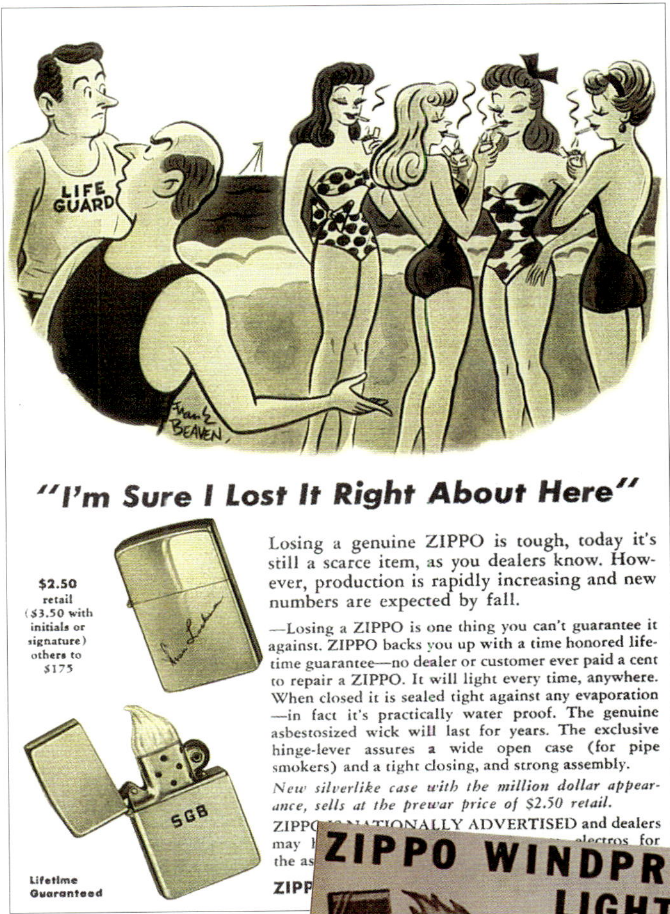

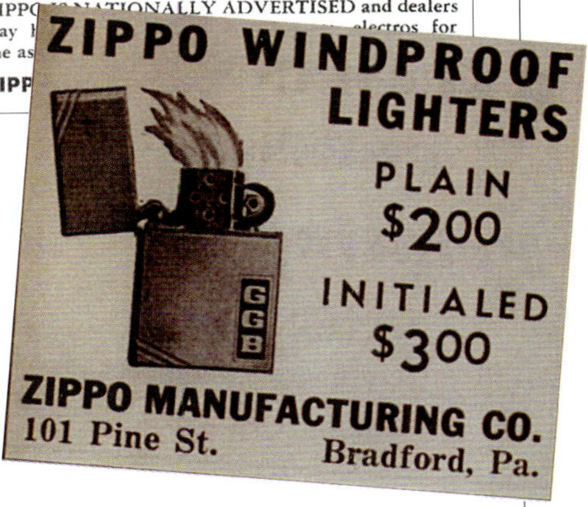

ABOVE: 'I'm sure I lost it right about here' – clever unisex advertising 1950s' style.

RIGHT: Advertisement placed in the American Motorist of September 1933. Note the Metallique initials on the lighter depictec are those of George G. Blaisdell.

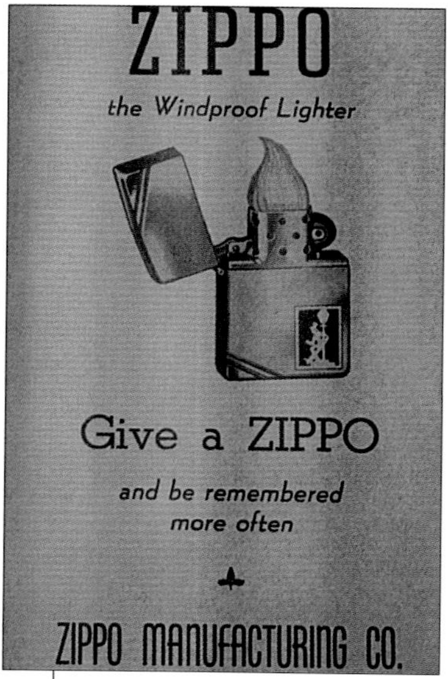

1940-41 Christmas season advertisement placed in the 'Inner City Bowling League.' *Photo A. R. Baer*

Christmas message to business owners trying to convince them to purchase Zippo lighters as gifts, with a company logo either engraved or affixed through the special metallique method. The more focused and directed advertising that Blaisdell had now centered on certainly seemed to work as by the end of the 1930s Zippo appeared to have a good following. The war did not help matters but Blaisdell used this devastating time to his advantage. He tried as best he could to get his lighter to our boys, both here in the United States as well as abroad. The lighter itself was never in fact endorsed by the U.S. Army, but became the most popular lighter among the troops. Blaisdell managed to get Zippo lighters to PX stores both at home, abroad and on U.S. ships. These lighters today are most sought after as many of them were emblazoned with personal messages, emblems and engravings, depicting the many situations that the soldiers found themselves in.

While during the war there was a shortage of most raw materials, including packaging products, Zippo had to keep its factory going. Steel was used instead of Brass for the lighters, and while advertising was reduced, the theme of such advertising was centered on the war. Many such advertisements depicted stories of one or more of our GIs far away from home, having a trusty 'friend' in their Zippo lighter. While Blaisdell probably did not know it at the time, this concept of his advertisements not only showing of his wares, but compelling his readers to look beyond just the pictures and

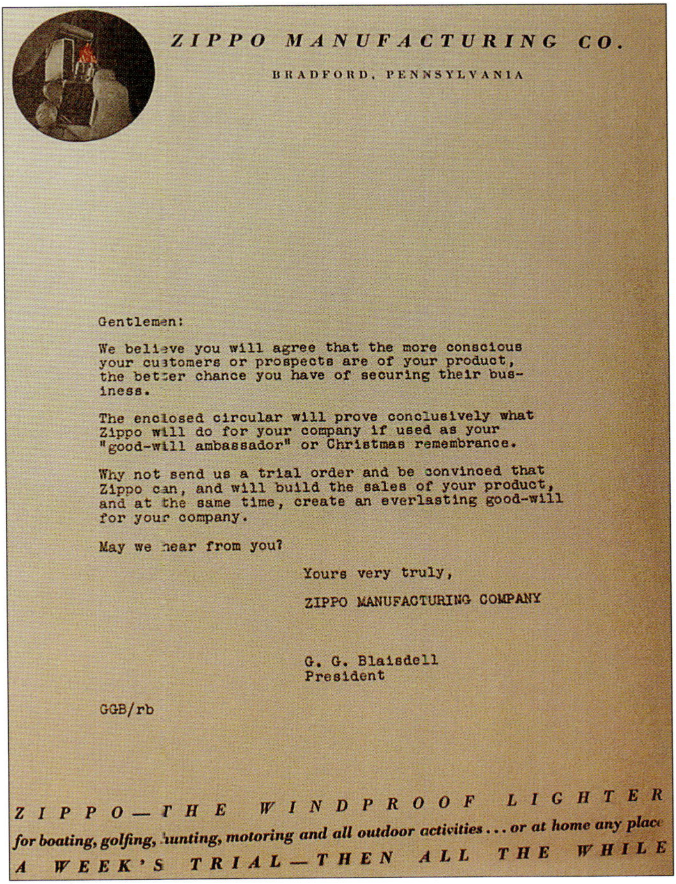

ZIPPO MANUFACTURING CO.

BRADFORD, PENNSYLVANIA

Gentlemen:

We believe you will agree that the more conscious your customers or prospects are of your product, the better chance you have of securing their business.

The enclosed circular will prove conclusively what Zippo will do for your company if used as your "good-will ambassador" or Christmas remembrance.

Why not send us a trial order and be convinced that Zippo can, and will build the sales of your product, and at the same time, create an everlasting good-will for your company.

May we hear from you?

Yours very truly,

ZIPPO MANUFACTURING COMPANY

G. G. Blaisdell
President

GGB/rb

ZIPPO — THE WINDPROOF LIGHTER
for boating, golfing, hunting, motoring and all outdoor activities . . . or at home any plac
A WEEK'S TRIAL — THEN ALL THE WHILE

Early undated letter from G. G. Blaisdell. Note the footer of the letterhead depicting many uses for the Zippo lighter. *Photo A. R. Baer*

read the factual stories, was to become the mainstay of Zippo advertising for the next 30 years. As the war in Europe came to a close our boys were returning, with hundreds of stories of war. Zippo lighters with their lifetime guarantee, were coming home and being sent to Bradford to the Zippo repair clinic for repair. Along with these lighters came the letters, the stories, the happy tales and the sad realities of war. While many of these lighters were repaired, those with bullet dam-

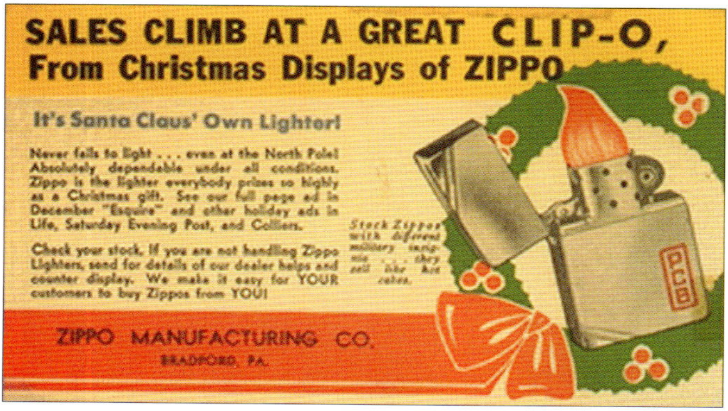
SALES CLIMB AT A GREAT CLIP-O,
From Christmas Displays of ZIPPO
It's Santa Claus' Own Lighter!
Never fails to light . . . even at the North Pole! Absolutely dependable under all conditions. Zippo is the lighter everybody prizes so highly as a Christmas gift. See our full page ad in December "Esquire" and other holiday ads in Life, Saturday Evening Post, and Colliers.
Check your stock. If you are not handling Zippo Lighters, send for details of our dealer helps and counter display. We make it easy for YOUR customers to buy Zippos from YOU!
Stock Zippos with different military insignia . . . they sell like hot cakes.
PCB
ZIPPO MANUFACTURING CO.
BRADFORD, PA.

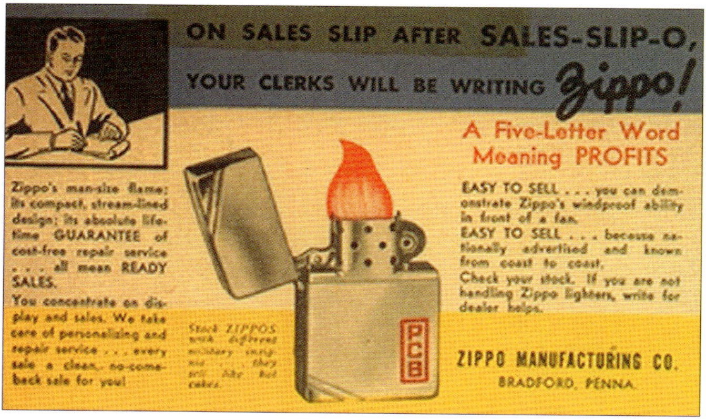
ON SALES SLIP AFTER SALES-SLIP-O,
YOUR CLERKS WILL BE WRITING Zippo!
A Five-Letter Word Meaning PROFITS
Zippo's man-size flame; its compact, stream-lined design; its absolute lifetime GUARANTEE of cost-free repair service . . . all mean READY SALES.
You concentrate on display and sales. We take care of personalizing and repair service . . . every sale a clean, no-come-back sale for you!
Stock ZIPPOS with different military insignia . . . they sell like hot cakes.
PCB
EASY TO SELL . . . you can demonstrate Zippo's windproof ability in front of a fan.
EASY TO SELL . . . because nationally advertised and known from coast to coast.
Check your stock. If you are not handling Zippo lighters, write for dealer helps.
ZIPPO MANUFACTURING CO.
BRADFORD, PENNA.

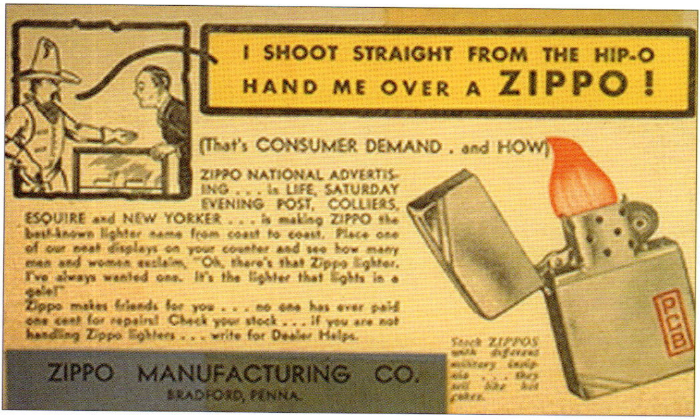
I SHOOT STRAIGHT FROM THE HIP-O
HAND ME OVER A ZIPPO!
(That's CONSUMER DEMAND . and HOW)
ZIPPO NATIONAL ADVERTISING . . . in LIFE, SATURDAY EVENING POST, COLLIERS, ESQUIRE and NEW YORKER . . . is making ZIPPO the best-known lighter name from coast to coast. Place one of our neat displays on your counter and see how many men and women exclaim, "Oh, there's that Zippo lighter. I've always wanted one. It's the lighter that lights in a gale!"
Zippo makes friends for you . . . no one has ever paid one cent for repairs! Check your stock . . . if you are not handling Zippo lighters . . . write for Dealer Helps.
PCB
ZIPPO MANUFACTURING CO.
BRADFORD, PENNA.

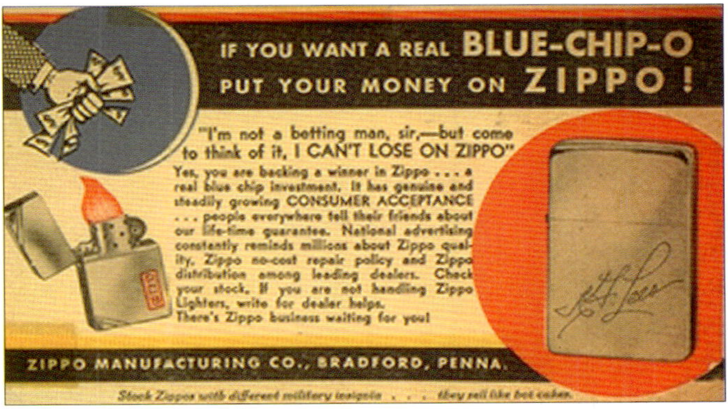

OPPOSITE AND ABOVE:

Early advertising concentrating on the rhyming qualities of 'Zippo.'

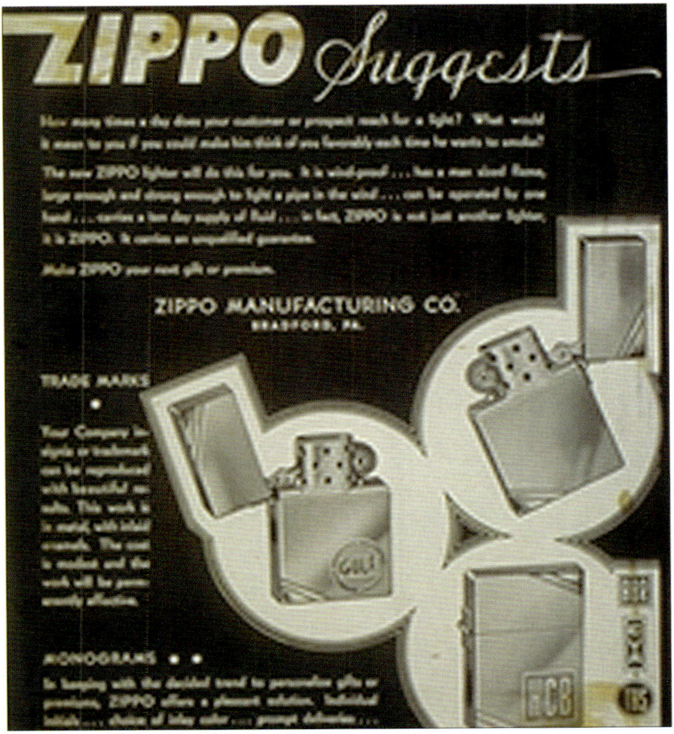

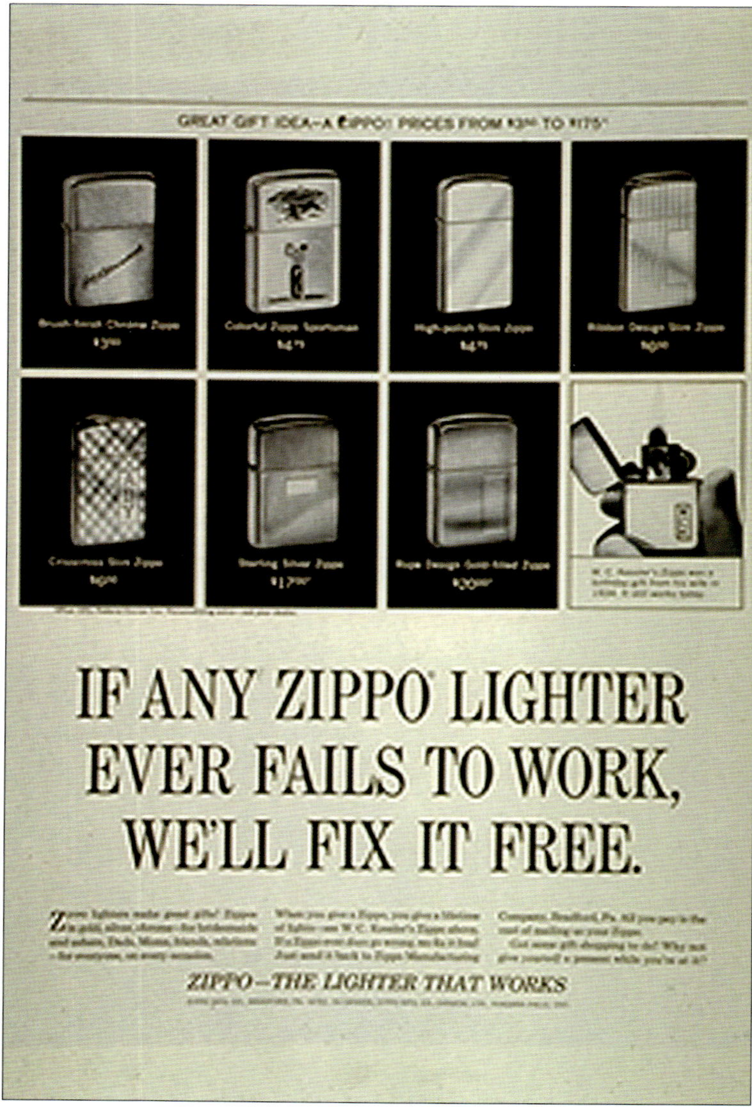

ABOVE AND RIGHT: Much advertising concentrated on Zippo's strongest sale's point: free repairs.

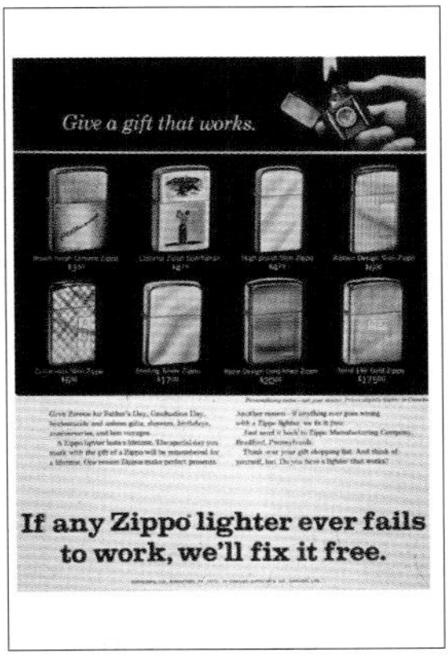

age were replaced. The owners always received their lighters back in pristine working condition. The important fact for Zippo at the end of the war was that they had managed to spread the word of their windproof, 'work-or we will fix it free' lighter to all corners of the earth.

Many of the letters told amazing stories, Zippos at Pearl Harbor, Zippos in Germany, Zippos shot down in Italy. Many of these stories became part of a post-war advertising campaign, depicting a black and white photograph of a lit Zippo lighter, usually the actual item with its slogan below, i.e., 'This Zippo lighter was at Pearl Harbor, Dec. 7, 1941. It still works today.' These advertisements were hugely popular and effective as they played on the minds of the millions of men and women who had sacrificed their time and in many cases the lives of many loved ones. It was around this post war era that in fact Zippos began to be collected. Soldiers and service men held on to theirs dearly, and Zippo recognizing this fact started to produce items with collectors appeal. The advertisements, continued to depict interesting stories, while at the same time introducing new and exciting models.

Essentially, early advertising centered around the wind or fan test. 'Try the fan test!' was an enormous campaign for Blaisdell, from this type of advertising so, 'Windy' was born, again playing upon the concept of a lighter working no matter what. The concept could very well have been based on the fact that Blaisdell ardently marketed his lighter as great for the outdoors. The sports series can attest to this, and this along with the fan test concept, campaign built the lighters brand to even greater fame.

With the above brand explosion, Zippo continued for the next 20 years to really work upon the fact that its lighter had

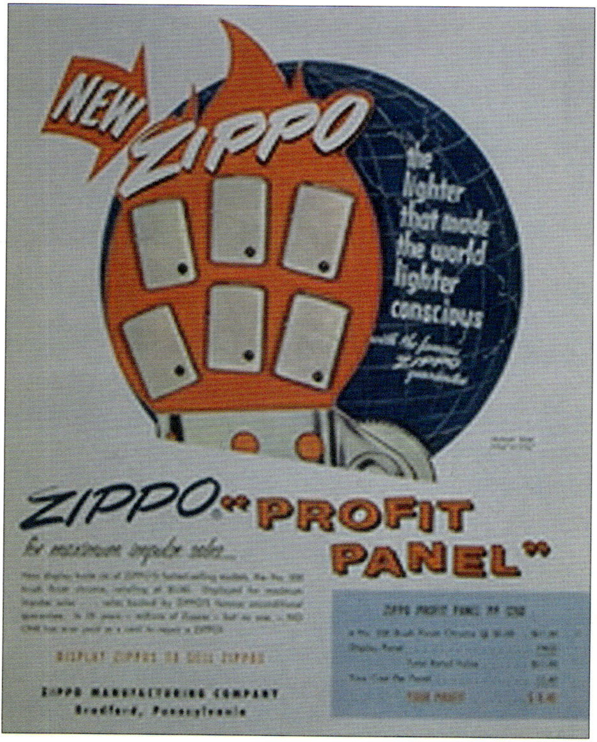

Advertisement that appeared in *Partners* in 1956. While Blaisdell spent an enormous amount of time marketing to the public, he never let up on the retailer, hoping to ensure that all were adequately stocked.
Photo A. R. Baer

seen so many great historical happenings, and used and researched these events to their advantage. The lifetime guarantee now became Zippo's slogan. 'It works or we fix it free.' Many advertisements depicted this slogan along with battered and 'battle weary' Zippos in full working condition. One of the all time classic ads from this campaign was the 1970 Advertisement featuring famous World War II photographer, Joe Rosenthal's Zippo still working. Joe Rosenthal probably took some of the finest heart rendering photographs ever, of World War II. Some of his unforgettable images will be cast in

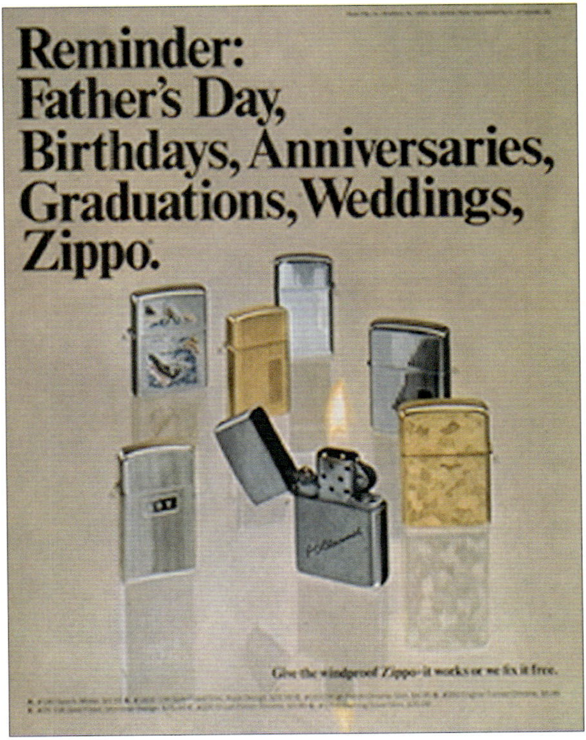

Father's Day promotions

the minds of American for decades to come. His image of American GIs hoisting the Stars and Stripes atop Mt. Suribachi, the most strategically important hill in the battle of Iwo Jima, did more than boost the morale of each and every American, it brought home the power, the glory, and more than that the hope that with this new capture, the war would soon be over.

Much of Zippo's advertising was to its business partners, retailers as well as its salesmen. Blaisdell could not impress more upon his people the importance of knowing exactly how to sell his product. Many leaflets and advertisements were never to be seen by the public, but were in fact created solely for the purpose of selling his lighters to the wholesalers and retailers. The pamphlets and sales materials created for the

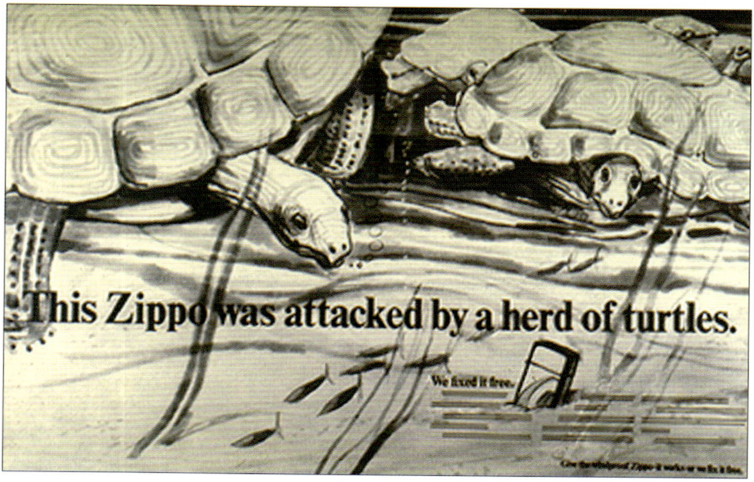

Proposed advertisement layout telling the story of a Zippo that survived being attacked by a herd of turtles.

Zippo sales teams all over the world were also of the highest standard, not to mention some of the early mail order concepts developed by Zippo.

In 1948 Zippo launched its biggest advertisement campaign to date. In an internal publication called the Zippo Zip, intended for business partners and retailers Zippo mapped out a campaign that was to reach an audience of 50 million. Starting in September, Zippo was to break advertisements in huge national magazines such as *Life*, *Look*, *The Saturday Evening Post*, and the *New Yorker*. The new colorful advertisements were meant to reach the gift buying public at the height of the holiday season. Essentially Zippo was ready to capitalize on the huge success they had made in terms of branding during the war years.

As more and more stories flooded into the Zippo repair Clinic, accompanied by letters, Zippo continued to publish the stories in its advertisements. Advertisements included stories of a Zippo that fell 1,100 feet into a Hawaiian pineapple field, another memorable advertisement told the

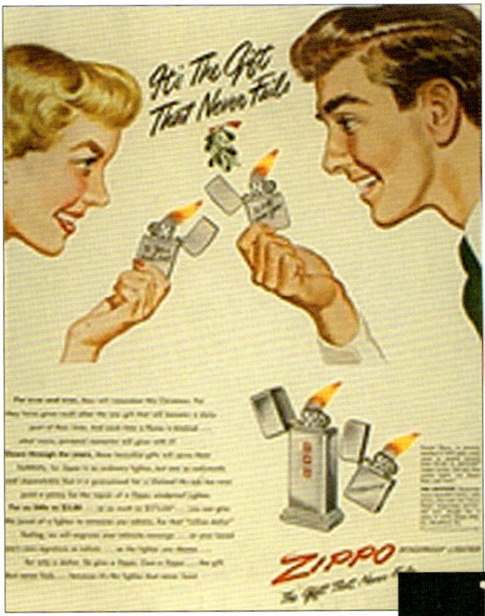

THIS PAGE AND FOLLOWING PAGES: Christmas advertisements were — and still are — an important part of Zippo's promotional spending as is evidenced with these ads.

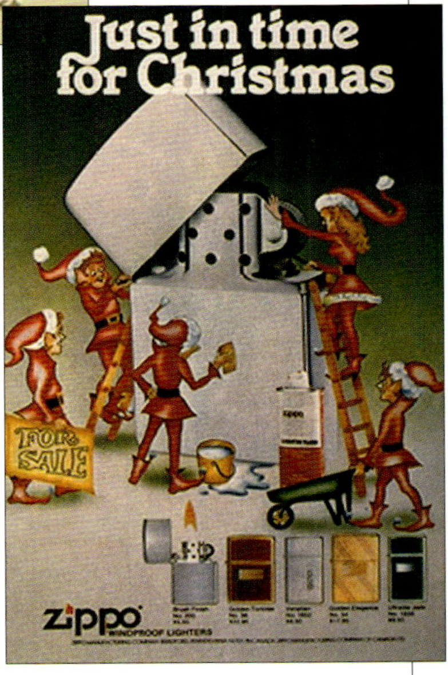

story of a Zippo frozen for four months in a -30°F ice cream storage room, that lit first time, once recovered.

Another famous advertisement told the story of how a Zippo had once been attacked by a herd of turtles — this was certainly among one of the most memorable yarns. Such 'story telling' advertisements continued well into the 1970s.

In the 1950s when Zippo first launched its slim lighters, the advertising campaigns of the day were colorful and exciting — and even now, the freshness and excitement portrayed in these advertisements remains timeless.

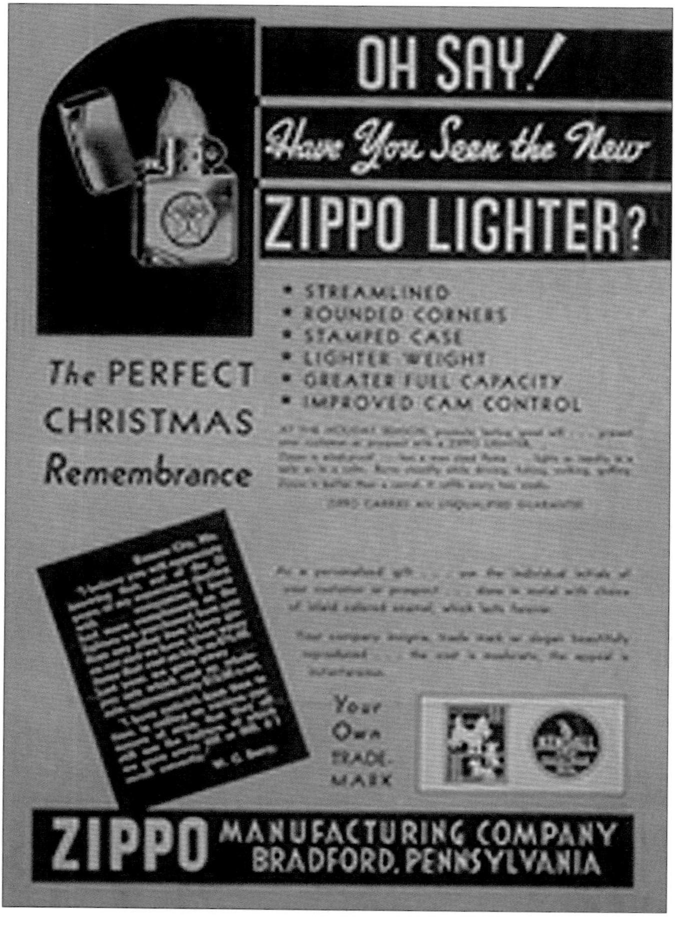

The concept of 'giving a Zippo' as a gift became a big part of Zippo's advertising, and as Christmas was the real time for giving, many of Zippo's campaigns were centered around this holiday. Some of the most striking advertisements came from the Christmas period over the years, and were seen in the national magazines and newspapers as well as in the local papers.

The Zippo advertisement of Santa's helpers around a huge Zippo was one of these, and it seemed at one time that every

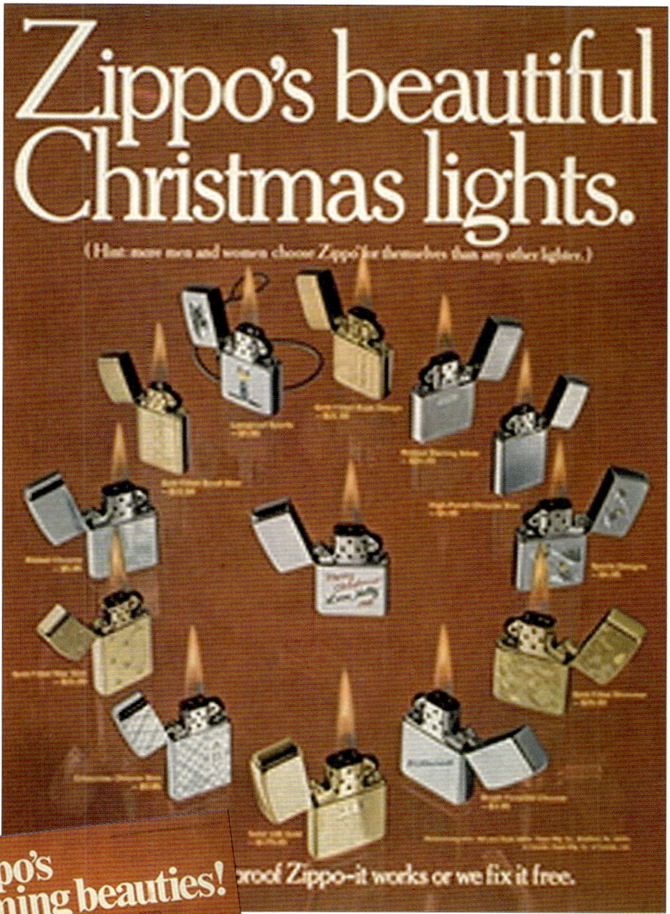

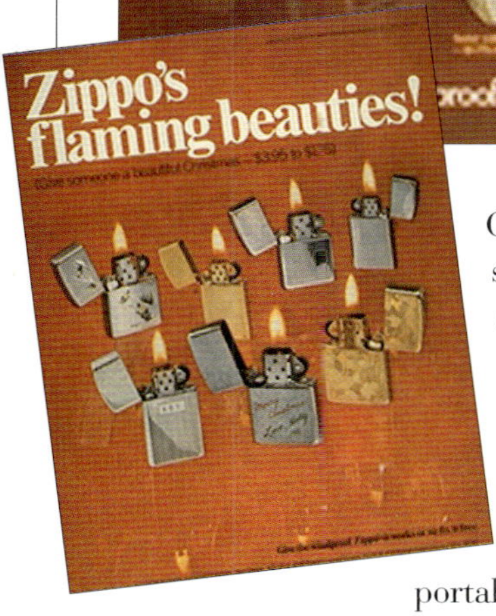

Christmas Zippo brought out a special advertisement. But it ran its course and the Christmas-themed campaign was dropped in 1996 after many successful years. Today Zippo does not actively market its lighter as specifically a cigarette lighter — but rather as a reliable, portable source of flame.

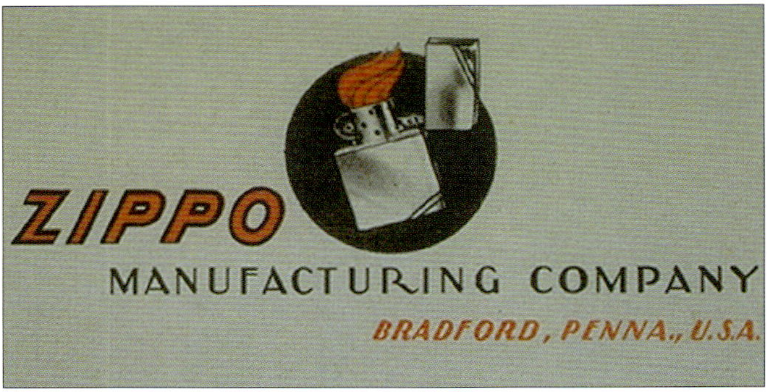

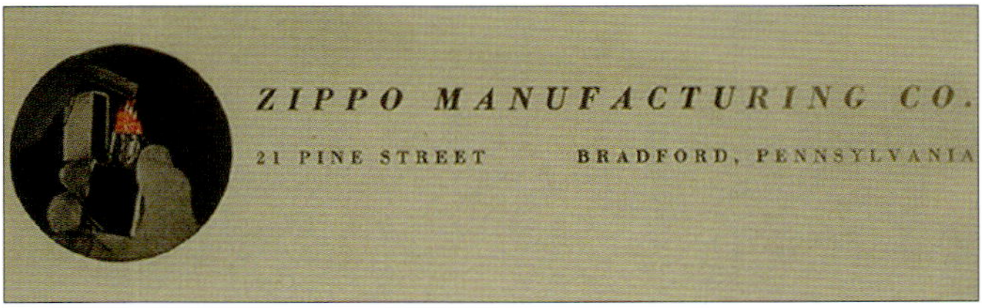

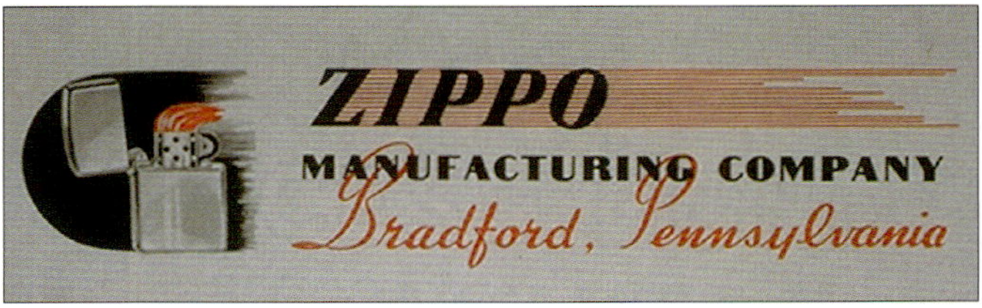

Early Zippo logos and letterheads.

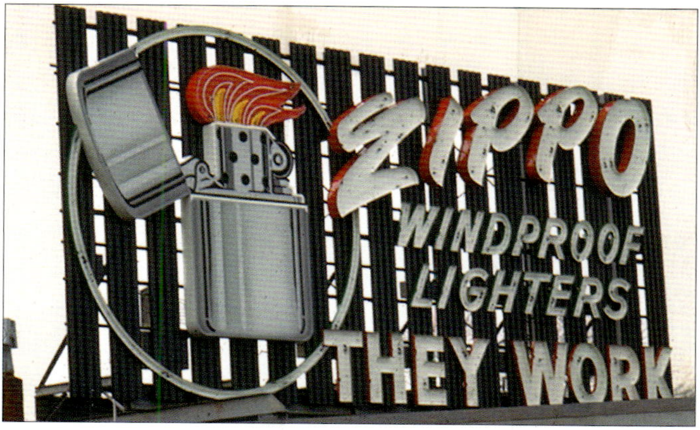

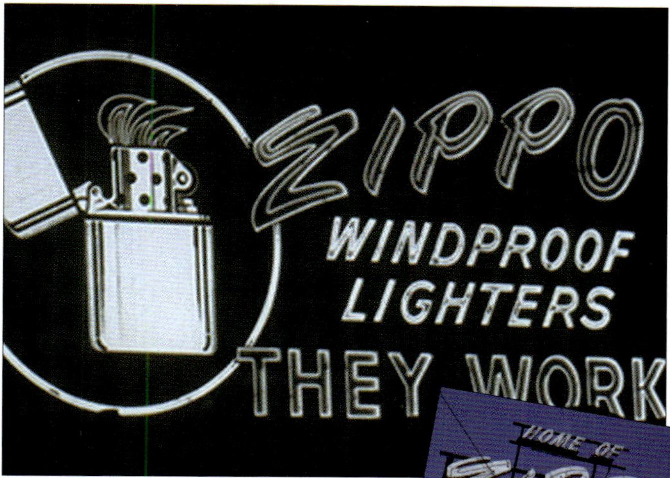

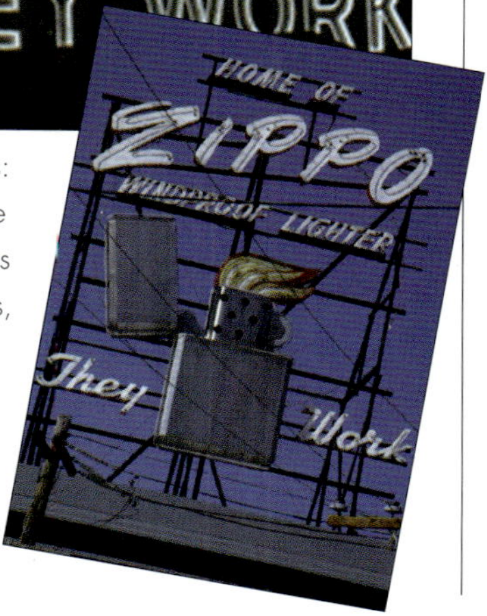

Zippo has been famous for its roof signs: here are three classic images. Above are day and night views of the rooftop signs at Zippo's Canada, Niagara Falls works, and right, the rooftop sign above the corporate headquarters in Bradford. These signs were installed in the 1950s and have not been changed since, except for repair.

CHAPTER 10

ZIPPO MILITARY LIGHTERS AFTER VIETNAM

U.S. NAVY

While today, every vessel in the United States Navy, from patrol boats and submarines, through to battleships and aircraft carriers has its own Zippo lighter, the association between Zippo and the Navy goes back a long time.

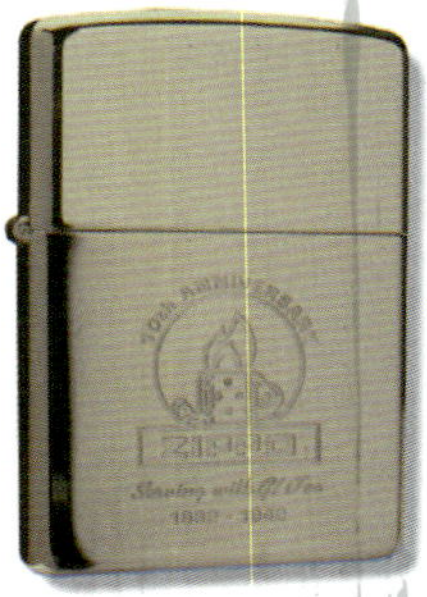

Serving with GI Joe – a celebration of Zippo's World War II legacy.

The tradition dates back to World War II, when sailors had naval insignia attached to their Zippo lighters.

Prior to 1947, and during World War II, the U.S. Navy did not permit the use of engravings that could identify the individual unit.

The now basic design of naval Zippos was created in the post war years 1947-1950, when standard silhouettes were sanctioned by unit commanders in the United States Navy, and engraved for each class of naval vessel.

The Korean War saw a further proliferation of lighters with representations of naval vessels, and more were manufactured during the Vietnam period.

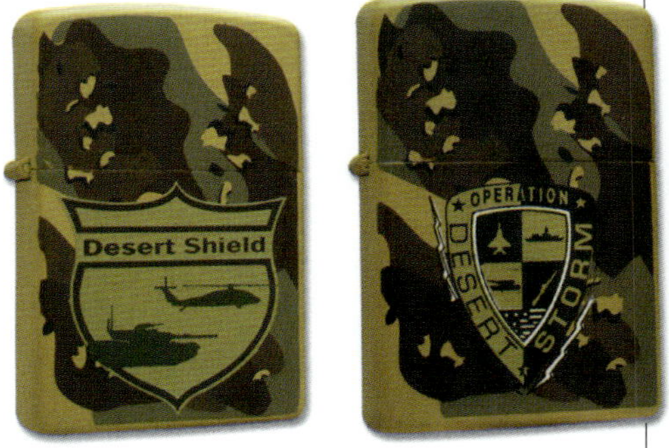

'Desert Shield' and 'Desert Storm' lighters, 1991.

A lighter commemorated the end of the war with

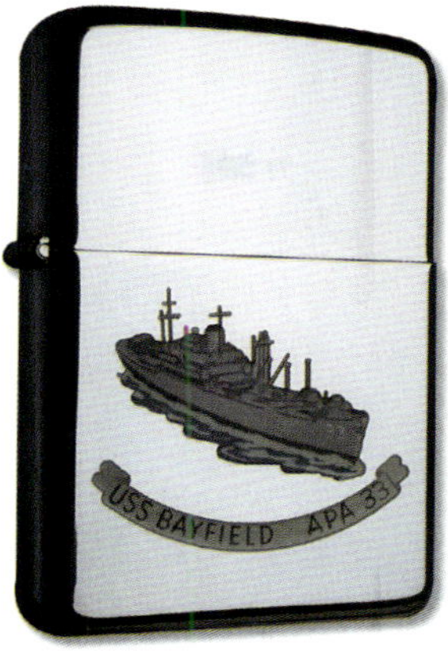

U.S. Navy ship's lighter for APA-33 U.S.S. *Bayfield*.

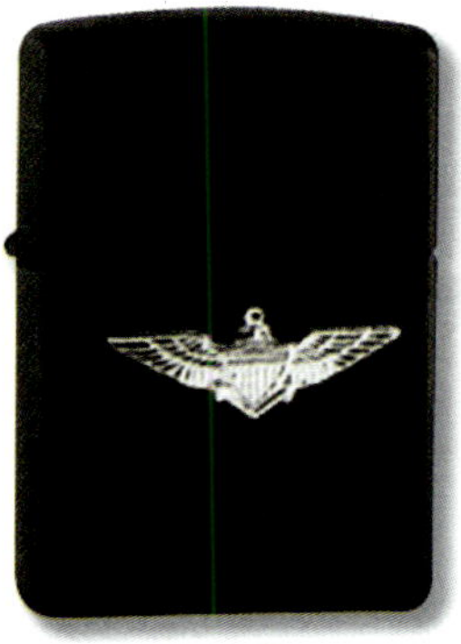

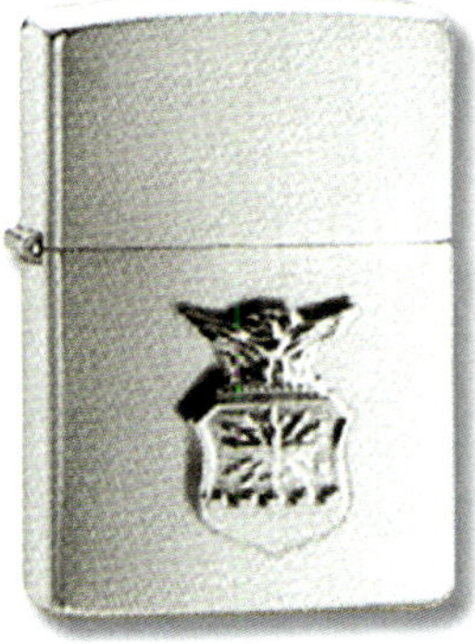

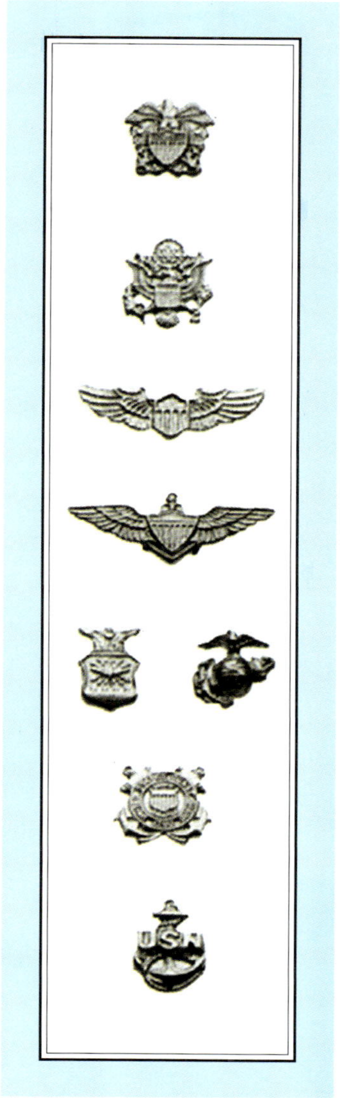

Members of today's services can order lighters in black and chrome with crests and wings etc.

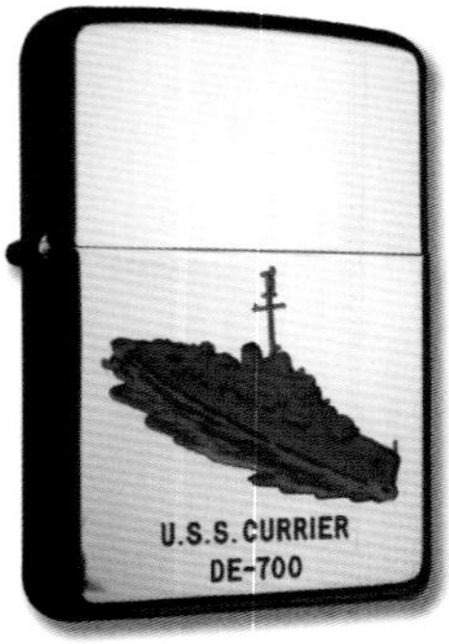

Lighter for crew of DE-700 U.S.S. *Currier.*

Japan, and the signing of the unconditional surrender agreement on board the U.S.S. *Missouri*, and bearing General MacArthur's signature was presented to all new officers trained in 1949.

The earlier lighters were etched in black on chrome-plated brass, while the ones manufactured later introduced colors to the etchings on the lighters.

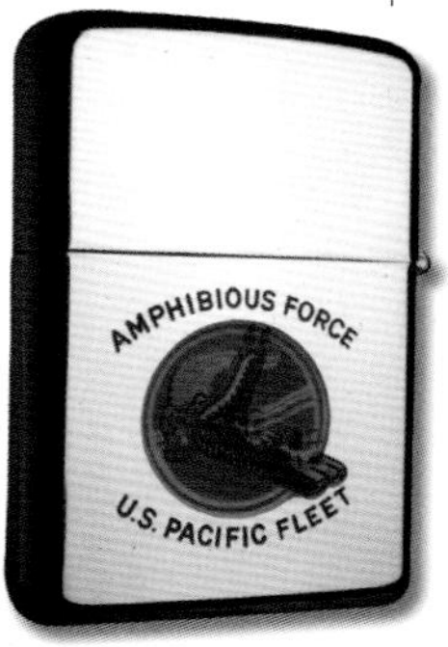

Zippo for the U.S. Pacific Fleet Amphibious Force.

Major occasions are honored by lighters commemorating naval participation. The aircraft carrier U.S.S. *Ranger* is depicted on a camouflage lighter issued to soldiers and sailors in Operation 'Desert Shield.'

Orders for U.S. Navy lighters are placed with independent companies, (two for waterborne, and one for land based forces), which after collating the individual vessel's requirements, forward the orders to Zippo.

What makes naval, (and other military) lighters such desirable collectors items, is that all the lighters manufactured for the Navy, are for purchase only by naval personnel, and are not available for sale to the general public.

FRANCE

As in the U.S., France's navy, army, airforce, and Foreign Legion have commissioned their own Zippo lighters.

Again, as in America, the lighters are not available to the public, and are sold directly to members of the French armed forces. This fact has helped to make the French military Zippo

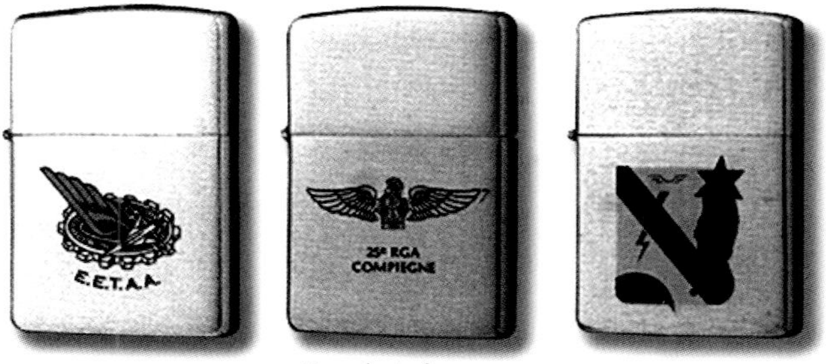

French Airforce

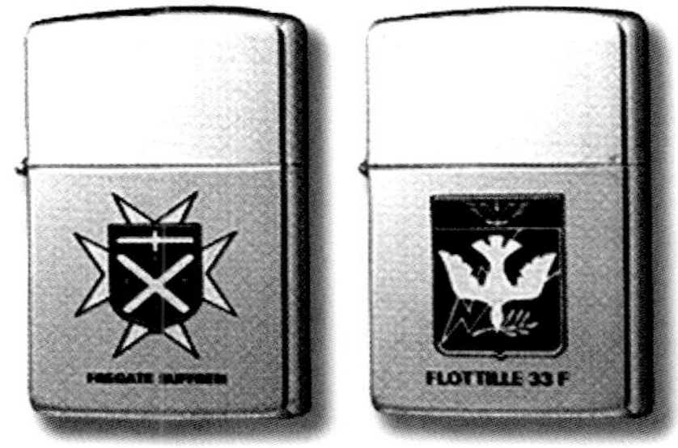

French Navy

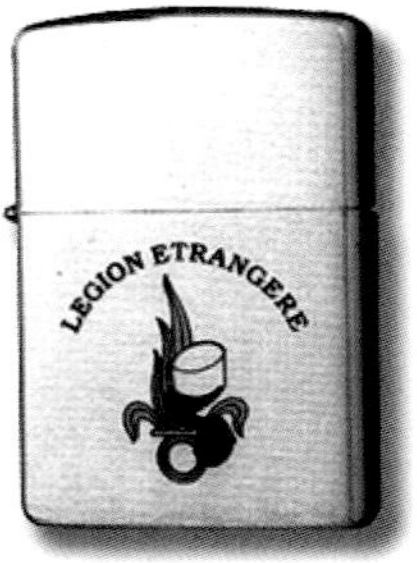

French Army

a relatively rare, and therefore desirable collectors piece.

In spite of Charles De Gaulle's withdrawal of France from military involvement in NATO , and the insistance that all things military, including 'The Bomb' remain under French control, the Gallic aversion to *'objets'* from the *Etats Unies* succumbed to the lure of the Zippo. Nowhere else could they find an icon as sturdy, reliable, and identity confirming as the Zippo. Nowhere else were they able to obtain a military symbol with a lifetime guarantee, and an endless supply of the perfectly executed artwork that boosts the Zippo legend.

Where else but from Zippo?

Wherever the French armed forces are stationed, whether in overseas 'départements,' such as Reunion, or former French colonies like the Ivory Coast, Zippos are admired and coveted by the local inhabitants, and demand for Zippo, the American Legend, continues to grow.

CHAPTER 11

ZIPPO MANUFACTURING

RIGHT: 'The Story of the GIs' Old Flame' – an article from *Popular Science* (1961) that showed the manufacturing process in the early 1960s.

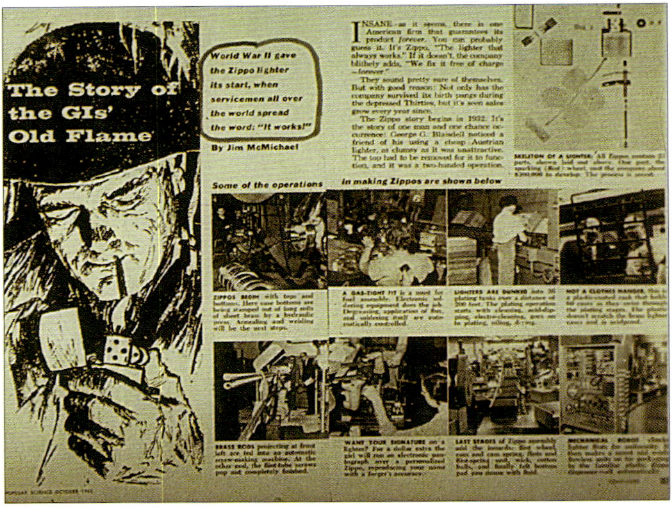

The Story of the GIs' Old Flame

World War II gave the Zippo lighter its start, when servicemen all over the world spread the word: "It works!"

By Jim McMichael

INSANE—as it seems, there is one American firm that guarantees its product *forever*. You can probably guess it. It's Zippo, "The lighter that always works." If it doesn't, the company blithely adds, "We fix it free of charge—forever."

They sound pretty sure of themselves. But with good reason: Not only has the company survived its birth pangs during the depressed Thirties, but it's seen sales grow every year since.

The Zippo story begins in 1932. It's the story of one man and one chance occurrence: George G. Blaisdell noticed a friend of his using a cheap Austrian lighter, as clumsy as it was unattractive. The top had to be removed for it to function, and it was a two-handed operation.

SKELETON OF A LIGHTER.

Some of the operations in making Zippos are shown below

ZIPPOS BEGIN with tops and bottoms. Here case bottoms are being stamped out of long coils of sheet brass by a hydraulic press. Annealing and welding will be the next steps.

A GAS-TIGHT FIT

LIGHTERS ARE DUNKED

NOT A CLOTHES HANGER.

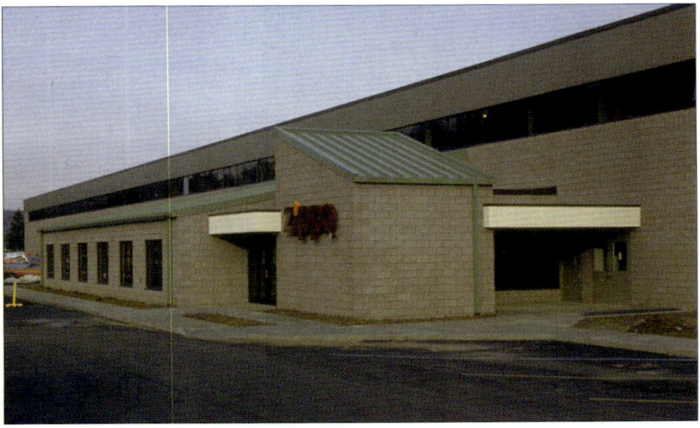

BELOW: Zippo's manufacturing plant, 1992.

BELOW: Scenes from inside the manufacturing plant.

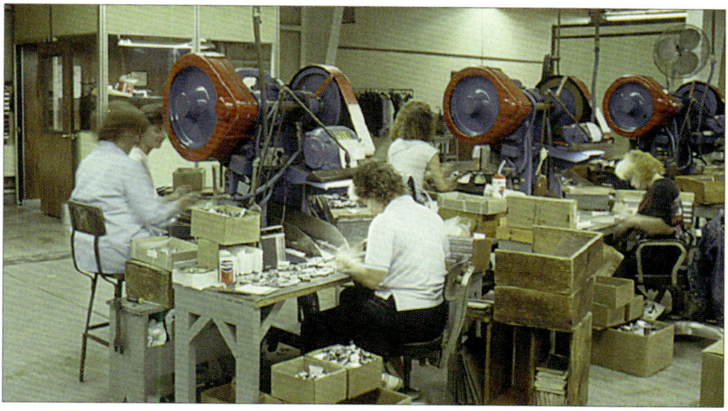

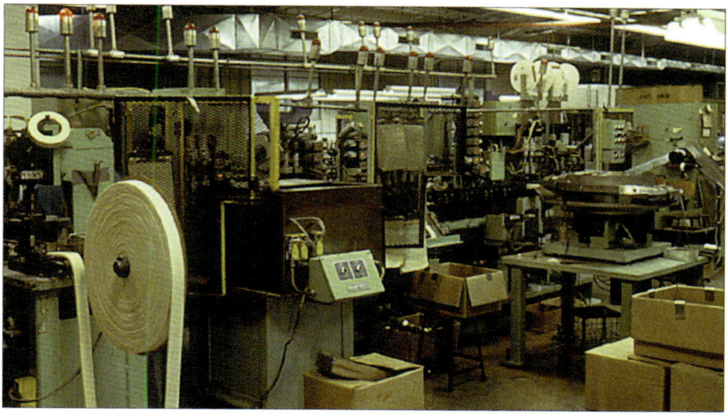

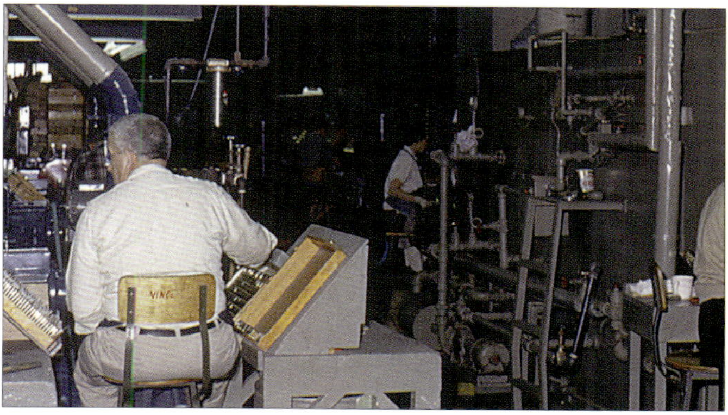

The way it used to be! The components and manufacturing steps required to make a Zippo lighter from the 1940s to the late 1970s.

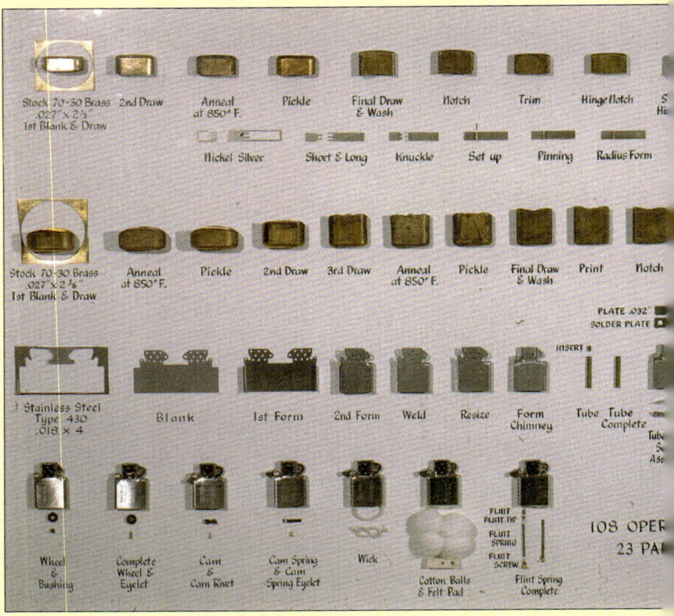

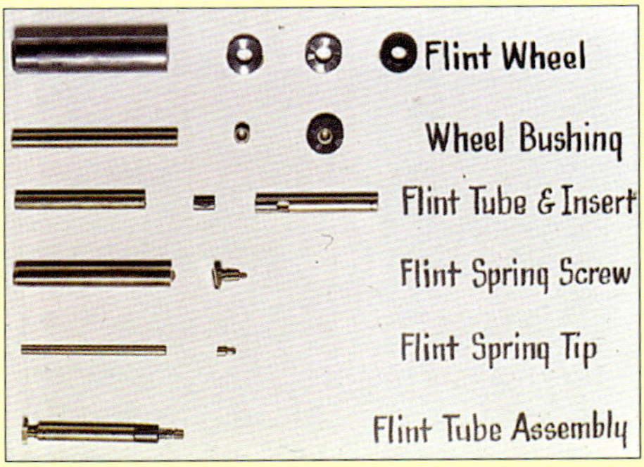

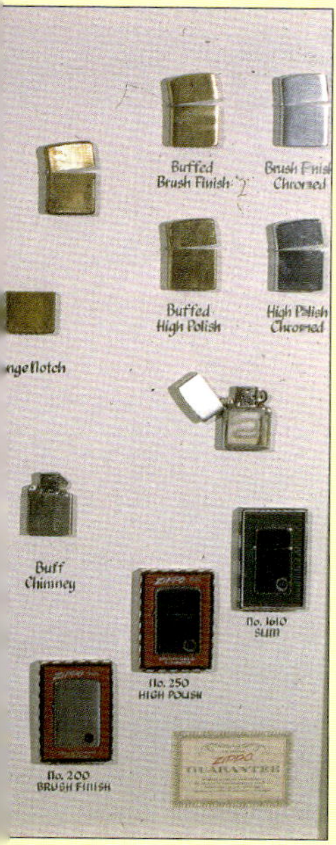

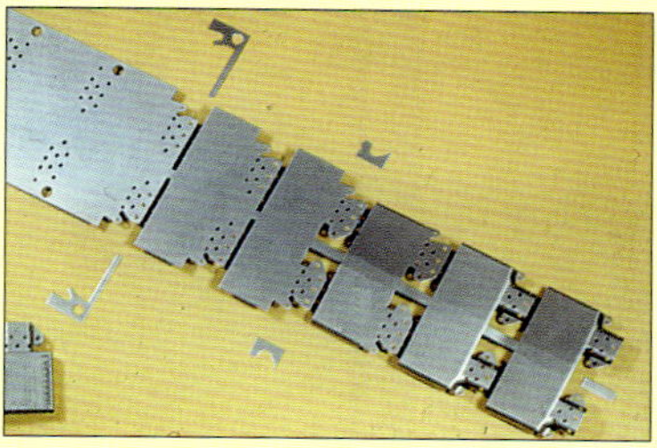

Today the insert is manufactured on an automated line that presses, perforates and cuts the metal to the correct shape and size.

The flint wheel and rayon and felt pads were hand-inserted until the 1970s when automation was introduced.

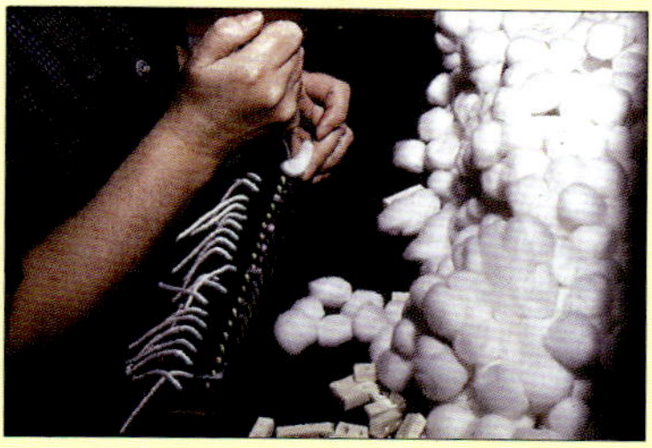

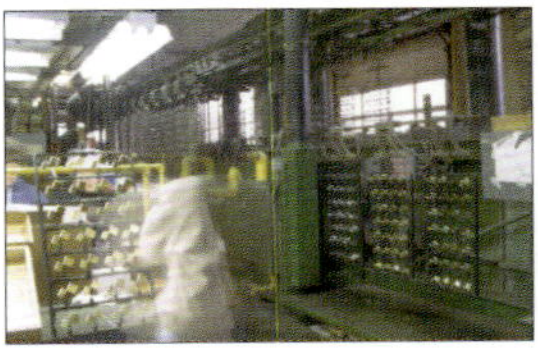

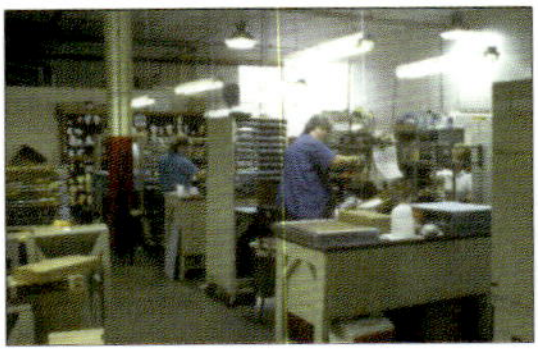

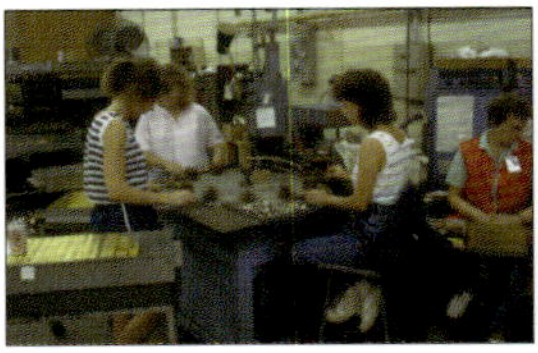

Scenes from the manufacturing process. Zippo has spent much time and money on improving this side of the business — until the 1970s much of the procedure was labor-intensive. Today insert, casing, and flint wheel assembly are automated and human involvement is mainly limited to quality control, packaging, and hand testing of the hinge.

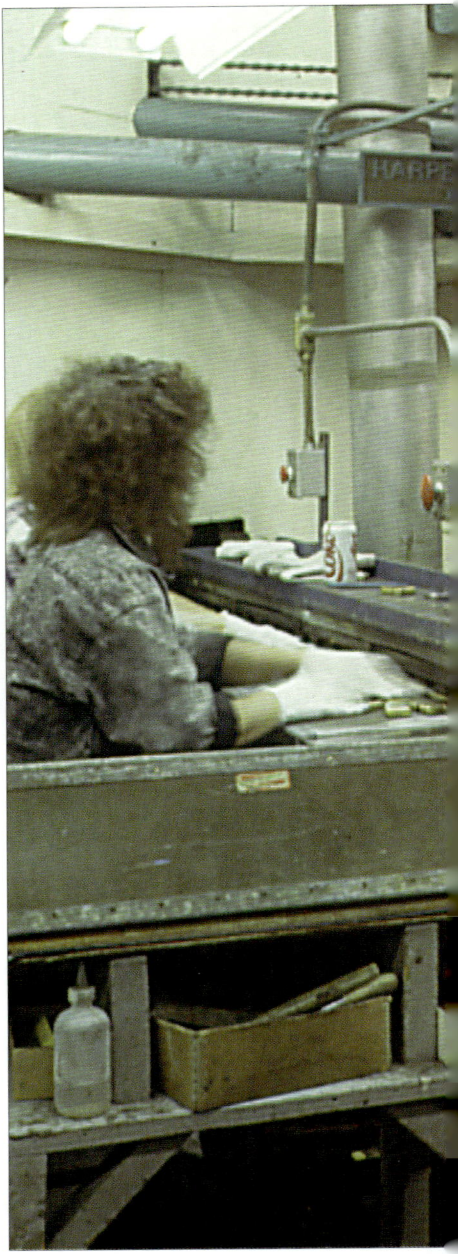

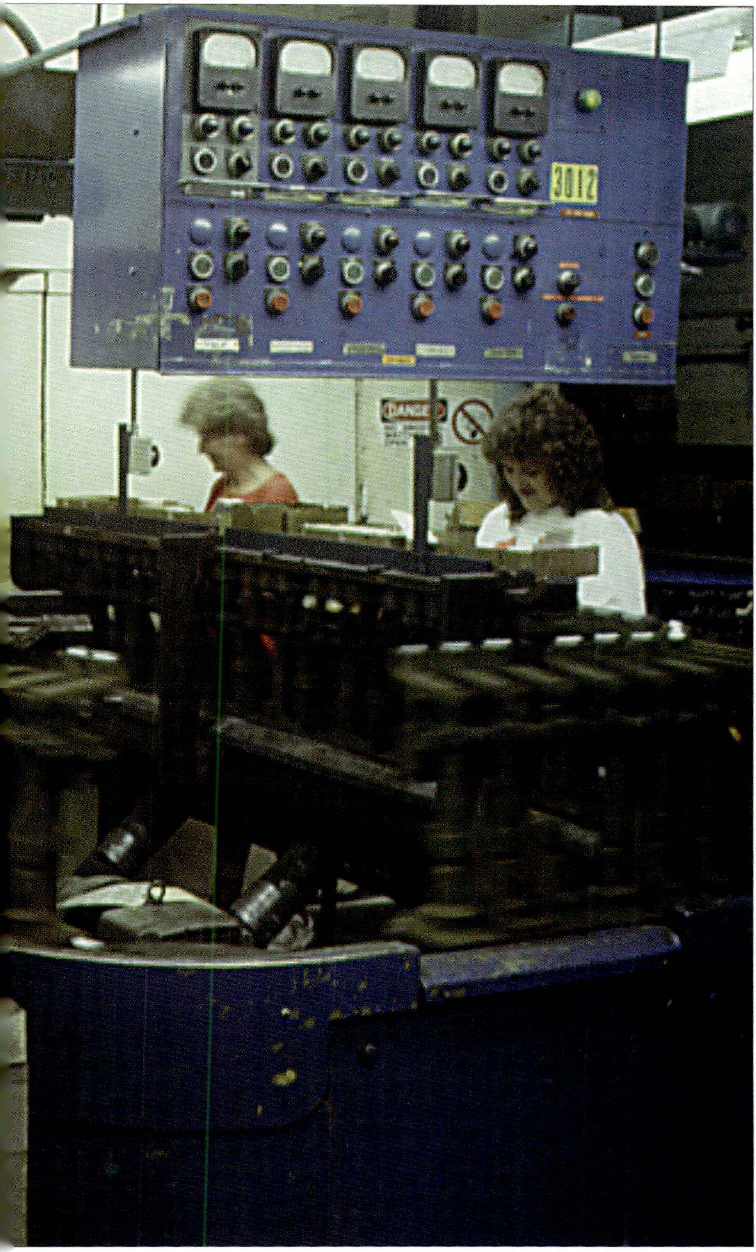
3012
DANGER

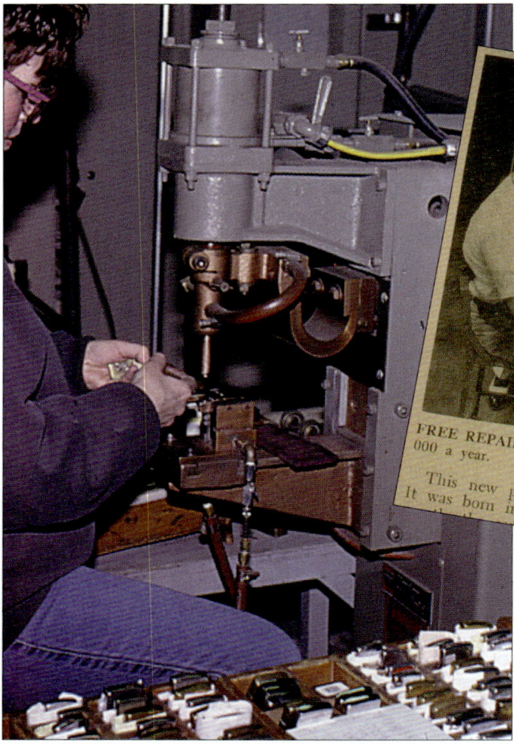

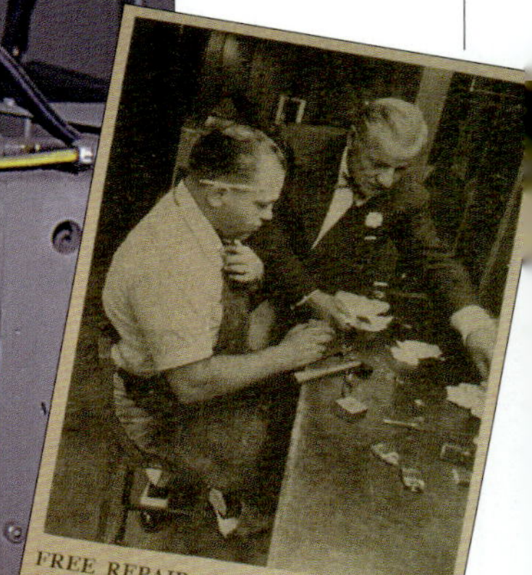

FREE REPAIR costs Zippo around $125,-000 a year.

This new product was the Zippo. It was born in 1933, remains almost

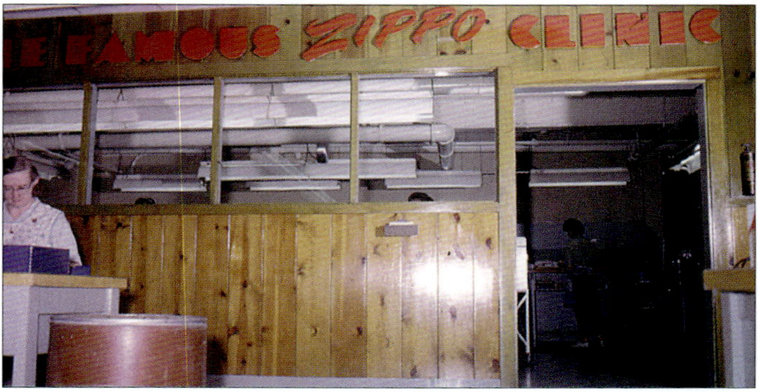

The repair of Zippos is an important part of the company's business. The photographs above show how little this has changed since George Blaisdell (top right) was alive. However, the old Zippo repair clinic (above) was moved into the new Zippo/Case Visitors Center in 1997.

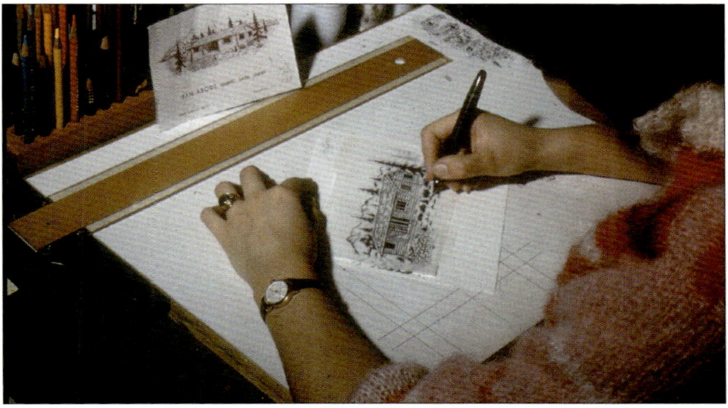

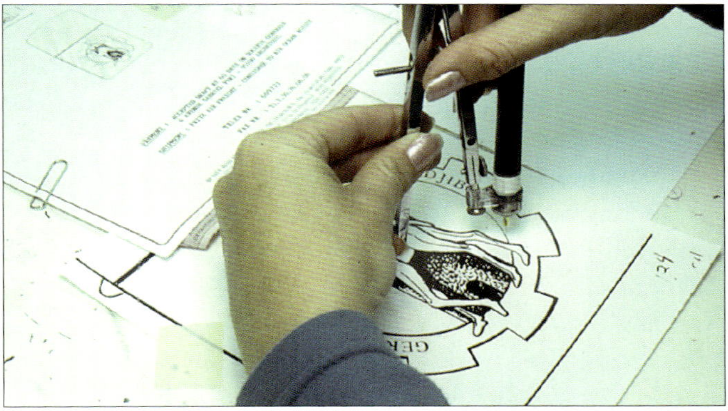

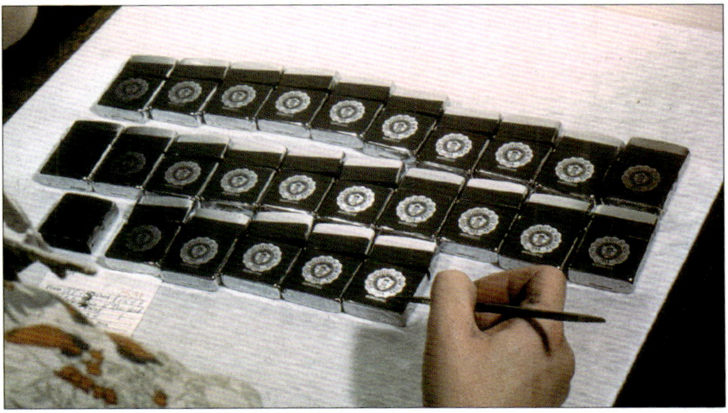

Today, most Zippos carry a motif and the success of the design procedure is a significant part of Zippo's continued market position.

CHAPTER 12

THE ZIPPO/CASE INTERNATIONAL SWAP MEET

The first Zippo/Case swap meet took place in 1995 in Zippo's hometown of Bradford, Pennsylvania. The idea was conceived at the first National Zippo Day, in July 1994, at the Zippo Family Store and Museum, in Bradford. National and international advertising ensured that Zippo enthusiasts world wide were made aware of the occasion. A three-week contest, with a winner's prize of an all expenses paid trip for two to Bradford and Niagara Falls, NY, also sparked interest among newcomers to the world of Zippo. Visitors flocked to Bradford from almost every state in the USA, and from countries all over the globe.

Judith Sanders of On The Lighter Side (OTLS) collectors' club divulged in a radio interview, that her club had 1,000 members, from 18 different countries. Media coverage was substantial including NBC television coverage, national press articles, and broadcasting by 150 radio stations.

Registered collectors enjoyed a barbecue, car show, and dancing on opening day, while many took a private tour of Zippo and Case manufacturing premises. The combining of Zippo and Case at this swap meet, led to knife collectors becoming interested in, and adding Zippo lighters to their collectibles, and the reverse took effect on Zippo lighter collectors. One Case collector admitted that since coming into contact with Zippo, in 1994, he now had collected 200 of their lighters. Dealers also attended the swap meet, to add to their inventory of Zippo lighters for the enthusiasts in their hometowns.

The two United States collectors clubs, OTLS, and Pocket Lighter Preservation Guild (PLPG), gained new members, who were enthralled by their display of history, politics, and business recorded on Zippo lighters since the 1930s, and found many

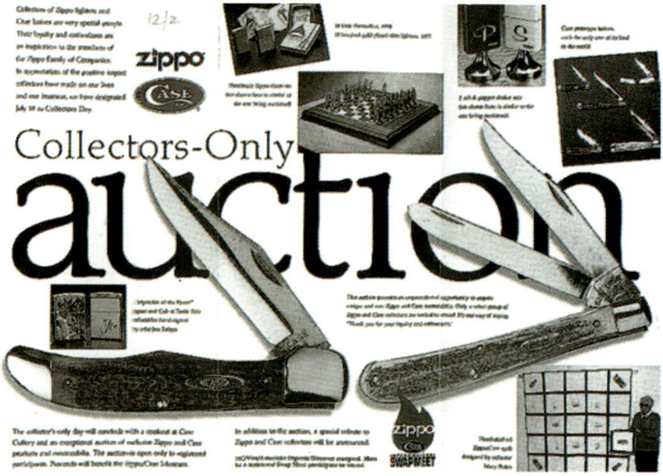

Collectors play a significant role in Zippo's marketing plans and the Swap Meet would not be complete without an auction.

categories of interest for starting their own collections. Prime collectibles were early Zippo lighters with outside hinges, and some of these changed hands for large sums of money.

Planning began immediately for the succeeding swap meets and they have become annual fixtures. The 1996 International Zippo/Case Swap Meet, held in the mini-city created for it, was a roaring success. Visitors and exhibitors mingled happily in the sea of tents, marveling at the items on show. An eye opener for many old established collectors, and even for Zippo officials, were lighters that previous to this meet had not been known to exist. One of only two red crackle lighters ever made was on display, while there was talk of a beige crackle lighter, of which one only is known. Both of these lighters date back to the early days of World War II, when a suitable finish was being investigated for the wartime steel Zippos.

Visitors had an opportunity to acquire one of the limited edition (250), of Olympic Games Commemorative lighters, which were offered for sale at the Zippo, Family Store. They also met Joan, the Pinup of the Year, who aptly hailed from Chicago, the 'Windy' city.

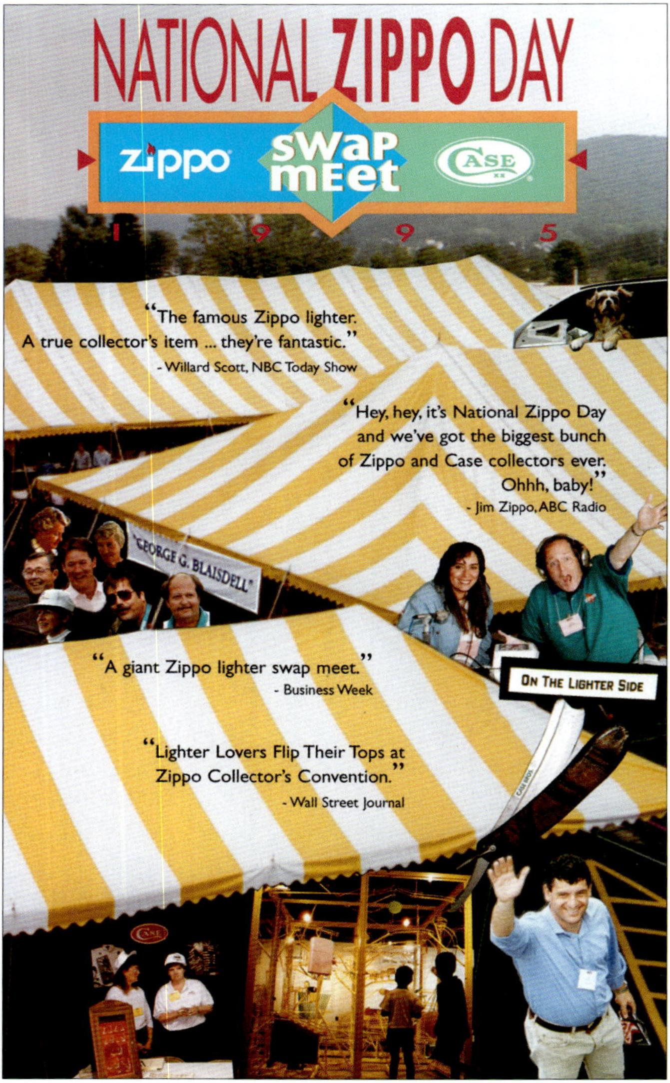

One of the highlights was the auction, the proceeds of which went to the new museum fund. One-of-a-kind items were auctioned, including a chess set made of Zippo Handilites, sold to a Japanese telephone bidder for $13,200.

Collectors agreed that their search for collectibles will never end for the elusive rarities that turn up from time to time. Rarities like the 1930s Zippo with a hook cam, and lighters bearing the names and logos of businesses that no longer exist. They left 'collector heaven' with the promise and commitment that they would be back in Bradford for the 1997 swap meet.

The new Zippo/Case Visitors Center was officially opened in July 1997, at the third annual swap meet. The Zippo/Case Visitors Center is located at 1932 Zippo Drive, just off Route 219 in Bradford, PA. 14 custom-made Zippo 'street-lighters' line the drive leading up to the building. Over the entrance towers a 40-foot Zippo lighter with a pulsating neon flame, and an enormous three-bladed Canoe pocketknife, symbol of the Case Collector's Club.

The 1998 Meet continued not only the run of success but also had an official centerpiece — in this case the unveiling of the new Zippo Car, a reproduction of the 'productmobile' driven by the company's salesmen in the late 1940s and 1950s.

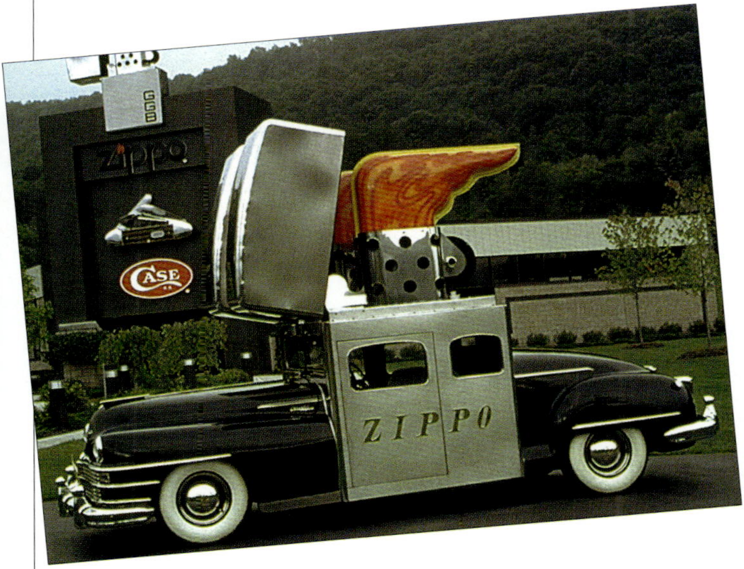

The Zippo Car at the 1998 Swap Meet.

It Happened in Bradford

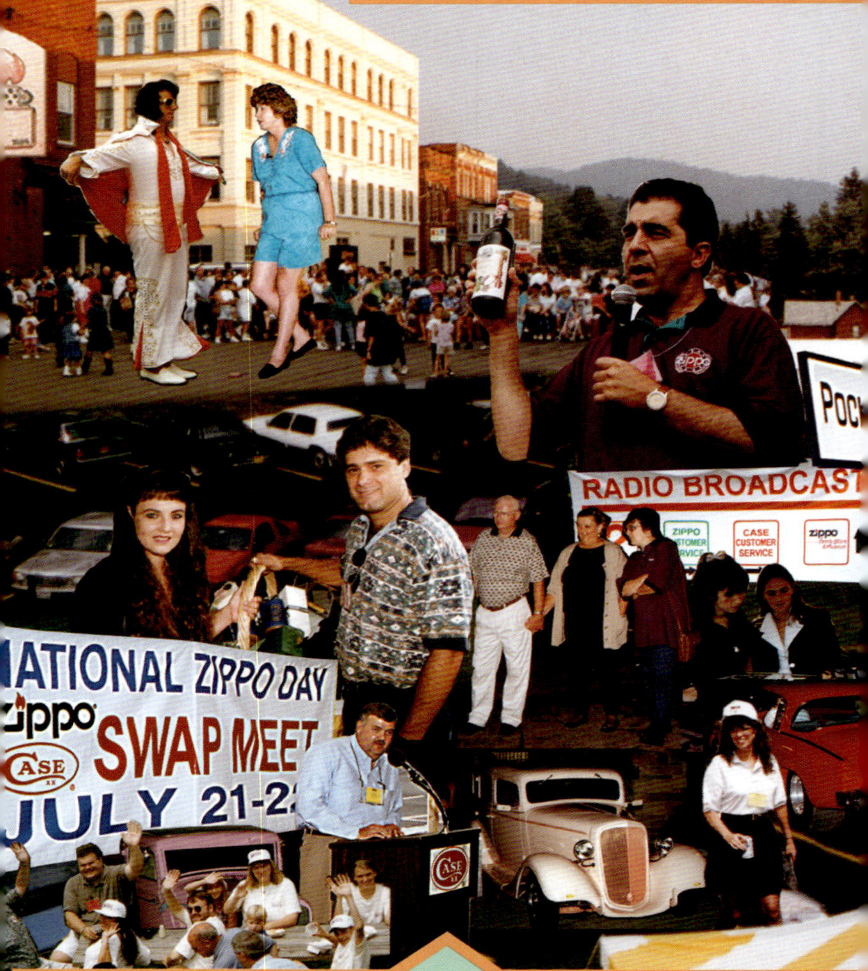

Thousands of Zippo lighter collectors and Case knife collectors traveled to Bradford, PA, the home of Zippo and Case, to celebrate National Zippo Day and the first-ever Zippo/Case Swap Meet.

This 30 minute video collage captures a cross-section of the events of July 20-22, 1995, characterized by fun, festivity and friendship.

Zippo

Case XX

A Zippo Company

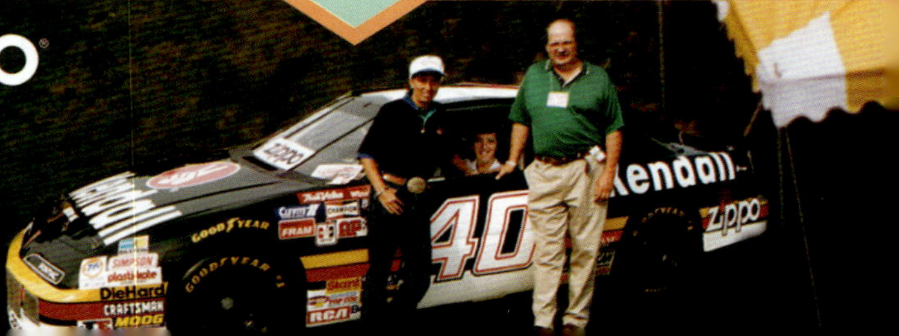

COLLECTORS CLUBS

On the Lighter Side (OTLS)
International Lighter Collectors
P.O. Box 1733
Quitman, TX 75783-1733
USA
Attn: Judith Sanders
Tel: (903) 763-2795
Fax: (903) 763-4953

Pocket Lighter Preservation Guild (PLPG)
380 Brookes Dr, Suite 209 A
Hazelwood, MO 63042
USA
Attn: Ronald Eyerkuss
Tel: (314) 731-2411
Fax: (314) 731-2903

Lighter Club of Great Britain
Oliver House
243 Selhurst Road
London SE25 6XP
England
Attn: Richard Ball
Tel: 44-181-653-4548
Fax: 44-181-768-0046

Zippo Club Lebenslicht
Eggersweide 61
22159 Hamburg
Germany
Contact: Norbert Dolck
Tel: 040-6-43-66-77
Fax: 040-6-45-45-15
E-mail: lebenslicht@cityweb.de

Funke und Flamme (FUF)
International Lighter Collectors' Club
Postfach 121
CH-9413 Oberegg
Switzerland
Attn: Rolf Muller
Tel/Fax: 14-71-891-1322

Zippo Club Deutschland
Saalburgstrasse 3
Berlin Germany
Tel: 49-30-6066055

The Lighter's Academy
Chino Pozzi
Mail Boxes Etc.
n. 221 - Via Oriolin 10
31100 Treviso
Italy
Tel: 39-422-579961
Fax: 39-422-579890

Lighter Club of Japan
3-39-2 Nakano
Tokyo, Japan
Attn: Kazuo Tsuboi
Tel: 81-3-5385-5801
Fax: 81-3-5385-5804

Zippo Club Italia
Int. 295
Via Ciro Menotti 2/A
20129 Milano
Italy

Sendenhorster Zippo-Club "Flames"
Germany
Attn: Brian Sobal
Tel: 49-2526-3868

Zippo-Club Iron Flame
Lindenstrasse 40
47551 Bedburg-hau
Germany
Attn: Andre Loussee
Fax: 49-2821-40767

Spark International
P.O. Box 41
CH-5412 Gebenstorf
Switzerland
Tel/Fax: 41-56-223-52-65

Zippo Collectors Club
American Original Magazine
P.O. Box 115
3730 ZN Maartensdyk
The Netherlands
Tel: 31-346-213690
Fax: 31-346-213584

CHAPTER 13

ZIPPO ON LINE

The millions of Internet users around the globe have at their fingertips easy access to the many Zippo related websites on the World Wide Web. In May of 1997 there were 62,644 sites which were either wholly or partially devoted to Zippo, or made much or little mention of the Zippo lighter and its companion products.

Here is a selection of some of the more pertinent websites:

www.zippo.com

The official website of Zippo Manufacturing Company is packed with award-winning interactive content. The large site includes multimedia features about everything in the Zippo universe. Included is the history of the company, along with the complete product catalog. Zippo news and events are continually updated and posted. The collectible nature of Zippo lighters is spotlighted, along with the Collectibles of the Year. An ad specialty section details Zippo promotional products. Also of interest is customer service information, including how to return a Zippo lighter for repair and the complete details of the extraordinary Zippo/Case Visitors Center.

www.zippocanada.com

The official website of Zippo Canada is a highly interactive site, featuring the history of Zippo Canada, distinctive Canadian souvenir lighters, and the complete product catalog. Of special interest is a section highlighting the unique collectible nature of Canadian Zippo lighters.

RETAILERS

www.smokeking.com

This is a retail site offering shopping on the net, and also features current Zippo collectibles, including pinup of the year, The 4 Seasons, the Olympic Games, and some of the Barrett-Smythe series. On offer as well, are Smokeking's own licensed designs.

www.theconnections.com

The Thinset Connection of Miami, Florida, is another retailer offering a vast selection for sale of current, vintage, and own designs.

www.thezippostore.com
www.vintagelighters.com

A New York based retailer.

www//movingpictures.com

This retailer has put a lot of work into creating a very interesting site. Unfortunately it is flawed by some incorrect information. It refers to the 'Austrian' lighter that provided George G. Blaisdell with his original inspiration, as an 'Australian' lighter!!

www.sidelines.com

Website of Sidelines International.

www.dantiques.com
www.arrowweb.com
www.axiscom.com

Website of Cloud Nine

http://netmar.com/mall/shops/studio/zippo/1997.htnl

A well laid out and informative website

COLLECTORS' SITES

http://ourworld.compuserve.com/homepages/Frank_Schulte
The collector here is Frank Schulte, who also includes links to other sites of Zippo interest.

http://n3.zippo.de/zippo
Provides links to German websites

http://web.inter.nl.net/hcc/m.j.dekker
A particularly well researched site of Netherlands collector M. J. Dekker, whose excellent layout includes links to many other sites.

http://home.t-online.de/home/zippo- germany/fuf.htm
This site provides a link to Funke und Flamme, a Swiss collectors' club website.

www.2a.meshnet.or.jp/ - hoho/index.html
We love Zippo. A very good Japanese collector site with lots of interesting and useful links, such as Zippos Over Tokyo, and Burning Warehouse.
Please note that some links are in Japanese only.

www.zippolighter.com
Avi Baer's website, which is on hold by arrangement with the Zippo Manufacturing Company.

CHAPTER 14

ZIPPO IN ENTERTAINMENT

TELEVISION AND CINEMA

Whether setting spooky events in motion in *Hocus Pocus* with Bette Midler or providing a clue to Gerard Depardieu's character in *Green Card*, the Zippo fills its role with unobtrusive professionalism. It holds its own with, and never upstages, such luminaries as Robert DeNiro (*Midnight Run*), Mel Gibson and Goldie Hawn (*Bird on a Wire*), and Chevy Chase (*Fletch*). In films as diverse as *The Thomas Crown Affair*, *Jurassic Park*, *The Right Stuff*, *JFK*, *Top Gun* and *Out Of Sight*, the Zippo lighter has proven its versatility and enduring appeal. But then, reliable performance is a Zippo hallmark. From Hollywood to television to Broadway, Zippo has been sharing the limelight since the 1930s, when

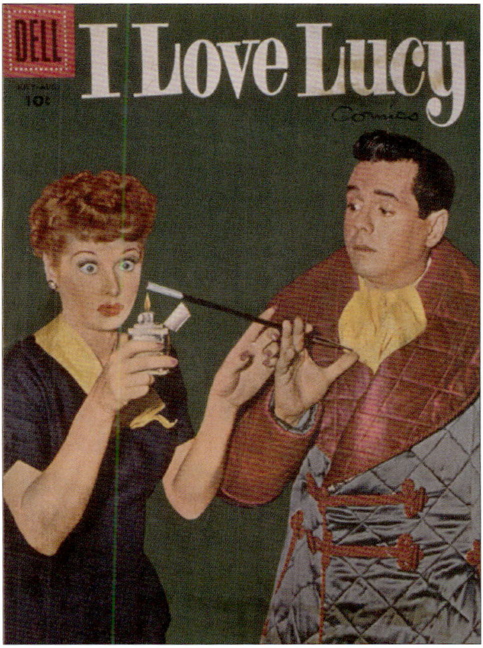

The *I Love Lucy* show saw early product placement in the form of a Zippo Lady Bradford on the coffee table and in related merchandise – as here on a comic.

it became almost mandatory equipment for the 'tough guys,' who with their raincoats, and hats perched on the back of their heads, always had a Zippo on hand.

Wartime movies featured Zippos as standard equipment for GIs, and Zippos abound in movies of the 1990s.

On television, Zippo played a cameo role in *Mad About You*, (May 1997), when Bruce Willis used his Zippo to guide Paul Reiser through the ducting system of a hospital, to the maternity section, where his wife (Helen Hunt) was in labor — this was actually a 'spoof' of the same scene he played in *Die Hard*.

Early TV featured a Zippo table lighter on the Ricardo's coffee table in *I Love Lucy*.

The musical Stomp, which has toured the United States, Canada and Australia, from Britain, features Zippo as a musical instrument in a number performed with Zippos by the eight member troupe.

Eric Clapton, composer of *It's Probably Me*, included the rhythmic click of the Zippo in the background of the video.

A Zippo helped to save Sean Connery and Harrison Ford, in *Indiana Jones And The Last Crusade*, and few moviegoers will forget Arnold Schwarzenegger saying 'Hasta la vista, Baby' as he flicked his Zippo in *Terminator 2*.

Other noteworthy films featuring Zippo, are *Apocalypse Now*, and *From Here To Eternity*, in which Donna Reed lights Montgomery Clift's cigarette, and the John Wayne movie *The Green Berets*, which introduced a camouflage Zippo.

ZIPPO IN FAST COMPANY

For the seventh year running, in September 1999 Zippo sponsored the Zippo US Vintage Grand Prix of Watkins Glen, an event that has grown to become one of the most anticipated weekends in motorsport.

Racing began at Watkins Glen in 1948, and the Zippo U.S. Vintage Grand Prix weekend relives the excitement of the past. The new Zippo Car, launched at the 1998 swap meet, will serve as the honorary pace car for the event.

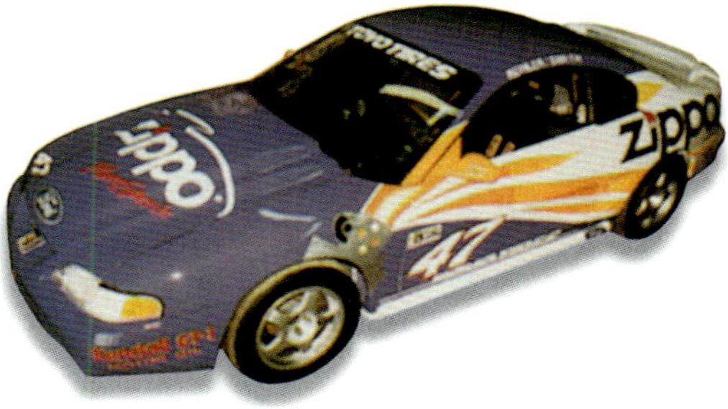

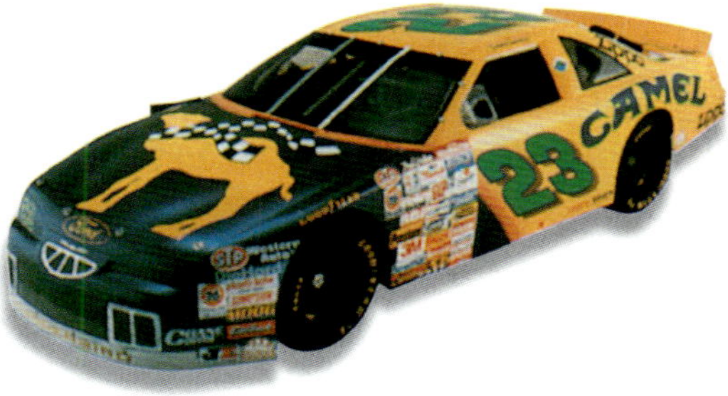

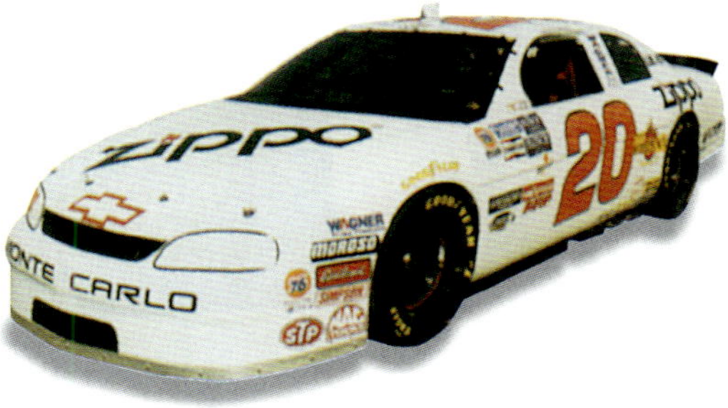

Zippo has been involved in motorsports for some years now. The company has sponsored the Zippo U.S. Vintage Grand Prix of Watkins Glen for seven years, and has had sponsorship arrangements with a number of drivers of both cars and motorcycles, the latter an arrangement with Harley-Davidson. Illustrated are the vehicles sponsored by Zippo that appeared at the 1997 swapmeet: John Kohler and Gary Smith's International Motorsports Association Street Stock Endurance Championship vehicle; and Jimmy Spencer's Winston Cup Camel car and his Busch Grand National car.

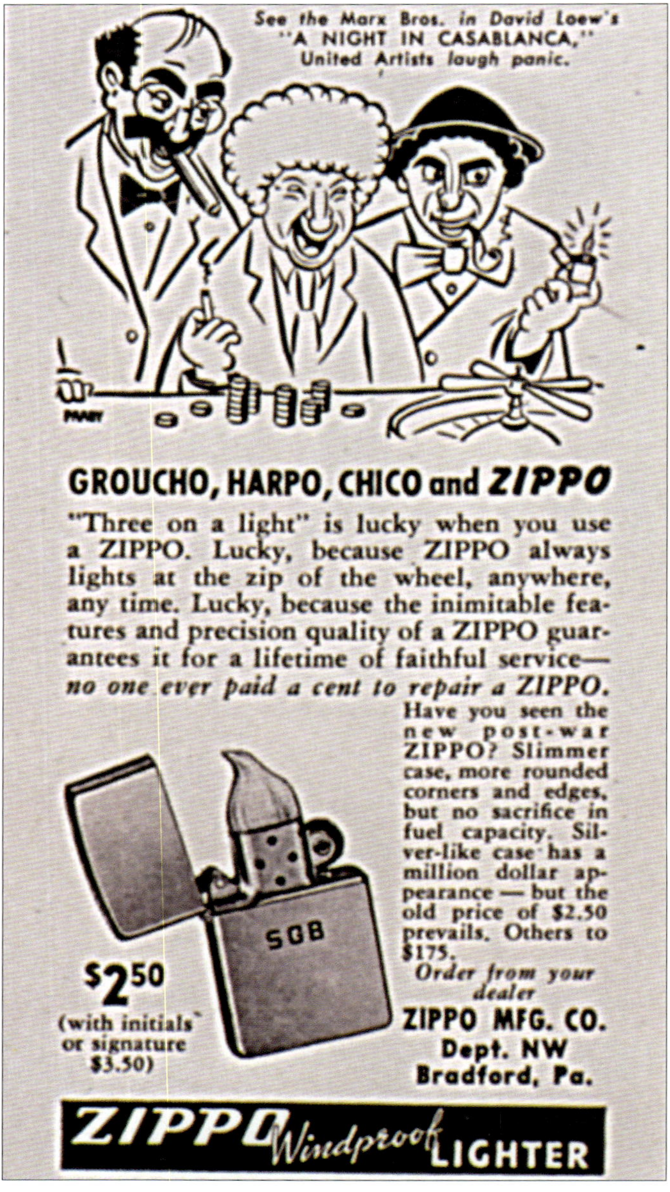

Links with the cinema weren't all one way:
here Zippo advertising makes use of the Marx Brothers.

CHAPTER 15

ZIPPO TRIVIA

☆ Zippo will have produced over 325 million lighters this year, and is aiming to produce 60,000 lighters a day, and still struggling to keep up with demand.

☆ Zippo is sold in 120 different countries of the world.

☆ A Zippo lighter saved the life of a Chicago student, Nikolaos Patronis, when the lighter stopped a bullet intended to kill him.

☆ A Zippo lighter was recovered from the stomach of a bear, in the 1940's, and still worked!

☆ A Zippo lighter was present at Casablanca, when Franklin D. Roosevelt and Winston S. Churchill met in 1943.

☆ Nobody has spent a cent to repair a Zippo lighter.

☆ Zippo bought W.R. Case and Sons Cutlery in 1993.

☆ 50,000 Zippo D-day commemoratives were bought in Germany in 1994.

☆ Zippo exports account for nearly 60 percent of sales.

☆ There are Zippo collectors clubs in Japan, Italy, England, Switzerland, Germany, the Netherlands and the United States of America.

☆ Judith Sanders, of On The Lighter Side collectors' club, owns nearly 700 Zippos, and her club has members from 18 different countries around the world.

☆ Zippo is the world's largest manufacturer of refillable lighters.

☆ Zippo produces more than 100 new designs every year.

☆ Even Fidel Castro (above) uses a Zippo.

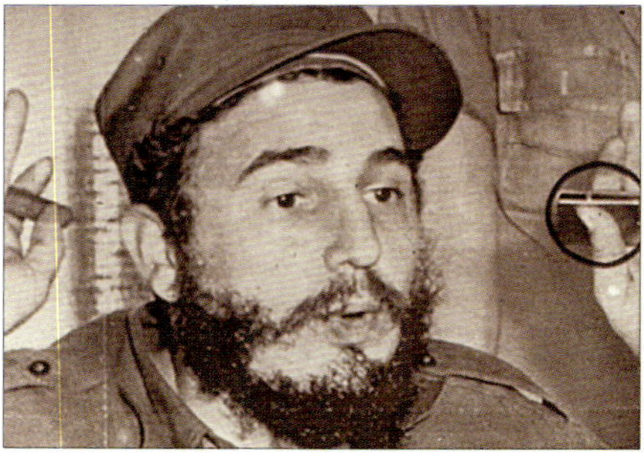

THE 1930s

☆ The original model was introduced in 1933. It had a rectangular shape with a protruding hinge holding the lid to the body and three barrels.

☆ Company records show that the first table lighter model was introduced in 1938; however, a Zippo pamphlet from 1938 describes a Barcroft model with a single-tier base as the 'No. 10 Table Lighter'.

☆ The retail price of the original windproof Zippo lighter was $1.95.

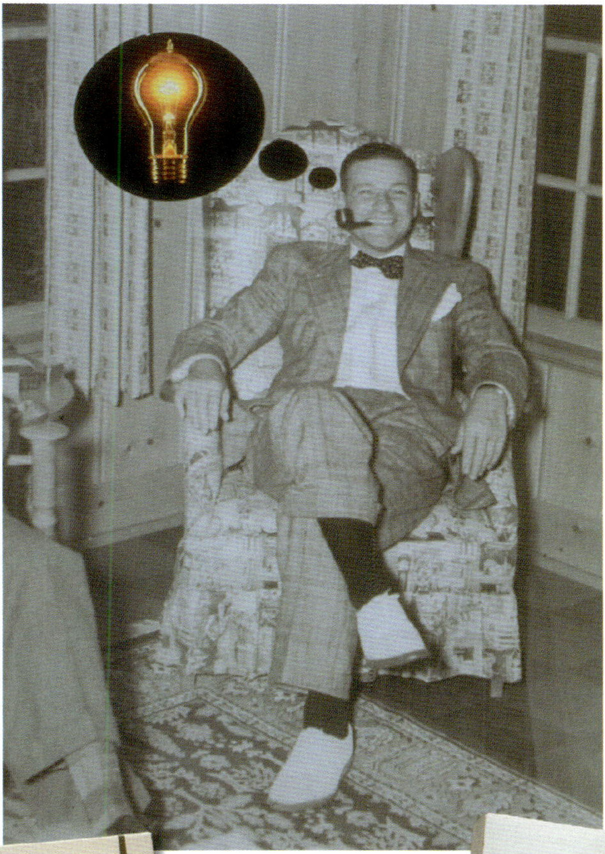

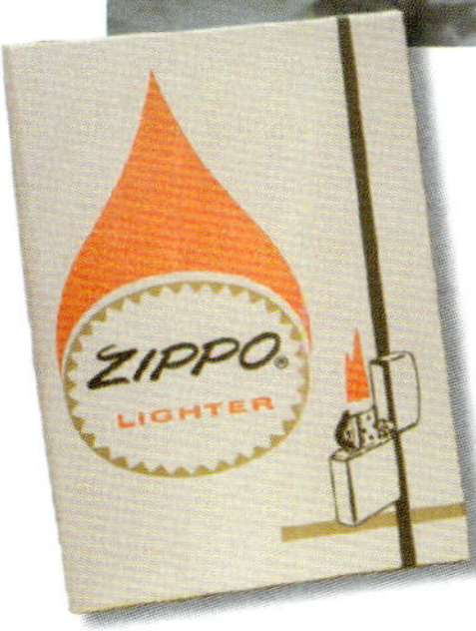

ABOVE: Blaisdell's idea – a Zippo promotional photograph.

RIGHT: Very early model – note external hinge.

LEFT: 1970s' packaging.

☆ Zippo models manufactured from 1933 onwards were decorated with two diagonal lines in the corner that were of different length from earlier models. Square models with no diagonal lines were manufactured up to 1940.

☆ In May 1934, Zippo applied for a patent for the manufacturing process. In 1936, the U.S. patent was approved and patent number 2032695, was engraved on the bottom to identify Zippo lighters until 1952.

☆ The Zippo was first introduced as a promotional item in 1936, when Kendall Refining Company ordered 500 Zippos, with the Kendall logo, for advertising purposes.

☆ The first sports model, the 275, appeared in 1937. This number represented the price: the model sold for $2.75.

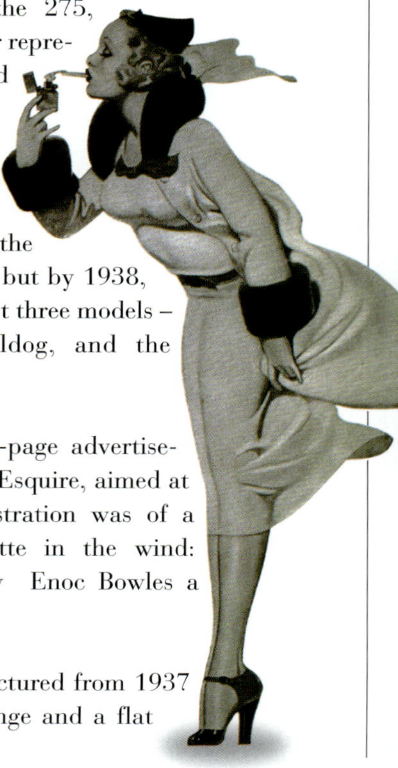

☆ Earlier decorated models included the Golfer, the Hunter, the Fisherman, the Bulldog, the Greyhound, and the Elephant, but by 1938, this list had been reduced to just three models – the Scotch Terrier, the bulldog, and the Fisherman.

☆ In 1937, Zippo ran a one-page advertisement in the December issue of Esquire, aimed at Christmas shoppers. The illustration was of a woman lighting up a cigarette in the wind: 'Windproof Beauty,' drawn by Enoc Bowles a popular illustrator of the day.

☆ Most of the Zippos manufactured from 1937 to 1943 have a four barrel hinge and a flat bottom.

THE 1940S

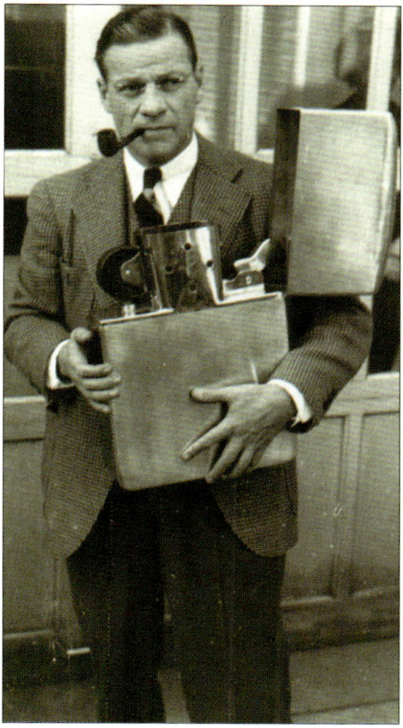

He never lit his pipe with that?! George Blaisdell and a promotional Zippo.

☆ Following World War II, 11 sports models were introduced, ranging from the 175A to the 175K. In 1949, this number increased to 17.

☆ The table lighter discontinued in 1938 was revived in 1947.

☆ The Zippos that were manufactured from 1943 to 1945 have rounded bottom and have a three-barrel hinge

☆ A large number of Zippos were shipped daily to soldiers all over Europe, Africa, and the Pacific regions during World War II.

☆ Once, a Zippo helped the pilot and crew of a damaged U.S. Army fighter plane return safely to base. The plane's electrical system was non-functional, and in the darkness of night the crew could not determine the plane's position. With the naked flame of the Zippo, the pilot was able to light up the instrument panel and direct the plane to safety.

☆ Zippo saved life of a U.S. soldier fighting on the Belgian front. The lighter and a bible in the soldier's chest pocket stopped the enemy bullet.

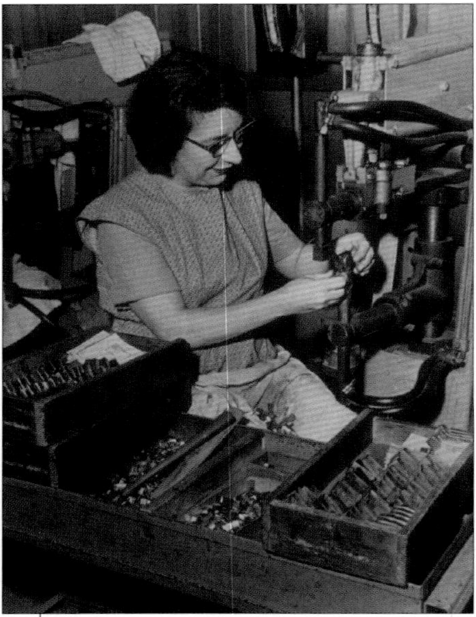

Early manufacture shot.

☆ A Zippo lighter was present on each of these occasions: on December 7, 1941, a soldier witnessed the sinking of the U.S.S. *California* in Pearl harbor after being bombed by the Japanese; a female soldier ran successfully from the attack of a V-2 rocket aimed at London; Joe Rosenthal, a wartime photographer, caught the U.S. Marines raising the American flag on Mt. Suribachi on Iwo Jima, Japan with his camera in 1945; and a soldier witnessed the signing of the Potsdam Declaration in 1945 by President Truman, Prime Minister Churchill, and Premier Stalin.

☆ A Zippo with a commemorative medal of the unconditional surrender of Japan, and the signature of General MacArthur, was given to all young officers trained on U.S.S. *Missouri* in 1949.

☆ Of all the Zippo table lighters, the original #10 was the tallest lighter, measuring over 4.5 inches. It had a large interior unit and could hold four times more lighter-fluid than a pocket lighter.

☆ In 1949, the Lady Bradford, with its elegantly curved silhouette, was announced. It was followed the next year by an improved #12 Lady Bradford. Both models were priced at $10.00, but, production was discontinued in 1951.

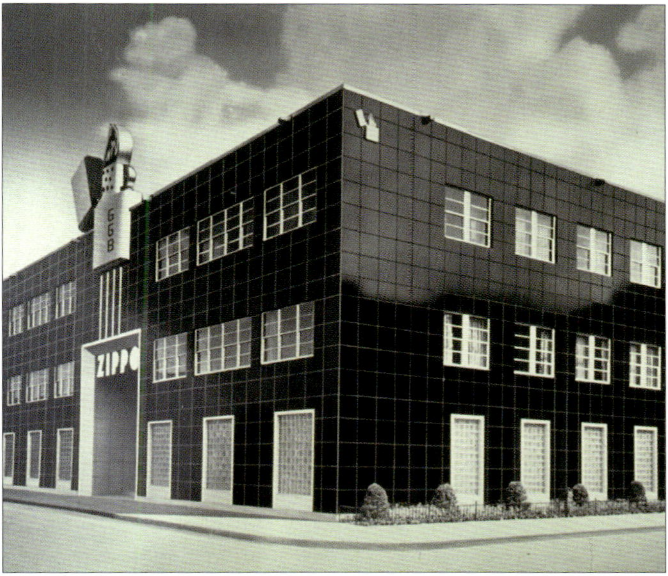

33 Barbour Street —
as it appeared 1954-1991.

THE 1950s

☆ The Coca-Cola trademark was engraved on a Zippo as an advertising medium in the 1950s.

☆ Phillip Morris has been using Zippo along with the image of a cowboy in the ads of Marlboro since 1954.

☆ Zippo's made from 1953 to 1957, included many companies in the aerospace industry. These companies used Zippos for promotional gifts or retailing.

☆ The Zippo fully covered with leather was manufactured only in 1950 and 1951. It has gold-leaf Zippo logo on the bottom. Thus today these are highly sought after items by collectors.

☆ From July of 1953, both 'PAT. 2517191' and 'PAT.

PEND.' were engraved on the bottom of the Zippo lighter.

☆ In 1954, the number 10 table model was renamed the Barcroft, and its production continued until 1979.

☆ Models in the New Sports Series, launched in 1959, displayed designs on both the bottom and the lid; these were the so-called two-faced Zippos. This series featured six models-five regular models depicting five types of sport and their players, and the Slim Zippo Lighter, which depicted a woman bowling. The series ran until 1970.

THE 1960s

☆ The Moderne and the Corinthian table lighters, with their slim bases were marketed between 1960 and 1966. Both were discontinued in 1966.

☆ In 1969, a Zippo with copper case appeared; it's a very rare model and was manufactured for a very brief time. The copper was bought from Kennecott Copper.

☆ Zippo's NASA Series with decorations of spaceships, rockets, lunar landers, space shuttles, and flight emblems documented all of mankind's journeys into space since 1960's.

☆ According to collectors, 200,000 Zippos were used by American soldiers in Vietnam.

☆ As the patent expired on August 1, 1967, the inscription of 'PAT. 2517191' which has been engraved beneath the Zippo logo was deleted.

☆ As the new press machine was introduced, the indent of the bottom became deeper in 1969. Also, the typeface of 'Z' in the Zippo logo was changed.

THE 1970s

☆ From 1970 to 1981, another Sports Series, this time without any design on the lid, was introduced. Some models shifted from their earlier affiliation with the Sports Series to their more recent membership in the Town and Country Series.

Many of the animal designs, such as hunting dogs, are now part of the Wildlife Series.

☆ In 1978, George Blaisdell dies.

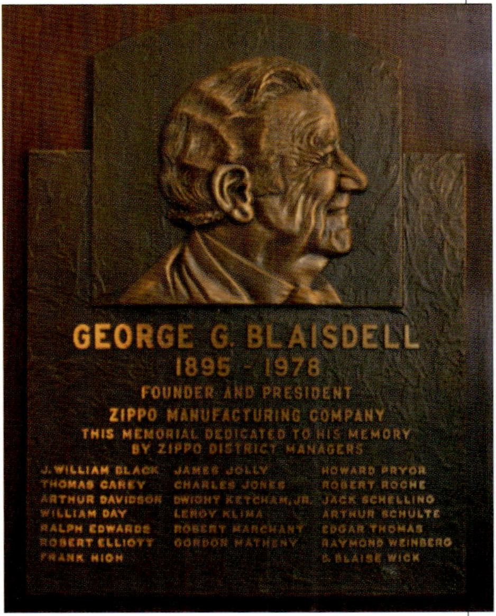

☆ In 1979, the Handilite a pocket lighter with an attached pedestal base, was introduced into the market.

THE 1980s

☆ The Sport Series models from 1981-83 had fewer colors, and in 1984, a series of designs featuring a circular picture area was introduced. The snowmobile design, however, has not changed since 1981.

☆ In 1980, the Zippo logo was changed and the inscription of 'BRADFORD, PA.' was moved beneath the logo.

☆ Contemporary range of Zippo butane lighters made between 1985 and 1989. There were 18 styles in the line.

☆ In 1982, the 50th anniversary of its inception, Zippo produced a replica of an early model for the first time. This lim-

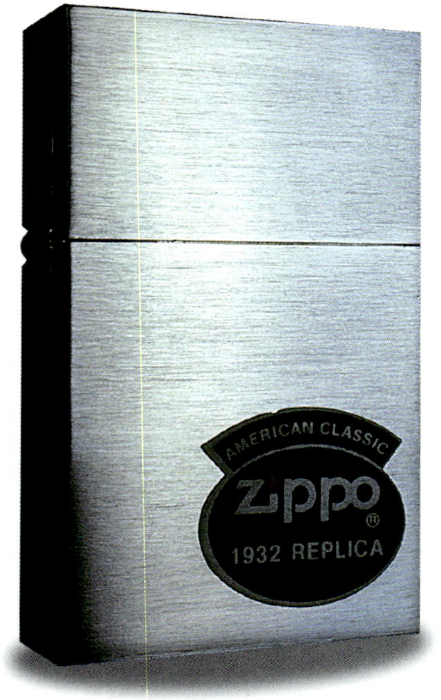

First model replica.

ited-edition lighter was sold very quickly as collectors all over the world were quick to snap them up.

✲ In 1988, reproduction of the 1932 replica model were offered through subscription, a method that had not been used before.

✲ Between 1985 and 1989 Zippo created the Contemporary range of Butane lighters. The line was discontinued primarily because this was the only line of Zippo lighters not made in the U.S.

THE 1990s

✲ 1997, the 65th anniversary of Zippo Manufacturing Company. Zippo releases a handsome 65th anniversary lighter depicting an art deco style.

☆ In 1999, Zippo releases the Millennium Lighter.

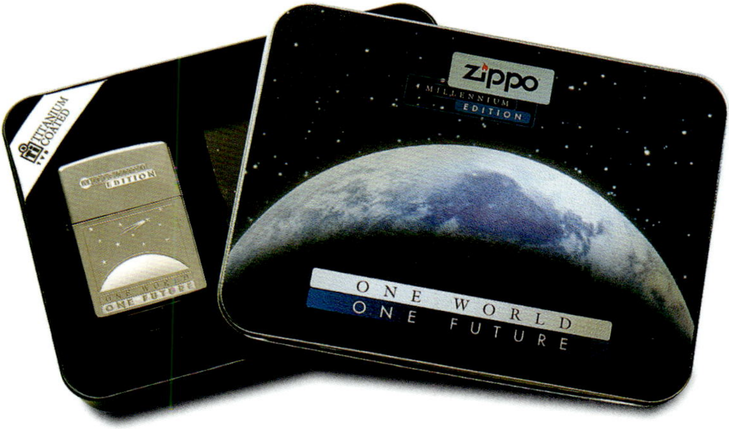

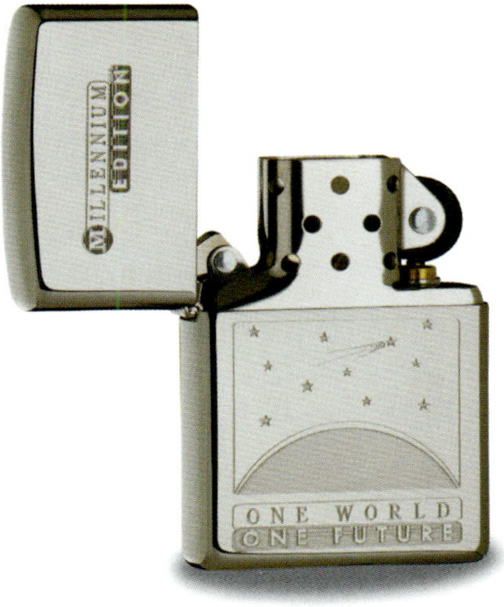

The Millennium has led to a series of lighters, including the limited edition Collectible of the Year for 1999, shown in its packaging.

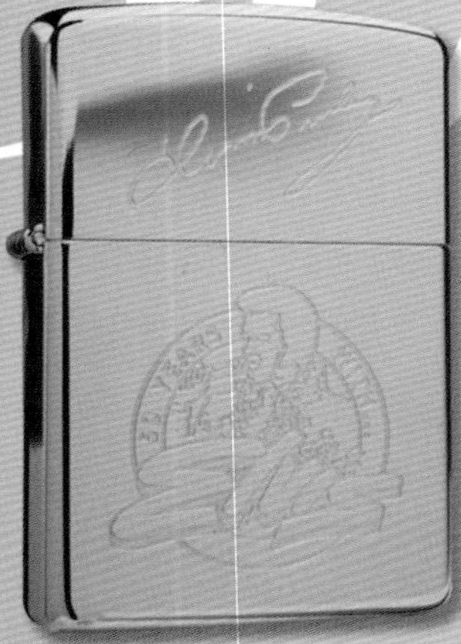

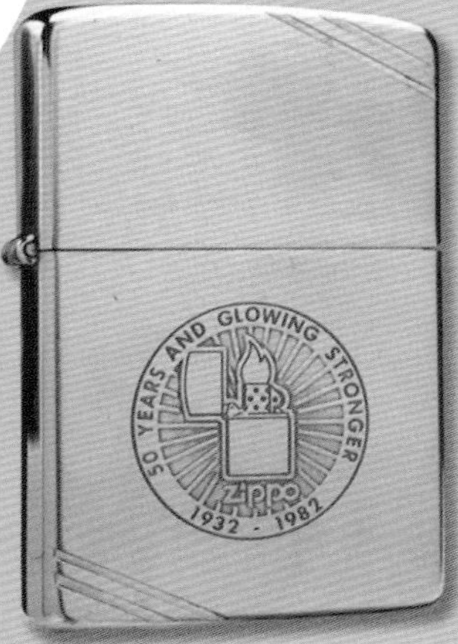

Anniversaries are often commemorated by the release of a Zippo. Here are three interesting ones: 50 years of Elvis (Above Left), 50 years of Zippo (Above Right), and 60 years of Zippo (Below Right). The other lighter (Below Left), as engraved on its face, is the 200 millionth Zippo created since 1932. The date it was reached was April 24, 1988 – after 57 years of production. The next 100 million lighters were produced in less than a decade, proof – if any were needed – that the company goes from strength to strength.

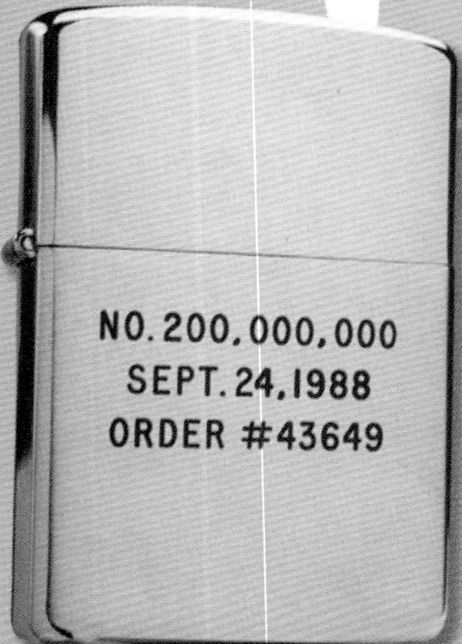

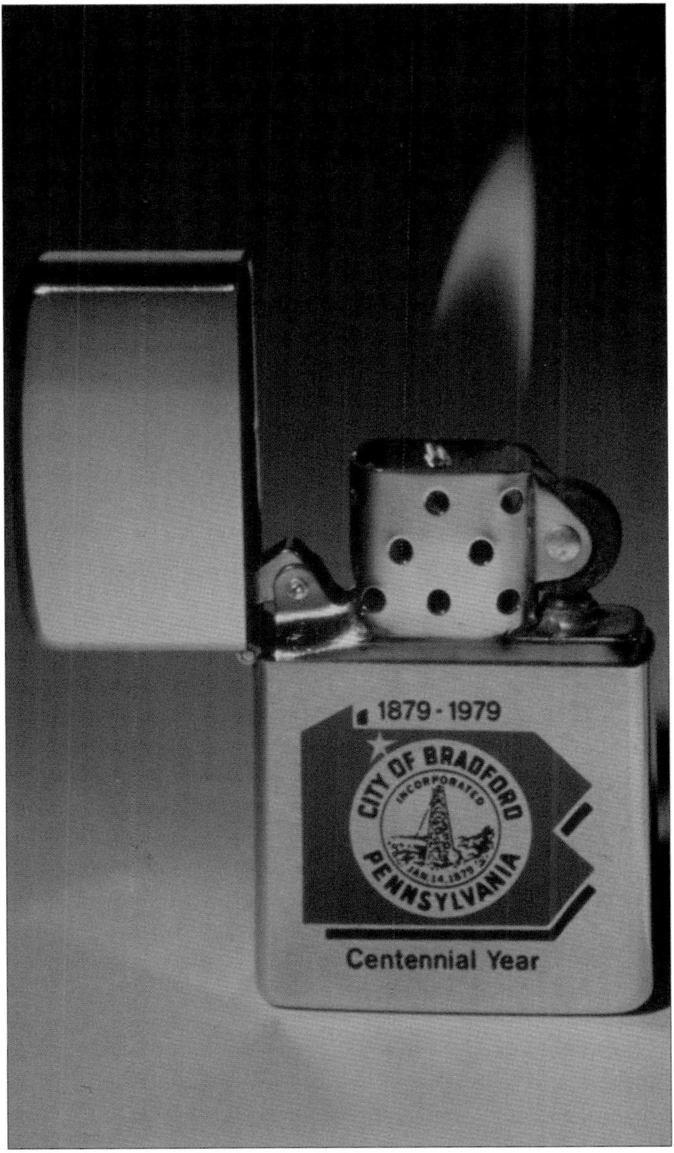

Celebrating the centenary of their hometown,
Zippo's City of Bradford Centennial lighter.

CHAPTER 16

DATING YOUR ZIPPO

The following listing shows how you can use the information on the base of a Zippo to identify its date of manufacture. When trying to determine the date of your lighter look at the base and match the lettering and styles to those shown below. While this is straightforward from 1958, before then it can be more difficult. Zippo records indicate an overlap of bottom stamp configurations from 1949 to 1957. Also, some lighters produced 1955–57 were date-coded although specifics remain unclear. Date coding was fully in effect by 1959

1933 ZIPPO MFG. CO. BRADFORD, PA.
ZIPPO
PAT. PENDING. MADE IN U.S.A.

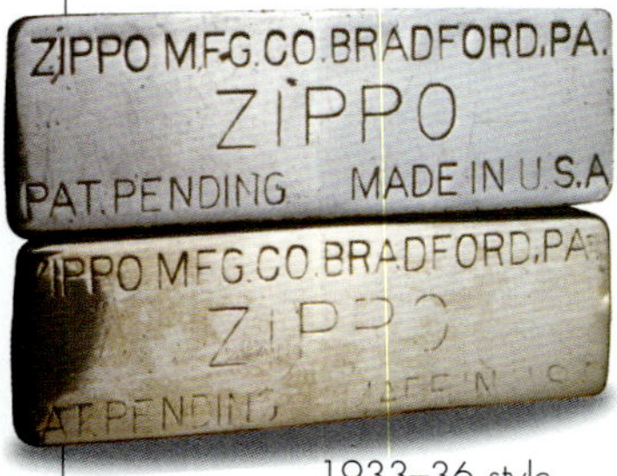

1933–36 style.

Late 1933 Decorative diagonal lines engraved on top and bottom of some lighters.

1934 Same as 1933. Lighter now shorter by one quarter inch.

1935 Same as 1934, Kendal oil ordered 500 units with their logo attached.

1936 ZIPPO MFG, CO. BRADFORD, PA.
ZIPPO
PAT. 2032695 MADE IN U.S.A.

The patent was issued March 3, 1936, so lighters manufactured only late in 1936 had the patent, otherwise the lighter was the same as 1935. The hinge was removed to the inside also late in 1936.

1937–46 ZIPPO MFG. CO. BRADFORD, PA.
ZIPPO
PAT. 2032695 MADE IN U.S.A

While much of the lighter remained the same over this period, there are a few points to note:

1. In 1938 a new press machine was introduced eliminating the soldering process, this introduced a new rounded design with the base marking remaining the same.

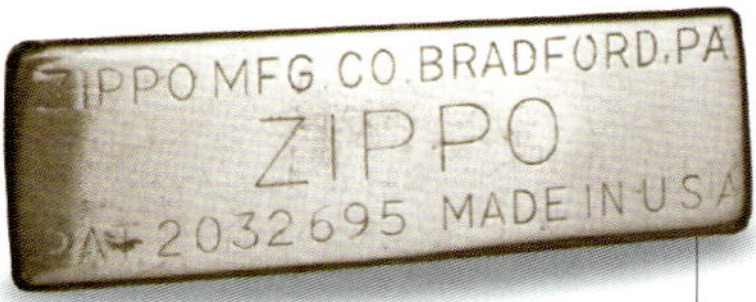

1937–41 style.

2. A four-hinge barrel was used until 1943 and then switched during World War II to a three-hinge barrel.
3. During the war lighters were made of porous steel due to a lack of brass. Most were finished with a black crackle finish, while there were some that were not finished.
4. In 1946 the new "canned bottom" was introduced and this saw the end of the flat bottom design.

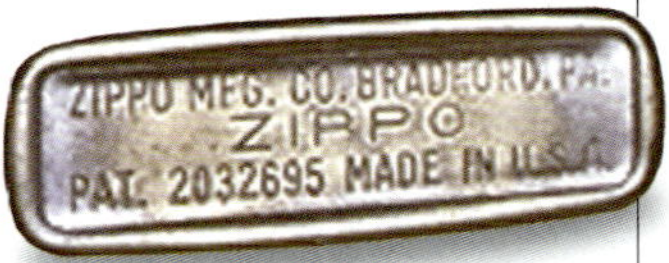

1947–51 style.

1947–48 Base remained the same as 1946.

1949–50 Base remains the same and five-barrel hinge adopted.

1953–57

ZIPPO MFG. CO. BRADFORD, PA.
MADE IN **ZIPPO** U.S.A.
PAT. 2517191 ® PAT. PEND.

1953–57 style.
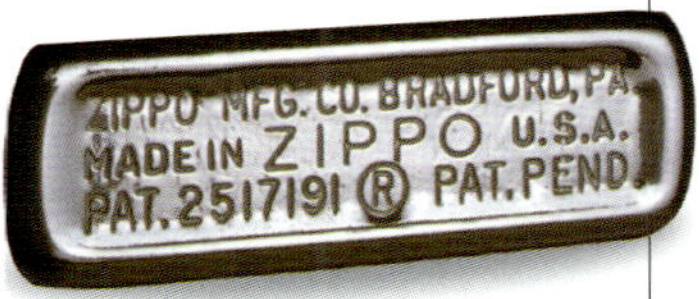

Application for Patent 2517191 on flint tube bushing was adopted on new lighters from 1953 and hence the changed number. At the end of 1957 a new etching process was developed that allowed for more detailed engraving. With this new technology came the new Zippo logo and the new series of codes to help identify the year of manufacture (note decreasing dots and dashes from 1958 to 1986). Note three 1958 styles as PAT. PEND. was removed and then centered.

1958 BRADFORD, PA.
. . . . ***ZIPPO*** ® . . . .
PAT. 2517191 PAT. PEND.

BRADFORD, PA.
. . . . ***ZIPPO*** ® . . . .

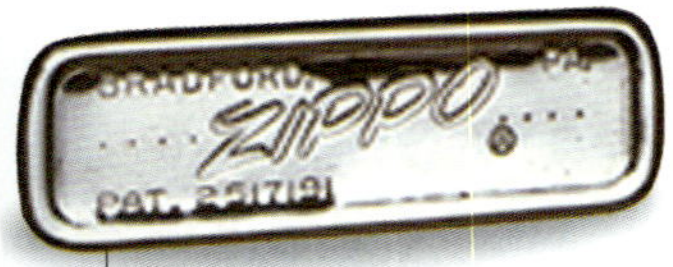

. . . . ***ZIPPO*** ® . . . .
=1958 (above).

. . . ***ZIPPO*** ® . . . .
=1959 (below); note some 1959 lighters were finished with PAT. PEND.

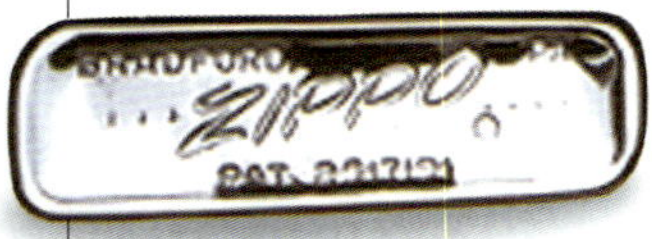

PAT. 2517191

1958 continued
BRADFORD, PA.
. . . . ***ZIPPO*** ® . . . .
PAT. 2517191

1959
BRADFORD, PA.
. . . . ***ZIPPO*** ® . . .
PAT. 2517191 PAT. PEND.

BRADFORD, PA.
. . . . ***ZIPPO*** ® . . .
PAT. 2517191

1960
BRADFORD, PA.
. . . ***ZIPPO*** ® . . .
PAT. 2517191

1961
BRADFORD, PA.
. . . ***ZIPPO*** ® . .
PAT. 2517191

1962
BRADFORD, PA.
. . ***ZIPPO*** ® . .
PAT. 2517191

1963
BRADFORD, PA.
. . ***ZIPPO*** ® .
PAT. 2517191

1964
BRADFORD, PA.
. ***ZIPPO*** ® .
PAT. 2517191

1965
BRADFORD, PA.
. ***ZIPPO*** ®
PAT. 2517191

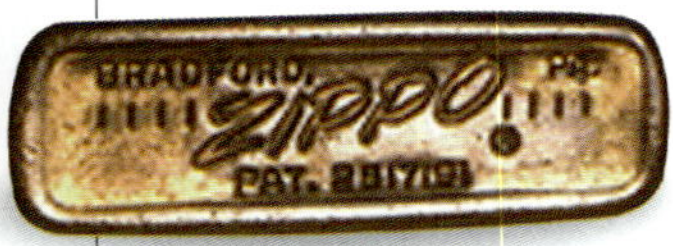

| | | | ***ZIPPO*** ® | | | |
=1966.

1966
BRADFORD, PA.
| | | | ***ZIPPO*** ® | | | |
PAT. 2517191

1967
BRADFORD, PA.
| | | | ***ZIPPO*** ® | | |

PAT. 2517191

1967 continued

BRADFORD, PA.
| | | | ***ZIPPO*** ® | | |

1968

BRADFORD, PA.
| | | ***ZIPPO*** ® | | |

1969

BRADFORD, PA.
| | | ***ZIPPO*** ® | |

1970

BRADFORD, PA.
| | ***ZIPPO*** ® | |

1971

BRADFORD, PA.
| | ***ZIPPO*** ® |

1972

BRADFORD, PA.
| ***ZIPPO*** ® |

1973

BRADFORD, PA.
| ***ZIPPO*** ®

1974

BRADFORD, PA.
/ / / / ***ZIPPO*** ® / / / /

1975

BRADFORD, PA.
/ / / / ***ZIPPO*** ® / / /

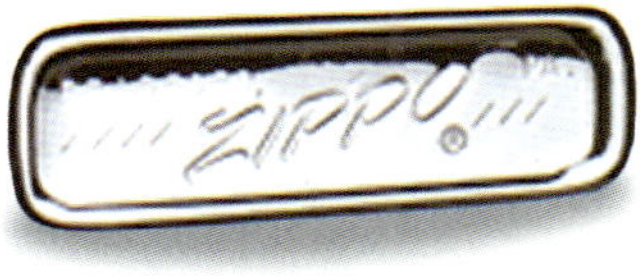

/ / / / **ZIPPO** ® / / /
=1975.

1976

BRADFORD, PA.
/ / / ***ZIPPO*** ® / / /

1977

BRADFORD, PA.
/ / / ***ZIPPO*** ® / /

1978

BRADFORD, PA.
/ / ***ZIPPO*** ® / /

1979

BRADFORD, PA.
/ ZIPPO ® //

1980

/ ZIPPO ® /
BRADFORD, PA.

1981

/ ZIPPO ®
BRADFORD, PA.

1982

**\ \ \ \ ZIPPO ® \ \ \ **
BRADFORD, PA.

1932 **ZIPPO** ® 1982
COMMEMORATIVE
BRADFORD, PA.

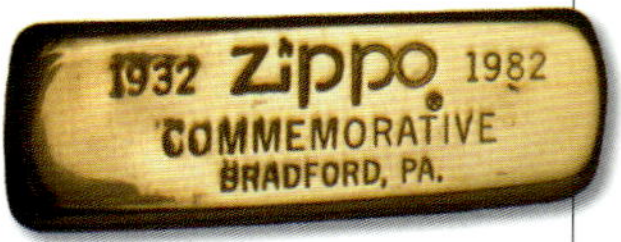

50th anniversary lighter introduced in1982 and produced subsequently with year of manufacture at right of Zippo name. The "Commemorative" was dropped after 1982.

1983

**\ \ \ \ ZIPPO ® \ \ **
BRADFORD, PA.

1932 **ZIPPO** ® 1983
BRADFORD, PA.

1984

**\ \ \ ZIPPO ® \ \ **
BRADFORD, PA.

1932 **ZIPPO** ® 1984
BRADFORD, PA. (Brass Lighters)

1985

**\ \ \ ZIPPO ® \ **
BRADFORD, PA.

1932 **ZIPPO** ® 1985
BRADFORD, PA. (Brass Lighters)

ZIPPO MFG. CO. BRADFORD, PA.
ZIPPO
PAT. 2032695. MADE IN U.S.A.

This lighter was the first of the Vintage series and was modeled after a 1937 type. This method of dating is still in use today along with a letter from A to L on the left-hand side indicating the month of manufacture. All lighters made after June 1986 have the month code stamped on the bottom of the lighter. The only exceptions to this are replicas and special editions that almost always are modeled on the originals.

1986

**\ \ ZIPPO ® \ **
BRADFORD, PA.

Note G for July **G ZIPPO ® II**
BRADFORD, PA.

1932 **ZIPPO ®** 1986
BRADFORD, PA.

1987

A ZIPPO ® III
BRADFORD, PA.

B *ZIPPO* ® III
BRADFORD, PA.

1932 **ZIPPO ®** 1987
BRADFORD, PA. (Brass Lighters)

ZIPPO MFG. CO. BRADFORD, PA.
A ZIPPO III
PAT. 2032695. MADE IN U.S.A.

D=April
IV=1988.

1988

A ZIPPO ® IV
BRADFORD, PA.

B *Zippo* ® IV
BRADFORD, PA.

1932 **ZIPPO ®** 1988
BRADFORD, PA. (Brass Lighters)

1988 replica.

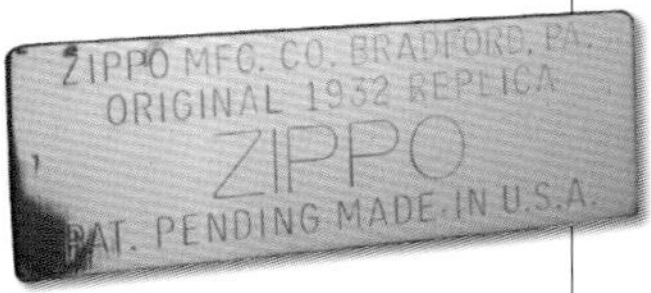

ZIPPO MFG. CO. BRADFORD, PA.
A ZIPPO IV
PAT. 2032695 MADE IN U.S.A.

ZIPPO MFG. CO. BRADFORD, PA.
ORIGINAL 1932 REPLICA
ZIPPO
PAT. PENDING. MADE IN U.S.A.

J=October
V=1989.

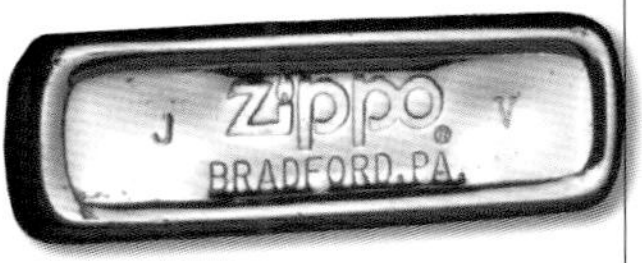

1989

C ZIPPO ® V
BRADFORD, PA.

1932 **ZIPPO ®** 1989
BRADFORD, PA. (Brass Lighters)

1989 continued

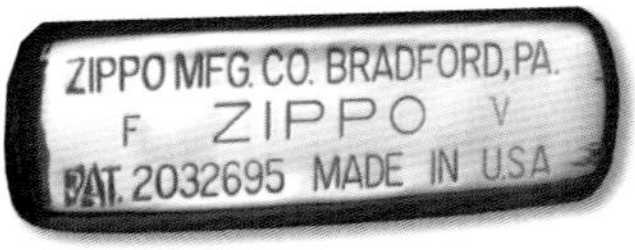

F=June
V=1989.

ZIPPO MFG. CO. BRADFORD, PA.
C ZIPPO V
PAT. 2032695 MADE IN U.S.A.

ZIPPO MFG. CO. BRADFORD, PA.
ORIGINAL 1932 REPLICA
ZIPPO
PAT. PENDING. MADE IN U.S.A.

1990

E ZIPPO ® VI
BRADFORD, PA.

1932 **ZIPPO** ® 1990
BRADFORD, PA. (Brass Lighters)

ZIPPO MFG. CO. BRADFORD, PA.
E ZIPPO VI
PAT. 2032695 MADE IN U.S.A.

ZIPPO MFG. CO. BRADFORD, PA.
ORIGINAL 1932 REPLICA
ZIPPO
PAT. PENDING. MADE IN U.S.A.

1991

D ZIPPO ® VII
BRADFORD, PA.

D ZIPPO ® VII
BRADFORD, PA. MADE IN U.S.A.

D *ZIPPO* ® VII
BRADFORD, PA.

1932 **ZIPPO** ® 1991
BRADFORD, PA. (Brass Lighters)

ZIPPO MFG. CO. BRADFORD PA.
D ZIPPO VII
PAT. 2032695 MADE IN U.S.A.

ZIPPO MFG. CO. BRADFORD, PA.
ORIGINAL 1932 REPLICA
ZIPPO
PAT. PENDING. MADE IN U.S.A.

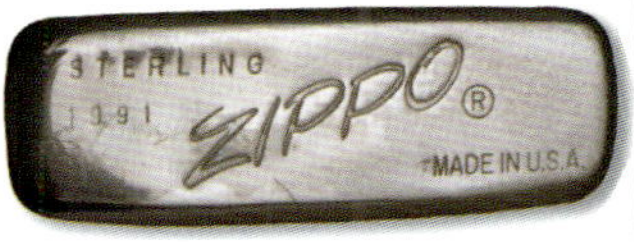

1991 Sterling silver edition.

1991 saw the addition of Made In U.S.A to the base of the lighters, and now a pattern was emerging, that exists through to today. The first two 1991 lighters in the above list have markings that are attributed to all regular models. The next lighter has the old italic brush stroke logo and was used on all flat bottom models. The next lighter's markings were applied to all solid brass products and the second last lighter's markings were (and still are) used on the Vintage series. The last, being the commemorative lighter, had no markings as to the year of manufacture on the outside, but on the casing inside it is marked accordingly with a letter denoting month of manufacture and a roman numeral for the year of manufacture. All these markings above apply to models produced today.

The following entry of lighters for 1992 can be applied to lighters up until 1999 with the exception of the roman numeral changing from VIII for 1992 through to XV for 1999.

1992

H ZIPPO ® VIII
BRADFORD, PA. MADE IN
U.S.A.

1932 **ZIPPO ®** 1992
MADE IN U.S.A.
(Brass Lighters)

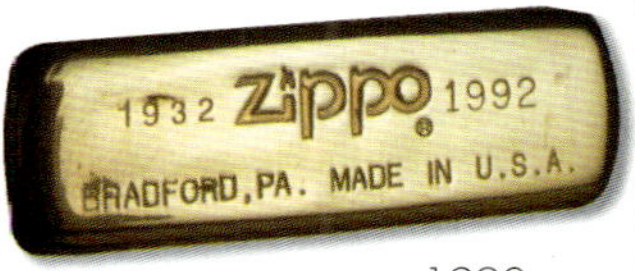

1992.

D *ZIPPO* ® VIII
BRADFORD, PA.

ZIPPO MFG. CO. BRADFORD, PA.
H ZIPPO VIII
PAT. 2032695 MADE IN U.S.A.

ZIPPO MFG. CO. BRADFORD, PA.
ORIGINAL 1932 REPLICA
ZIPPO
PAT. PENDING. MADE IN U.S.A.

CHAPTER 17

THE ZIPPO FAMILY

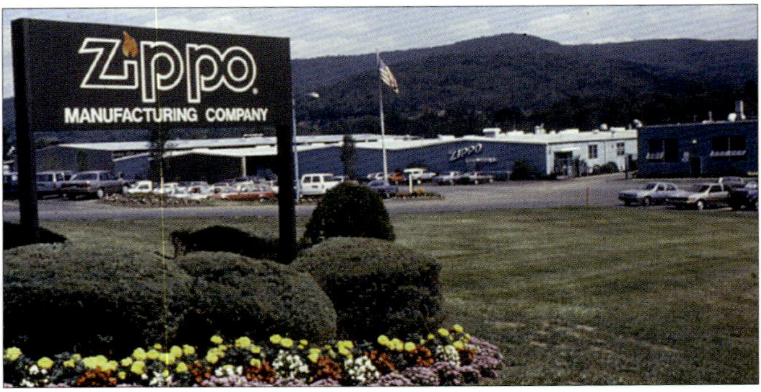

Zippo's manufacturing plant prior to 1992.

The ubiquitous Zippo lighter is not the only product bearing the famous Zippo name. Zippo's head office on Barbour Street, Bradford, Pennsylvania, oversees a host of other Zippo relatives.

Newly arrived in 1996 is the ZipLight™, pocket flashlight, a battery-pack powered mini-light that can fit into any standard Zippo case. There are Zippo pen and pencil sets, money clips, key rings and key holders, cigar cutters, compact pocket tool kits, named Fixxit, a pipe smoker's pocket cleaning and tamping kit, and a wide selection of pocket knives.

Zippo offers tape measures, belts and belt buckles, pouches for lighters, and pouches for knife/lighter combinations.Also available are chrome and gold base stands, which convert any Zippo lighters into table lighters.

There is, in the U.S., a line of clothing, consisting of, golf shirts, jackets, sweaters, T-shirts and caps, bearing the Zippo name and logo.

OPPOSITE: Head office on Barbour Street as it looked between 1954-1991. Today the lighter is still there, but the façade is different.

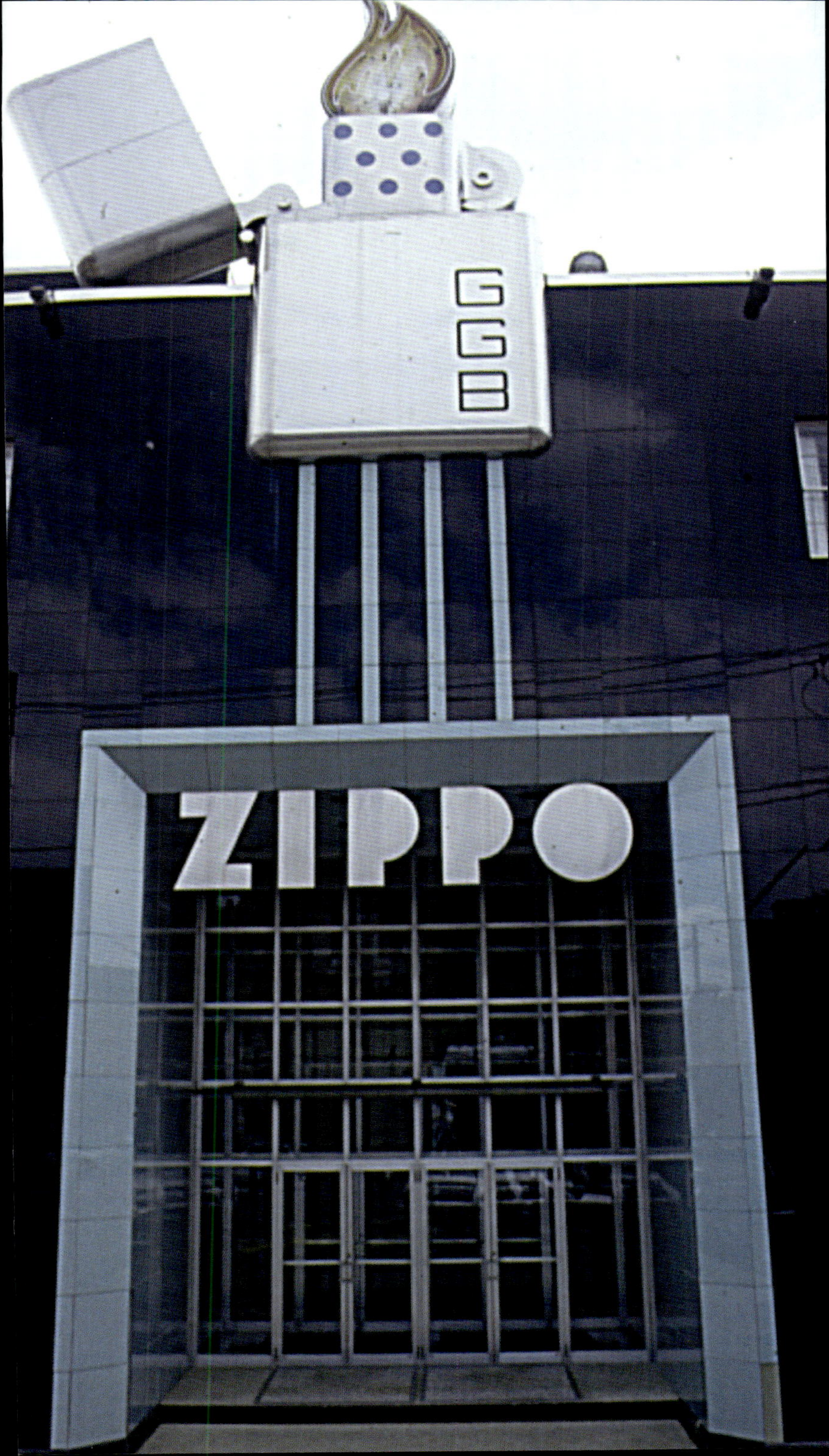
GGB
ZIPPO

A clothing manufacturer in Japan, is licensed to produce jeans, gloves and leather jackets, featuring the Zippo name.

With the exception of clothing items, which are not manufactured under Zippo's control, all other Zippo products are covered by the famous Lifetime Guarantee.

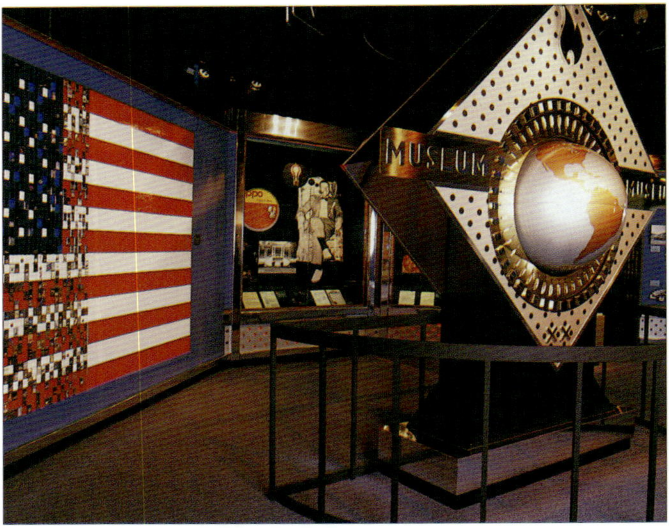

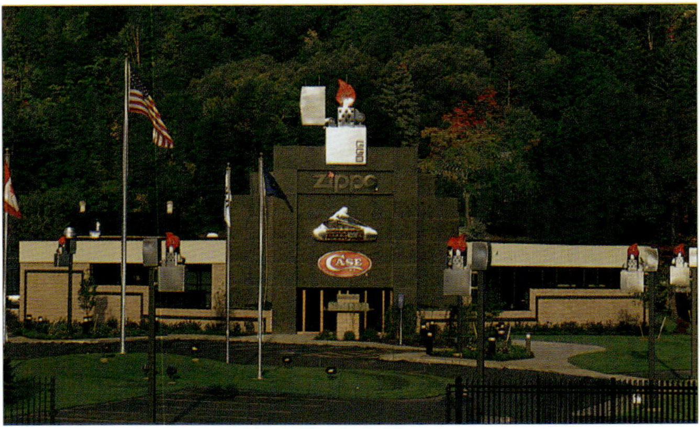

The Zippo/Case Visitors Center.

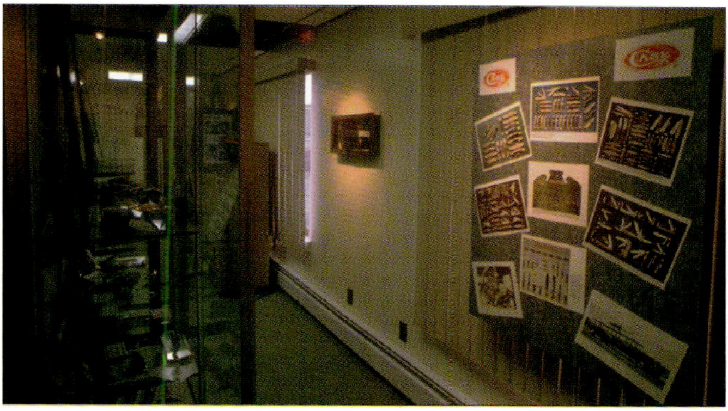

Inside the former Zippo museum.

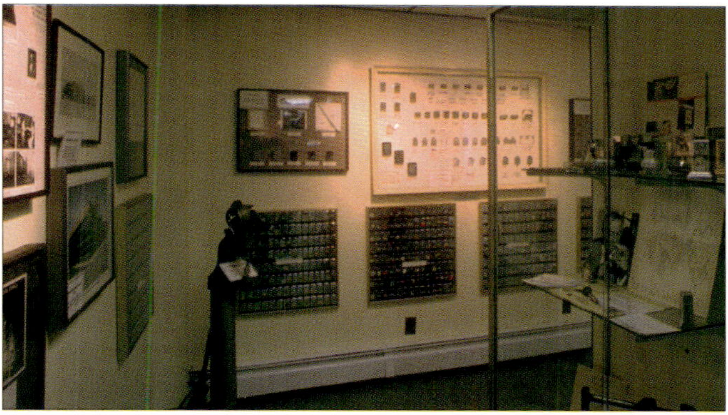

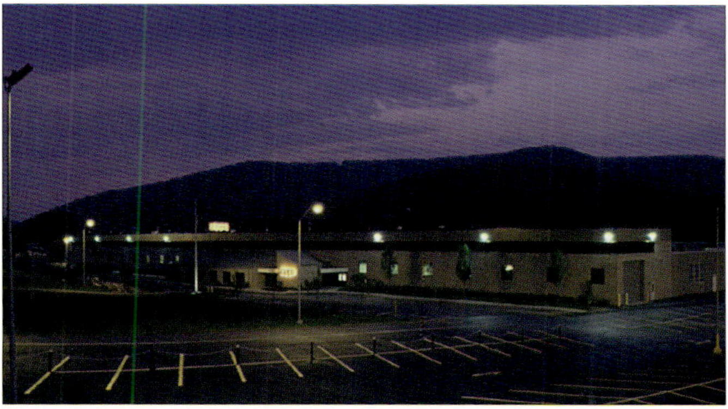

Zippo Manufacturing at night.

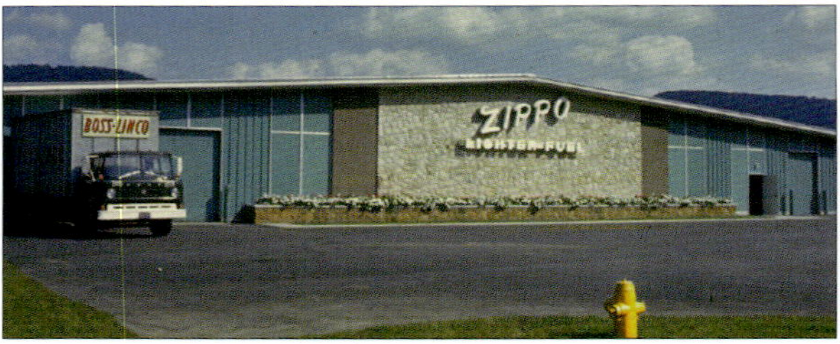

Zippos need fuel, and the Zippo fuel plant is an important part of the Zippo empire. It's also one of the few parts of the Zippo campus in which smoking is forbidden!

BELOW AND BELOW RIGHT:
1950s Zippo fuel advertising.

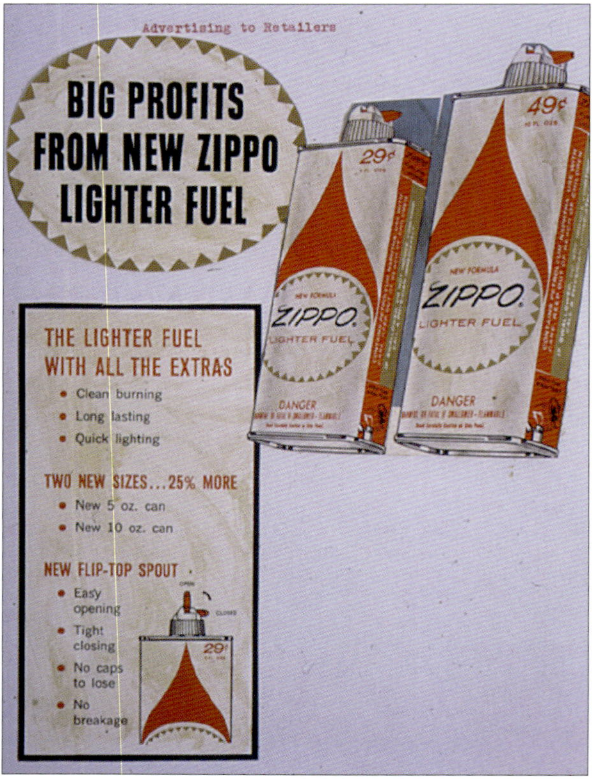

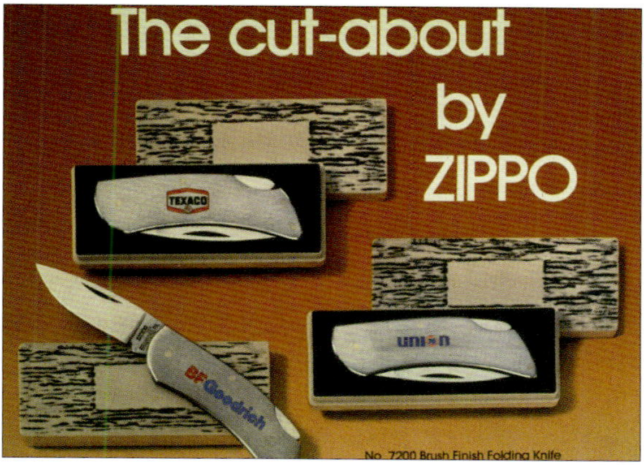

Zippo knives. Since 1993 Case has been part of Zippo.

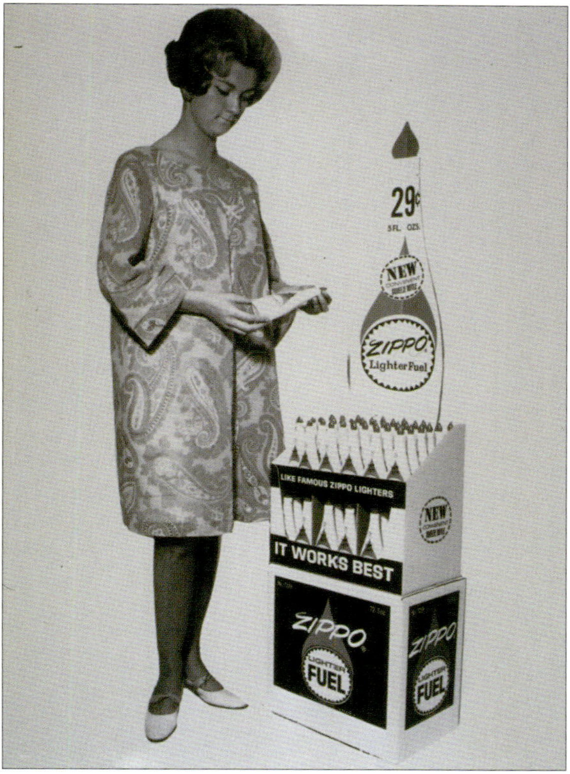

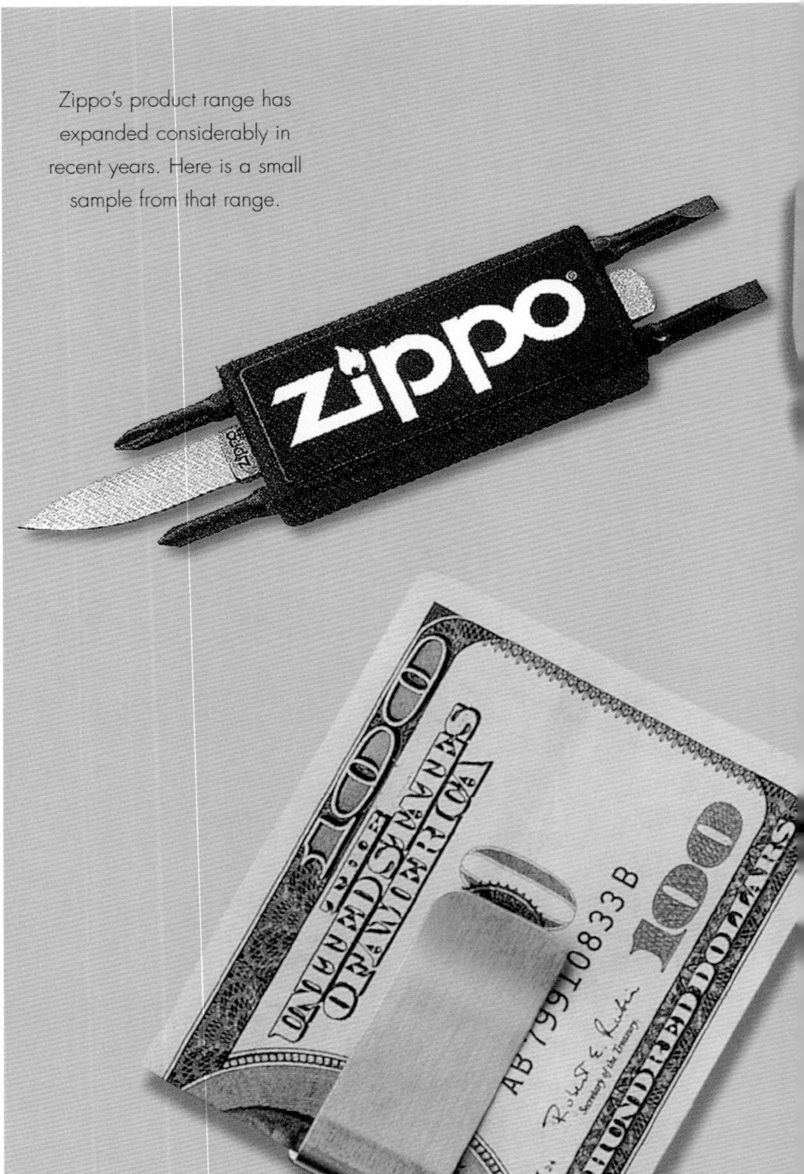

Zippo's product range has expanded considerably in recent years. Here is a small sample from that range.

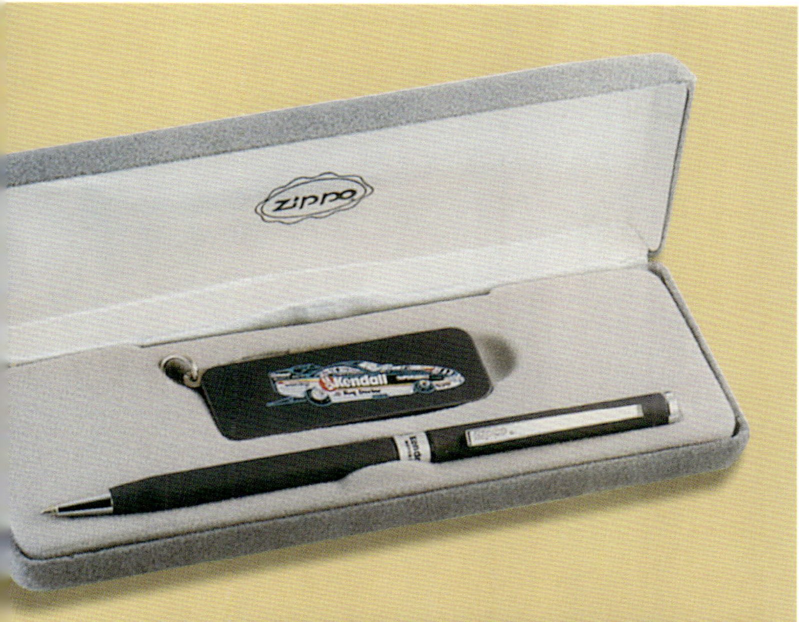
Zippo
Kendall

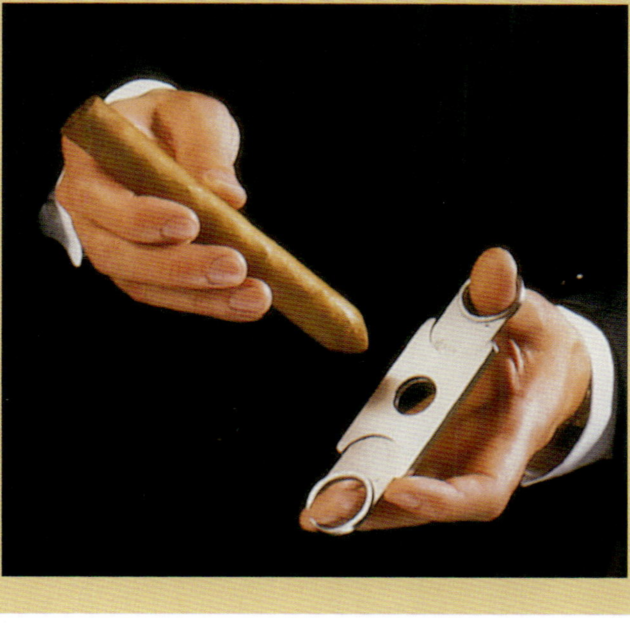

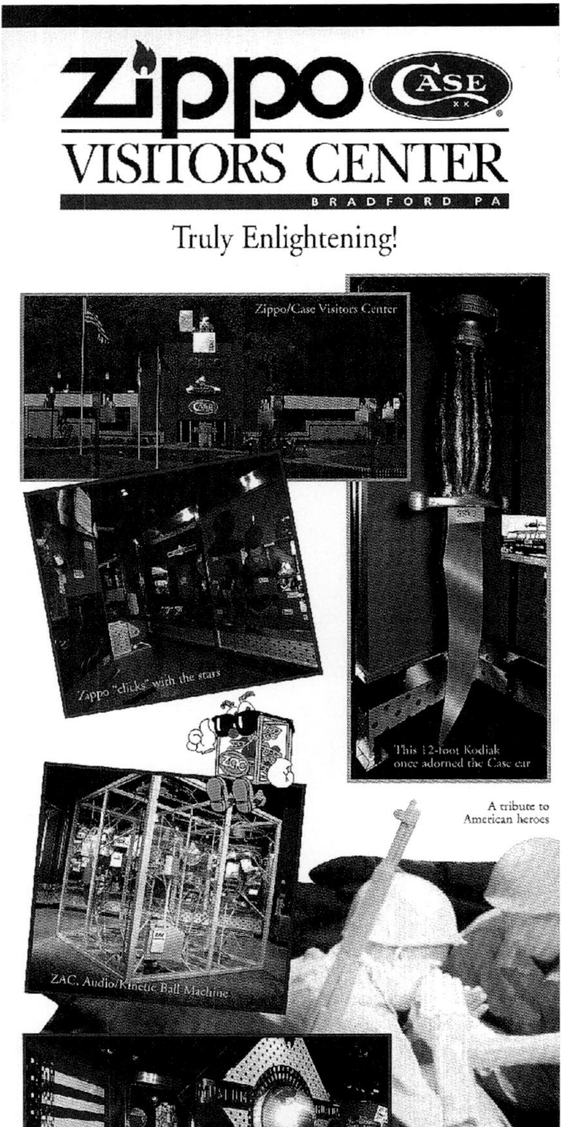
Zippo
CASE
XX
VISITORS CENTER
BRADFORD PA
Truly Enlightening!
Zippo/Case Visitors Center
Zippo "clicks" with the stars
This 12-foot Kodiak once adorned the Case car
A tribute to American heroes
ZAC, Audio/Kinetic Ball Machine
Fascinating displays of Zippo/Case art and history

BIBLIOGRAPHY

Archives of The Zippo Manufacturing Company.

Business Week, July 23, 1955.

Forbes Magazine, November 18, 1996.

Hoosier Heritage-http://www.spcc.com/ihsw/pyle.htm.

Johnston, Mary Ann; *A Pocket of Peace*; Pennbank, 1979/Integra Bank 1994.

Poore, David; *Zippo A Great American Lighter*; Schiffer, 1997.

Popular Mechanics, August 1994.

Pyle, E. T.; *Brave Men*; Henry Holt & Co Inc, 1944.

Pyle, E. T.; *Last Chapter*; Henry Holt & Co Inc, 1946.

The Bradford Era; December 15, 1962.

The Orange County Register, February 23, 1997.

The Zippo Lighter Collector's Guide; The Zippo Manufacturing Company, annually.

Zippo – A History of Progress; The Zippo Manufacturing Company, July 1995.

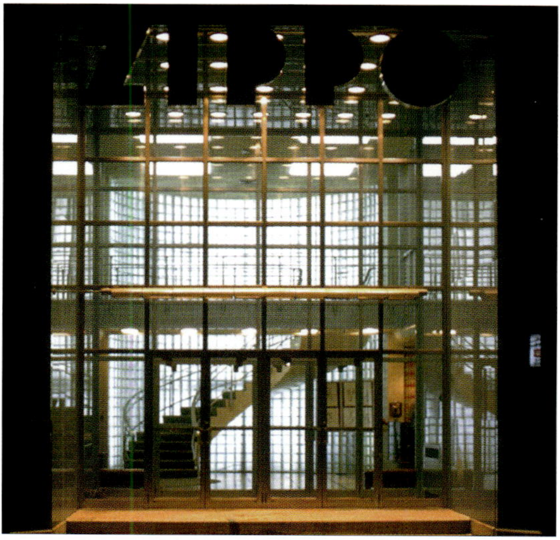

View of the Zippo building at night.

INDEX